Integrity in a Changing World

Charles O. Bennett

Audit Bureau of Circulations

Integrity in a Changing World

Charles O. Bennett

Seventy-Five Years of Industry Self-Regulation
Through the Audit Bureau of Circulations

Audit Bureau of Circulations

The Mobium Press • Chicago • 1989

Library of Congress Catalog Card Number: 89-61918

ISBN: 0-916371-10-7

Designed by Mobium Corporation for Design and Communication
Chicago and New York

Printed in the United States of America

R. R. DONNELLEY & SONS COMPANY
Chicago and Crawfordsville

This book is dedicated to the ABC auditors
and those who, through the years, have
given meaning and direction to their work.

Contents

Foreword

Circulation is the foundation of advertising and publishing success. It is the avenue of contact between the advertiser and the readers that sales messages seek to attract. Primary sources of revenue and services provided by a publication, to make it an indispensable medium and a financial success, are based on circulation. Circulation data are the starting point for print media research and the bases on which advertising rates are established.

Because circulation is a vital success element in the life of the advertising and publishing world, advertisers, advertising agencies, and publishers voluntarily joined together in 1914 to create the means through which both buyer and seller could benefit from uniform standards and reliable circulation data.

This is the story of that concept: It was given little chance of success at its birth, has fought the battles of evolution, and is today, 75 years later, so ingrained in the fabric of advertising buyer-seller relations that its existence is often taken for granted.

The Audit Bureau of Circulations rose out of the chaos of no effective standards for advertisers to know and evaluate the circulation products they were offered, and a publishing conscience that was largely not prepared to provide these data. Unlike regulations mandated for other industries by government edict, ABC's standards resulted from the cooperation of the tri-partite interests involved.

A 1965 history of the Audit Bureau, *Facts Without Opinion*, traced the development of the audited circulation movement and the first 50 years of the organization in detailed chronological order.

This book is actually a collection of histories. During infancy, the organization overcame the threats of ignorance, jealousy, and skepticism. In gaining experience and maturity, ABC weathered many controversial discussions as rules and practices were modified to mirror ever-changing conditions in the advertising and publishing marketplace, issues fueled by the diversity of member interests, competitive rivalries, changing attitudes, and new technology and sophistication.

Hopefully, this book will serve as a useful reference for future studies. The Audit Bureau has often been credited as being evolutionary, not revolutionary. Issues are revisited in the light of new marketing needs. Reviews are extensive, change is continuous. This book attempts to chronicle many of those changes in rules and philosophies. By exploring the histories of major individual subjects—their beginnings, their modifications, and the conditions and people who were involved in their evolution to today's standards—the hope is to provide a better understanding of how this remarkable organization has operated and matured over the years.

Throughout its history, members of the Audit Bureau of Circulations have dedicated this association to being the preeminent self-regulatory auditing association, responsible for the verification and dissemination of members' circulation data and other information, for the benefit of the advertising marketplace.

This dedication has never wavered, nor has the promise and commitment of objectivity and integrity; facts without opinion.

Recognizing circulation value • "Medicine men" lead the drive to organize advertisers • American Association of Advertisers introduces circulation audits • Association of National Advertisers effort too little, too late • Advertising Audit Association's scheme overcomes the odds • A shaky Audit Bureau of Circulations is born.

The formation of the Audit Bureau of Circulations in 1914 came during a period that produced some of the most profound changes in business practices in the history of North American industry. Pure food and drug, anti-trust, postal, and fair trade legislation were results of the reform mentality that also brought the Audit Bureau into existence.

Together, these efforts sought to bring order out of chaos. The uniqueness of the Audit Bureau is that it was established not under threat of government edict, but solely by advertiser, advertising agency, and publisher within the industry. As tribute to the association, never in its 75 years have the governments of the United States and Canada questioned ABC's efficiency or integrity. Rather, agencies and courts of both countries have frequently sought advice from this organization.

Changed many times to adapt to the pace of changing industry conditions, the Audit Bureau of Circulations is today the keystone of the audited circulation movement and an outstanding example of effective self-regulation in industry.

The Audit Bureau focused the attention of advertisers, advertising agencies, and publishers on the importance of circulation as the common denominator in their business relations. In addition to making available circulation facts, the Audit Bureau created standards upon which circulation analyses could be made, interpreted, and evaluated by the buyers and sellers of advertising space. It created and has maintained a language with which buyers and sellers of print media space can communicate with mutual understanding.

Historical Setting

The idea that advertising values and circulation were somehow related first emerged in the post-U.S. Civil War years, when manufacturers sought to open new markets. The industrial revolution, which ultimately recognized a need for audited circulation facts, covered many years. It wasn't until the end of the 19th century, however, that the elements of mass production and mass media were teamed to form a new selling force and new concepts of advertising.

Basic to this force were three parties. The manufacturer or advertiser with a product or service to sell had only recently begun to understand the potential of communicating sales messages through mass media. Publishers had only recently begun to realize that their circulations had an economic value beyond the simple sale of copies. The transition of advertising agencies, from advertising space brokers to suppliers of creative messages and counsellors on the use of that space, was just underway.

Long the sole property of publishers, circulation facts became of interest to all three parties. Cautioned by traditional business practices and the lack of uniform standards, publishers were reluctant to share these facts. Rising publishing costs forced them to reveal certain circulation data as a condition for obtaining advertising revenue. Fearing a loss of independence, most publishers hid the true nature of their circulations because of (or behind) the lack of common understanding of terms and definitions.

Concerned more with the production of a publication than with accounting for its distribution, comparatively few publishers kept records capable of producing reliable circulation data. It was also not economically feasible to provide actual figures in the light of competitors who would simply better them with their own.

These factors, along with the competition generated by the sheer numbers of publications, were seized upon by too many opportunistic publishers to inflate circulation figures and market coverage well beyond practical limits. Thus, circulation integrity was based on degrees of believability, and even religious publications were not above suspicion.

There were voices in the publishing wilderness, however. After months of holding off until actual circulation increased to the amount being quoted by its advertising salesmen, Victor F. Lawson's *Chicago Daily News* was one of the first newspapers to publish its press run

Returns were a perfectly legitimate component of a publication's circulation in pre-ABC days.

figures. The *Washington Star* followed by publishing circulation totals for each of the publishing days of the preceding year. Lawson went even further by establishing a circulation auditing company and offering its services to other newspapers.

The *New York Times* offered a $2,500 wager if an audit showed the *New York Herald*'s circulation larger than that of the *Times*, an offer the *Herald* ducked because "the practice of betting is immoral."

And there was W.J. Richards, *Indianapolis News*, who called his fellow publishers to court by saying, "In the whole range of the world's wide commerce, advertising space is the only commodity which refuses the purchaser test proof of the measure given. That hoary evil of the counting room, false statements of circulation, furnishes the loudest demand for rate practices of the advertising agent. And until the circulation liar is run out of business, there can be no stable rates."

If advertisers had reason to distrust publishers, they also contributed to the general chaos of the times. Claims for their products and services were frequently limited only by a copywriter's imagination. Publishers, who considered themselves the voices of the social conscience, editorially attacked the policies and products of manufacturers.

A partial list of advertising refused by many publishers included: "women's medicines; free-for-all cures; sensuous productions; all matrimonial; intoxicating liquors; cigarettes; messages liable to mislead;

messages reflecting upon another business; quack doctors; mail-order houses; fly-by-night merchants; messages deemed objectionable by good newspapers; fake financial; loan sharks; piano certificate; strikes or boycotts; cancer, tuberculosis, venereal disease cures; land speculations; political advertisements in opposition to the stated views of publishers; messages explaining un-American doctrines; and merchandise not carried and promoted by local businesses."

Cleverly written space contracts frequently guaranteed payment upon fulfillment of "small type" conditions no publisher (however honorable) could complete. "Dishonesty" discounts of circulation claims were used by many advertisers as a tool to control space rates.

Advertising agencies had long served as space brokers for publishers. By the turn of the century, the business split: The prototype of the modern advertising agency took on the function of creating, and later placing, advertisers' messages; the other "special" advertising agencies became the forerunners of today's publishers' sales representatives. But many of these agencies carried out both functions, placing the agency business betwixt and between and creating distrust on the part of the publishers and the advertisers.

This was the chaotic setting into which the audited circulation movement was introduced and from which the Audit Bureau of Circulations would emerge to substitute orderly self-discipline and confidence.

Association of American Advertisers

By the early 1890s, the single largest category of advertisers using print media space was manufacturers of medicinal products. Because of the unsupported and frequently fraudulent claims of most of these companies, they were also the most controversial. In an effort to deal with increasing editorial criticism and the threat of government intervention in their practices, they were the first to organize nationally—as the Proprietary Association of America.

Under the leadership of Frederick L. Perine, Hall & Ruckel, a circulation committee was established by the association in 1895 with the express purpose of "obtaining correct statements of newspaper and periodical circulations wherever and whenever required." Requests by the PAA committee met with sparse response from publishers. While they also sought the same results, advertisers in other fields were reluctant to support this effort by "the medicine men."

In January 1898, Perine gathered six advertising managers for a meeting to explore the feasibility of establishing a national organization to deal with the problem of obtaining correct statements of newspaper and periodical circulations. The study and planning continued off and on for the next 18 months. On June 5, 1899, representatives of 30 advertisers met in New York at Perine's invitation. These representatives surveyed the possibilities of a union of national advertisers for the promotion of interests common to all.

Speaking at this meeting, A. Cressy Morrison, Scott & Bowne, acknowledged the need for such a national organization directing its attention to "correcting national evils and creating a national code for advertisers." He left no question as to his views of problem priorities: "There are many other avenues of usefulness which this association can develop," but "the purpose which underlies this meeting is the question of circulation."

From this meeting came the Association of American Advertisers, with Perine as president. The group had numerous objectives, but it placed a proposed program of securing accurate information about the circulations of publications first. About the same time, a western organization, the American Society of National Advertisers, began a similar program, with C.W. Post, Postum Cereal Co., as a leading spirit. This organization was soon merged with the AAA.

In its first year, the AAA made exploratory inspections on the four magazines of the Frank A. Munsey Co. The Audit Company, conducting the audits on behalf of the organization, reported that "the figures of circulation claimed by Mr. Munsey have substantially been borne out by our testing." The audits cost the association $300. Financing audits in a volume sufficient to impact on the problem was a major concern to the AAA members until the auditors suggested that the association continue to specify outside auditing firms, allow publishers to pay the costs, submitting the results exclusively to the association, which, in turn, would provide a formal verification certificate. The paid association manager also served as its auditing staff, handling special situations. By the end of its third year, audits had been conducted on some 400 publications, and staff "inspection reports give more information on publications in 57 cities."

The advertisers first considered circulation to be the number of copies printed and prepared for distribution. Later they were to define circulation as the number of copies distributed in such a way that they were likely to be read, whether paid or not. Still later, the association restricted the definition so that net paid distribution was the important thing to be determined.

By 1905, a majority of members questioned the ethics of publishers paying for their own audits. Eventually the association added examiners to its staff to do its own field auditing work. The AAA mailed out statement blanks to publishers, requesting that they be filled out with basic circulation data, along with a brief explanation of the organization and its purpose. Along with the instructions for filling out the form was the following request:

"If you are willing to have one of the examiners of the association inspect your circulation records without cost to you and report thereon to the members, please fill in permission for examination at the end of the blank. Whether you do this or not, we ask you to submit statement of circulation, as requested."

After early difficulties, the Association of American Advertisers included the following stipulation:

"Before said examination shall commence, the examiner shall be furnished in writing with an agreement that any and all books, papers, etc., considered by said examiner as necessary to ascertain the fact as regards circulation of said publication, shall be placed at the command of the examiner, and that he shall have access thereto. Also an agreement that the publisher will submit to a re-examination if necessary."

Publishers who submitted to an examination were given a certificate, attesting to the average paid circulation for the period covered by the examination and the paid circulation for the last month of the period, both figures "excluding all returned, unsold, and waste copies." One of the faults for which the AAA was most criticized was the fact that while it audited for paid circulation, its rules never included a definition for paid circulation.

While the purpose of the organization was generally acknowledged to be a good one, support from the advertising community was not as expected. At no time did the AAA have more than 100 advertiser members and, through most of its existence, probably averaged around 50. Publishers were slow to submit circulation statements. In 1907, statements were received from 279 publishers and, in 1908, 331. During 1909, the association issued 126 certificates covering the examinations of publishers' records by the three staff examiners.

Despite its original intent to concern itself with the broad interests of the national advertiser community, the association devoted itself and its funds almost exclusively to the problem of circulation reports. This singleness of purpose, plus dissatisfaction with the dominance of pharmaceutical advertisers among its members and officers, caused dissidents in June 1910 to call for the formation of a second national organization, the Association of National Advertising Managers (now called the Association of National Advertisers).

Publishers eager, but advertisers can't raise funds to make more than a few audits.

At least two AAA directors were dissatisfied with the leadership of Bert M. Moses, Omega Chemical Co. In the vanguard of the formation of the ANAM were E. St. Elmo Lewis, Burroughs Adding Machine Co., and L.C. McChesney, National Phonograph Co. Efforts to effect a merger between the two organizations only served to widen the breach, which was not healed for many years. The dispute did bring about the incorporation of the ANAM in May 1912, after Moses was re-elected AAA head, and a rivalry that ultimately led to the organization of the Audit Bureau of Circulations.

While the ANAM was in the throes of organizing, the AAA experienced increasing financial problems. Moses told the members, "Our weakness is that we can't make half the examinations called for by reputable publishers simply because the money isn't available to employ enough examiners."

At the 1913 AAA annual meeting, Moses reported a membership of 73 advertisers and an income of $15,000, the highest in the association's history. Several decisions were made at this meeting that were to have special importance on the course of later events.

Searching for new sources of revenue, non-voting associate memberships were approved for publishers "and persons engaged in bill board, painted sign, street car, and other branches of the advertising business," including both special and general advertising agencies. However, a suggestion that publishers assist in the financing of audits was not acted upon.

Another important decision concerned the election of officers. Since its inception, presiding officers of the Association of American Advertisers had been representatives of proprietary medicine companies located in the eastern part of the United States. Moses, who had held the presidency for five terms and who was under fire from dissident members, was encouraged not to seek another term. He had become extremely controversial in his efforts to kill the Richardson amendment to the National Food and Drug Act, aimed at prohibiting unsupported, misleading, and false labeling and advertising claims.

The easterners proposed a candidate. Since 32 out of the 52 advertisers at the 1913 annual meeting were from the Middle West, this candidate had little chance of election. The mid-westerners nominated and elected a full slate of candidates, headed by Emery Mapes, Cream of Wheat Co. Further, they agreed to move the association's headquarters to Chicago.

The members also agreed to tighten its auditing practices. "Circulation audits of some kind or other have been made for a number of years. That many

Mapes moved the association's headquarters to Chicago.

of them have failed to be satisfactory to advertisers is known to nearly everybody who has bought space. The AAA has been making circulation examinations ever since it was organized, currently at the rate of some 300 annually, but often under such conditions that it was impossible for its auditors to verify statements made to them by the publishers," the circulation committee chairman reported. Approved were the plan for regular annual audits and provisions for re-audits in the event of controversy surrounding an audit.

The committee chairman's report indicated that others, besides AAA, were making circulation audits. N.W. Ayer & Son, on behalf of its *American Newspaper Annual and Directory*, employed a circulation auditor to investigate publishers' claims in 1909. The extent of these activities was limited and discontinued in 1914. A number of publishers hired financial auditors to examine circulation claims. In addition to the AAA, at least five other groups claimed circulation audits in 1913.

Association of National Advertising Managers

New officers of the AAA had barely been installed and the move to
Chicago completed when, in March 1913, L.C. McChesney, president of
the Association of National Advertising Managers and a former director
of the AAA, called a group of representatives of various New York-
located segments of the advertising business together for a conference.
The purpose of the meeting was "to assist in the working out of a
uniform plan to make circulation audits, this plan, at the option of the
publisher, to take the place of all other forms of making examinations
now in vogue."

    The ANAM believed that publishers, agencies, and advertisers
"should arrive at an understanding as to the meaning of the word
'circulation' when applied to the several classes of publications carrying
advertising." It suggested that a simple,
uniform recordkeeping system be devised
so that audits could be carried out
quickly and at minimum cost, and that
audits could be carried out by designated
chartered accountants working under the
guidance of advertisers. "In our opinion,"
McChesney suggested, "publishers
should, at their own expense, have an
official audit made at least once a year,
the findings of such audits to be automatically sent to all associations representing agencies and advertisers."

    ANAM's circulation committee
chairman, Orlando C. Harn, National
Lead Co. and later a director, board
chairman, and managing director of
the Audit Bureau of Circulations, was
named to head up planning for the new
auditing program.

    Harn was quick to point out that
the major weakness of the AAA plan was
inadequate financing and, therefore, its
efforts "accomplished only a drop in the

*Harn was an early critic of
the effort he later headed.*

9

bucket." The costs should be collected at the most convenient spot, he said, "like an indirect tax and let the publisher distribute the tax by means of his advertising charges pro rata over all his advertisers. Pity for the poor publisher is out of place. He will not pay for it in the end."

AAA President Emery Mapes and others of the association's board firmly believed that a system of audits paid for by publishers would prove merely a whitewashing campaign. In a statement Mapes said "more in sorrow than in anger that this present move looks more like an attempt to establish elusive, rather than honest, audit of circulations."

Concern that ANAM would be any more successful than the AAA efforts had been was expressed by James Keeley, *Chicago Tribune*, at the June 1913 convention of the Associated Advertising Clubs of America. "I say to you that the accountant does not live who can go into the office of a publication and come away with the positive and absolute knowledge that he has obtained the facts. What these accountants certify to are merely totals of figures furnished to them by the actual publications themselves.

"A radical change in the method of examining circulations is needed if the advertiser is not to be swindled and the honest publisher is not to be handicapped by a dishonest competitor. Your official examination is not worth one battered cent." Keeley expressed the feeling that only government action against the "long and short distance circulation falsifiers who defraud the advertiser" could bring about any measurable improvement. The current circulation statement, he said, was meaningless and "entitled to the place of honor in any joke book. Certificates and circulation examinations only promote fraud and chicanery because one never knew whether to trust the methods used in securing attestations."

The convention of Associated Advertising Clubs of America wound up its meeting by accepting, "with considerable enthusiasm," a declaration that criticized "the present chaotic multiplicity of methods of arriving at verification of circulation statements," calling for "radical revision of these methods," and calling for support for the Bureau of Verified Circulations, as the ANAM program was known.

Advertising Audit Association

Not everyone who attended the AACA meeting was enthusiastic over the declaration. On his return to Chicago after the convention, Stanley Clague, the Clague Agency and president of the Western Advertising

Agents Association; an assistant of his by the name of Hugh Brennan; and client Arthur Lynn, Montgomery Ward & Co., discussed the action and, more especially, the fact that western interests had been completely overlooked in the Association of National Advertising Managers plan. They acknowledged that the AAA program was failing, and Brennan commented that he had formulated a plan for reorganizing it earlier. They discussed Brennan's plan, but took no action.

In New York, the Bureau of Verified Circulations began to send blank forms to publishers, asking not only for circulation but also advertising rate information. In Chicago, officers of the AAA met to discuss the criticism of its efforts and the association's lack of funds for carrying on further auditing operations. Another of Clague's clients was Fred W. Squier, Pabst Brewing Co. and chairman of the AAA's circulation examination committee. During a discussion, Clague outlined Brennan's plan to Squier. Squier was impressed and asked Clague to proceed informally.

In early July, he and Brennan met with William Field, *Chicago Tribune* and representative of the American Newspaper Publishers Association in the Bureau of Verified Circulations venture. He agreed to support the plan they outlined. While continuing to represent the ANPA in the eastern program, he was instrumental in delaying progress until much spade work had been accomplished in reorganizing the AAA. Clague and Brennan spent most of the summer months discussing the plan with publishers and lining up support.

In September, Squire called for an executive meeting of the AAA board "to consider the serious conditions confronting the association" and to inquire of Clague what part the Western Advertising Agents Association could take in a solution.

Clague outlined a plan of cooperation "whereby advertisers, agents, and publishers might lay down the foundation of a real institution." Clague proposed that advertising agents take the leading hand in a completely new auditing bureau, under the guise of the old AAA. To camouflage their efforts, the new organization would retain the initials of the AAA but would be called the "Advertising Audit Association" and would utilize the old organization's auditing staff.

In addition to advertisers, Clague proposed that the organization would include as full members the advertising agencies and publishers of magazines, farm publications, newspapers, and trade and technical publications. "A yearly volume of information would be issued on each

Clague's drive and leadership resulted in the formation of the Audit Bureau of Circulations.

publication, with a supplementary quarterly report from all publications made on affidavit, as well as a complete investigation made by inspectors for each publication once a year."

He suggested "that a board of directors be appointed on which the advertising agents will have two members, daily newspapers two members, magazines two members, farm publications one member, and advertisers six members, thereby preserving the majority view of the advertisers as planned by the Association of American Advertisers."

In presenting the plan to the western advertising agents, Clague pointed out that the Bureau of Verified Circulations provided for only one agency director on its board and specified that representative was to be from the Association of New York Advertising Agents. He also informed these agencies that the Associated Advertising Clubs of America would be asked to endorse the plan suggested by the ANAM as the sole organization to verify circulations at its meeting the following June. "There is no doubt that if this wish is realized it would be unjust to us as advertising agents, but unless some action is taken, we may wake up after the damage is done."

The western agencies gave Clague's plan their unanimous endorsement and agreed to work with the AAA officers in bringing it about. At a meeting of the Advertising Audit Association less than a week later, Clague, Mapes, and Jason Rogers, *New York Globe*, were directed to draw up a plan of action. The agencies were asked to raise the first $5,000 of what the organizers hoped would eventually be $100,000.

Organizers of ANAM's Bureau of Verified Circulations met in October to elect an executive board. The board, consisting of two advertisers, one advertising agent, and four publishers, was instructed to draw up a constitution and bylaws and report back to a full conference at an early date.

Erickson's work among easterners was vital to movement's acceptance.

In December, Clague learned that Russell R. Whitman, *Boston American*, was leaving his newspaper and was granted approval to approach him to take the job of organizing the new association and enlist the support of various interests. He agreed. During his visit to the East, Clague also met with Alfred W. Erickson, the Erickson Co. and president of the Association of New York Advertising Agents and its representative on the Bureau of Verified Circulations board. Erickson yielded to Clague's salesmanship, promising not to reveal the plans for the new association and, at the proper time, give the western movement his wholehearted support.

Meanwhile, Rogers was busy in Chicago, lining up the support of the Gilt Edge List of Newspapers and the Standard Farm Papers.

With these plans complete, the advertising trade press was filled in. *Printers' Ink* broke the news on December 13, 1913, that a "New Audit Movement Would Include All Advertising Interests." The article announced the formation of the Advertising Audit Association, with Louis Bruch, American Radiator Co., as chairman for organizing purposes, and the employment of Russell R. Whitman to aid in organizing memberships in the new association. *Editor & Publisher* followed with additional information two days later.

The constitution and bylaws of the new auditing organization provided that "Any advertiser, advertising agency, or publisher in the United States or Canada may become a subscriber. Each subscriber shall have one vote in the general conduct of any and all matters relating to the work of the association." Bert Moses, former AAA board chairman, called "this idea of equality damn foolishness. The agent mistrusts the publisher; while the publisher slanders the manufacturer and his fellow publisher, he mistrusts the agent; and the advertiser has no reason to believe either one of them, but he is in the unique position of owning the purse."

Bruch headed organization committee and was first chairman of the Audit Bureau.

The announcement caught Orlando C. Harn and other organizers of the New York effort by surprise. Within days of its publication, Harn wrote to members of the Association of National Advertising Managers urging a cautious attitude towards the western movement and also mentioned the possibility of permitting that group to merge into or serve as one of the auditing sources of the eastern effort. An invitation to this effect was extended in January 1914.

Now more fully underway than the Bureau of Verified Circulations, the organizing committee of the Advertising Audit Association replied, "It is the sense of the [organizing] meeting that this association will not amalgamate with the ANAM in its new movement to appoint auditing firms, but cordially invites them to join with the Advertising Audit Association."

When Clague offered to meet with the eastern group to personally present the AAA reply, Alfred W. Erickson, as temporary chairman of the eastern group, called a meeting of representatives of the eight associations participating in that effort. After a review of the plans and progress of the AAA, the group voted to consolidate its efforts with those of the western group. Through an exchange of telegrams two days later, terms of the merger were agreed upon.

At Harn's urging, the board of the Association of National Advertising Managers refused to support the united group. Erickson wrote Harn a blistering note that, in part, said, "I am both chagrined and grieved at the failure of your organization to endorse the work of its committee, and it seems too bad that the various advertising interests cannot work harmoniously on a movement as big and important as this." Harn replied, "It certainly is a very unsatisfactory situation which has come to pass in our efforts to get a solution of the auditing problems. I do not altogether blame the members of the ANAM who have opposed a prompt approval of the amalgamation plan."

While clouds of gloom and dissension hung over the East, the sun was shining brightly in Chicago. Membership promotions treated the consolidation as a *fait accompli,* and pledges towards the $100,000 start-up goal were being received. The old American Association of Advertisers, whose membership had increased from 73 to 151 during this critical year, gave "thunderous approval" to the new consolidated auditing organization at its 14th annual meeting and voted to turn over its full facilities, staff and all, to the new organization. The AAA continued on for several more months, if only on paper. But with its mission accomplished, this, the first association of national advertisers, passed out of existence.

Despite strong efforts to kill the plan, initial goal is over-subscribed and organization meeting called.

Despite efforts by the ANAM to sabotage the Chicago efforts, from openly urging its members not to participate to counseling publishers' representatives to recommend their publishers withhold support, Whitman told the consolidated group's organizing committee on April 30 (the same day ANAM was opening its annual meeting) that the fund of $100,000 necessary to effect the permanent organization had been pledged. Plans were laid "to arrange for a convention of members." In the East, the announcement of this accomplishment was "received with both shock and disbelief."

Realizing that the Associated Advertising Clubs of the World (formerly of America) was scheduled to meet in Toronto in June, and that the endorsement of this group was of major importance, the organizing committee called for a convention of members of the "Advertising Audit Association and Bureau of Verified Circulations." The convention was scheduled for May 20 and 21 in Chicago.

Audit Bureau of Circulations

When the first convention of the amalgamated bodies convened, 595 out of the 612 members who appear on the charter membership list were present or represented by proxy. Represented were 74 national advertisers, 49 advertising agents, 338 newspapers, 27 magazines, 52 farm publications, and 55 business publications.

In opening the meeting, Committee Chairman Louis Bruch, American Radiator Co., called it "the most striking movement in all the history of advertising. There has been for a long time a disbelief that such a thing could come about, as a combination or consolidation in an association of such divergent opinion and ideas as that of the buyer and the seller. But strangely, while it has been doubted for years that such a thing could be brought about, the answer is that we stand today an accomplished fact, having started this association by a charter membership of more than 600, and a total of subscriptions of about $118,000; that is the best answer of all the interests here that the buyer and seller can come together on a mutual foundation.

"I want to say for the organization committee that we are simply turning over to this meeting a wonderful foundation; we have bought the site, we have got the material here together, and it is up to you gentlemen to lay the cornerstone and the constitution today for a structure of which we shall be proud.

"And someday, maybe the advertising world in the future shall say of those men when they met on the 20th of May, 1914, that 'they builded better than they knew.' I hope that will be their verdict."

A constitution was adopted, and a board consisting of representatives of 11 advertisers, 2 advertising agents, 2 newspapers, 2 magazines, 2 farm publications, and 2 business publications was elected. Bruch was elected the first board chairman and president. An early order of business for the board was to select a new name for the organization—the Audit Bureau of Circulations.

The fierce tempo of progress that began less than a year earlier continued during the succeeding months. The vital endorsement of the Associated Advertising Clubs of the World was obtained in June. A board committee on standard forms and auditing practices, appointed at the May meeting, completed its work with the adoption of forms in mid-July. Standardized circulation statement forms were sent to publisher members two weeks later.

The board received notice on August 21 that the State of Illinois had approved the articles of incorporation for the Audit Bureau of Circulations. Early in September, Whitman reported that circulation statements had been received from more than 300 publishers.

On September 21, ABC's first five audits were initiated simultaneously in different parts of the United States. The Audit Bureau's initial auditing staff included the holdover auditors of the old Association of American Advertisers. Within two weeks, six new auditors were added to the field staff.

Overview

In spite of this evolution and preparation, the Audit Bureau of Circulations was introduced to a confused and often cynical industry. Everyone professed to believe in honesty and a "square deal," claimed to be practicing the golden rule, and blamed the competitor for practically all that was wrong with the world of business. Uniform standards and circulation accounting practices did not exist. With no little justification, mistrust was as basic to the industry as were advertisers, advertising agencies, and publishers.

Many, especially publishers, saw little hope for the Audit Bureau of Circulations and voluntary, cooperative self-regulation, preferring to believe the answer lay in government intervention.

That it succeeded in bringing order out of chaos in its initial years is tribute to those who believed in the importance of its mission. That it has succeeded over the years in adjusting to the changing and diverse viewpoints of its tri-partite membership, the divisiveness of competitive pressures within its membership, and the evolution of new marketing sophistication and publishing practices is tribute to the integrity and dedication of its members, directors, and staff.

Today, after 75 years as the foundation of buyer-seller relations in the advertising and publishing industry, the Audit Bureau's services are as relevant and as essential to the success of that industry as at any time in its history.

For this reason, while each member had an equal vote in the Audit Bureau's activities, advertisers were given a special oversight function. In the bylaws adopted at the organization meeting in 1914 it was specified that "The power to in any way alter these bylaws shall be vested solely in the board of directors, to be effective only after confirmation by a majority of Division A (advertiser) members, ratified by two-thirds of the membership of the Bureau voting upon such alteration."

Advertisers also were given the majority voice on the board of directors, and board chairmanship was limited to an advertiser representative. In 1919, the advertiser oversight reference was removed as unnecessary since the board's actions were controlled by advertiser directors. Advertisers maintained their majority on the board until 1935, adopting a shared majority with advertising agency directors. The provision that the chairman must be an advertiser was amended in 1941, sharing this distinction with agency representatives.

Throughout the 75-year history of the Audit Bureau, the guidance and support of advertisers have been keys to the organization's success. As directors, as individual members, and through advisory committees and allied association input, they have strongly influenced ABC standards and services.

Association of National Advertisers

One of the strongest supporters of the audited circulation movement in the United States over the years has been the Association of National Advertisers, the new name the Association of National Advertising Managers chose in 1914. Twenty-two ANA past chairmen and many of its directors have also served on the ABC boards, ensuring close cooperation between the two organizations.

This relationship got off to a rocky start, however. After the amalgamation of the Advertising Audit Association and the Bureau of Verified Circulations had been agreed to and announced, ANAM Secretary C.W. Patman issued a confidential bulletin to members of that organization cautioning them against supporting the joint effort.

While resentment existed over the speed with which the Chicago group was able to progress, a more important hang-up was the fact that the new organization had no plans to accept ANAM members in a gratis plan to provide them with report services. Patman pointed out that the new organization expected advertisers to pay membership dues of $200 (on top of the $50 dues to ANAM) to obtain "circulation reports which are rightly due buyers of space at no cost whatsoever." He further deplored the new organization's appeal to individual concerns, without regard to the support of those concerns to the Association of National Advertising Mangers, minimizing the probability of ANAM oversight of the new organization's function.

The issue festered for several years, despite the fact that several ANA members also served on the new ABC board. During the Audit Bureau's annual meeting in May 1917, Allan C. Reiley, Remington Typewriter Co. and chairman of the ANA, issued an ultimatum. "The only reason for the existence of a circulation auditing organization is for the purpose of furnishing authentic circulation information to national advertisers, and it is very desirable that such a service for national advertisers be under the control of organized national advertisers.

ANA ultimatum rebuked by ABC directors.

"In order that a working agreement may be effected between the ABC as an auditing organization and the Association of National Advertisers, the board of directors of the ANA propose the following plan—The entire membership of the ANA to become members of the ABC upon the payment of a nominal annual membership fee of five dollars per member—11 (the entire advertiser membership representation) of the 21 or a majority of the ABC directors to be elected from the ANA membership.

"We ask an answer before the close of your annual meeting in order that we may have some official advice from you before we present the matter for open discussion by our members in convention assembled."

ABC Chairman Louis Bruch, American Radiator Co., was unanimously instructed to reply "that apparently the ANA has not yet a full understanding of the services rendered by the ABC, and that we suggest a joint meeting of six directors of the ANA and six directors of the ABC for the purpose of considering the possibility of closer cooperation between the two organizations."

At a meeting of ABC and ANA directors, it was agreed to set up advertiser "steering" committees on business publications, newspapers, and farm publications to effect closer cooperation and liaison between the groups. Proposals for an amalgamation of ABC and ANA were presented at a special meeting of the ABC members in January 1918. The members adopted the following resolution:

"That the members of the Association of National Advertisers be extended a cordial invitation to become members of the Audit Bureau of Circulations in accordance with the terms of the bylaws of the ABC, and it is the sense of the meeting that the views and recommendations of the ANA toward the betterment of the service of the ABC will at all times be gladly received and considered."

A plan was announced whereby the two associations would meet in Chicago during the first week in June. The meetings were held, and the ANA formally endorsed the work of the Audit Bureau. Reiley told the ABC members, "Real good has been accomplished. When publishers understand the interest which advertisers take in ABC audits no publication with value to offer advertisers will feel that it can afford to stay out of the ABC."

At the October 1920 ABC annual meeting, the ANA directors even more emphatically endorsed the Audit Bureau's work. Speaking for the ANA, John Sullivan, its secretary, said, "There was a time when we

ANA and ABC no longer stand "on opposite hills."

stood on opposite hills. We didn't understand one another, and we were apt, pretty frequently, to tell each other where to go. We weren't getting very far. We are gratified to see the amount of progress that has been made the past two or nearly three years in the relations of the ANA and the ABC. We strongly support the Audit Bureau and congratulate you upon your great success."

Over the years, ABC has sought the counsel of ANA on issues of particular concern to advertisers. For many years, ABC was the major source of input data for ANA's series of *Circulation and Rate Trend* books. The close working relationship of the two organizations is reflected in the awarding of the ANA's Paul West Award to the Audit Bureau of Circulations in 1964. In part, the citation says:

"At its inception . . . the Audit Bureau of Circulations was the beginning of a promise for a higher degree of professionalism in the advertising world. And in 50 years of painstaking and totally objective analysis, the Bureau has fulfilled that promise.

"This organization has been the cornerstone against which all succeeding measurement procedures have been laid in order to erect what is now an imposing edifice of scientific evaluation of the effectiveness of advertising.

"ABC has been a leader and a spokesman in the cause of improving advertising measurement standards and in the practices of publishing as

After 50 years, ANA agreed that the Audit Bureau had fulfilled its promise.

well. It has been called 'The Publisher's Conscience,' and rightly so, for its more than 4,000 members belong on a voluntary basis, and represent an unbiased, tripartite, self-regulatory effort on behalf of publishers, advertisers, and agencies, of which our industry and nation can be proud.

"We cite the Audit Bureau of Circulations for all its achievements—and for its cumulative achievement, the attainment of greater effectiveness in advertising."

Association of Canadian Advertisers

When the Audit Bureau of Circulations was organized, its founders fully anticipated that it would serve the advertising and publishing industries in Canada as well as the United States. The January 1914 prospectus held out the hope that the new organization would include "every important medium of advertising in the United States and Canada." Eleven Canadian publications and one advertiser, the Canadian Pacific Railway Company, were among its charter members.

Circulation information was a key issue when advertisers first met to organize the Association of Canadian Advertisers in 1914, and it was still a major concern when that organization was incorporated three years later. One of the first projects undertaken by the ACA was to prepare "Circulation and Information Forms" for use by publishers in filing sworn circulation statements.

At the urging of its first chairman, L.R. Greene, Tuckett Tobacco Co., Ltd. and member of the Association of National Advertisers, ACA followed the ANA course of withholding full early support of the new auditing organization. At the November 1915 board meeting, ACA reported that "There was some discussion of the attitude which the association should take towards audits of Canadian publications made by the Audit Bureau of Circulations and it was the consensus of opinion that it should be announced immediately that the audits of this Bureau would prove satisfactory to the ACA." As was the ANA policy, ACA added the Audit Bureau's name to the list of approved auditors from whom it would accept publishers' circulation reports.

W.A. Lydiatt, secretary of the ACA, interpreted this action more enthusiastically. In informing the ABC board of the ACA action, he wrote, "You can count on the influence of the body of Canadian advertisers represented by this association (including over 80 percent of the big buyers of space in Canada) exerted toward getting Canadian publishers to submit their records to an audit by your Bureau."

Canadian buyers encouraged by audit progress.

Early in 1916, ABC agreed to institute a Canadian Advisory Board (committee) and invited ACA to name four of its seven members. The committee was constituted in March, and, as of mid-May, Canadian membership was announced at 89, including "all of the large dailies in Toronto and Montreal."

The effectiveness of the advisory committee's activities and the continuing interest of the ACA in encouraging the use of ABC reports are enthusiastically reported in the minutes of the ACA annual meeting in May 1917: "The daily newspaper situation is now pretty well cleaned up—to a degree which fully justifies the insistence of our organization. Of 127 daily newspapers in Canada, 53 dailies are now members or have applied for membership in the Audit Bureau of Circulations. Of the remainder, 25 dailies seem to have adopted the practice of furnishing reports on the ACA forms, reasonably complete as to the information furnished. The remaining 47 dailies, about whose circulation no satisfactory information is yet available, are chiefly those of small circulation which do not enter into the schedules of many of our members.

Two Canadians have served as ABC chairmen: C. Warren Reynolds (1968-1969) and Robert J. Galloway (1988-1989).

"We have reason to congratulate ourselves that the improved situation which exists in the daily newspaper field in Canada today is due in no small measure to the efforts of our organization—in which respect we have been of service to every advertiser using daily newspapers at present or in the future."

Through the years, cooperation between members of the Association of Canadian Advertisers and the Audit Bureau has been effective.

Since the first Canadian advertiser, B.H. Bramble, Canadian Chewing Gum Co., was elected to the ABC board in 1918, seven former ACA chairmen have also served as ABC directors. Robert J. Galloway, Campbell Soup Co. Ltd., was board chairman during 1988 and 1989.

Canadian advertisers have freely given time and talent to ABC affairs over the years, providing input on the special marketing conditions in that country. In 1929, ACA asked the ABC board to reconsider its paid circulation membership requirement adopted earlier in the decade. ACA's efforts on behalf of buyers seeking ABC-audited information on free distribution publications in Canada continued through 1936 when, with ABC's cooperation, ACA's trade and technical committee organized the Canadian Circulations Audit Board.

Membership

For much of the Audit Bureau's history, advertiser membership has been somewhat of an anomaly. Audited circulation facts came at the insistence and initial funding of advertisers. ABC's primary role has been the protection of advertisers' monies—ANA once suggested, "If the existence of ABC has saved the buyers of print media space only 10 percent, and this seems ridiculously low, by eliminating waste distribution, by providing a measure against which rates can be judged, and by making available reliable information upon which values can be determined, that organization deserves the support of all advertisers."

Yet, out of a charter membership of 978, only 51 national and 3 local advertisers were included. In 1934, during the waning days of the depression, the count was 44 national and 25 local advertiser members (most of these sponsored by local newspapers).

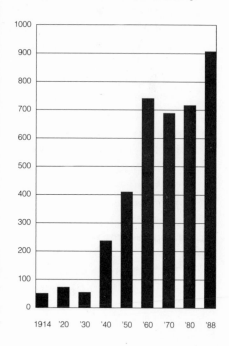

National Advertiser Membership

27

The post-depression period was one of growth in national advertiser membership in the Audit Bureau. Stimulated by an economic upturn and a succession of educational campaigns, membership jumped to 207 in 1935. While negative economic conditions and mergers have affected totals, the upward trend of national advertiser membership has continued, with a record high of 954 in 1986.

At the suggestion of newspaper publishers, the local advertiser membership category was created within the advertiser division in 1920 to bring more local merchants into ABC participation. It offered an opportunity for these merchants to become members with dues ranging from $5 to $15, depending upon the number of publications on

Regional Advertiser Membership

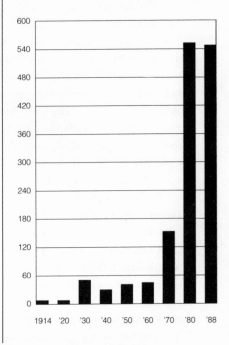

which reports were requested. Local advertiser membership totals went from 3 in 1920 to 207 a year later, almost all of the growth the result of newspaper sponsorship. Newspaper interest waned after 1926, and local advertiser membership totals dropped. It wasn't until educational efforts were instituted in 1965 that regional advertiser membership, as it became known, once again began to grow. In the 25 years following 1963, membership went from 59 to 548.

ABC's advertiser membership today is more broadly based, more representative of the industry, and individually more involved in the organization's affairs than at any point in its 75-year history.

Board Representation

The Audit Bureau's board of directors has increased over the years, from 21 in 1914 to the present membership of 33. In its initial concept, advertisers were given control of the board with a majority representation of 11 directors. When the board was expanded to 25 members in 1926, advertiser representation was increased to 13 directors.

Advertisers maintained their majority until 1935, when the board was increased to 27. Then, recognizing that the interests of advertisers and advertising agencies were comparable, as far as media evaluation was concerned, it was decided that the principle of buyer control could be maintained through a joint majority made up of advertiser and advertising agency directors. Advertisers relinquished one of their directorships to the agency members. In 1953, another of the advertiser directorships was given to the agencies. When the board was enlarged to 31 in 1956 and to 33 in 1969, no changes were made in the advertiser representation. The buyer majority was maintained with the addition of two advertising agency directors.

In an effort to recognize Canadian participation in the Audit Bureau and to ensure representation to members there, ABC voted in 1918 to designate that one of its advertiser directorships be filled from the Canadian membership. In 1987, a second advertiser membership was designated for Canadian representation, and another advertiser directorship was relinquished to agency members, to provide additional representation for that division's Canadian constituency. Both actions were taken without changing the board's 33-person size.

Involvement of U.S. and Canadian advertiser and advertising agency members, beyond board members, has long been the desire of ABC's directors. Particularly successful in adding more buyer input to ABC discussions were the task force efforts initiated by Board Chairman Charles A. Tucker, R.J. Reynolds Tobacco Co., in 1982, and the formalization of these groups as continuing buyer advisory committees by Chairman Don Goldstrom, Armstrong World Industries, in 1984.

Advertising Agencies: Providing the Energy for ABC Efforts

New allegiances and new functions • Chicago and New York groups active in planning • American Association of Advertising Agencies endorses ABC • Canadians support the association • Membership includes most major companies • Importance reflected in increased board voice.

It is difficult to consider today's advertising agencies in a role other than serving the interests of advertisers. The affiliation is so recognized in the Audit Bureau that the two membership groups share majority voice on its board, serve jointly on its buyer advisory committees, and share divisional programs at its annual meetings.

This clear-cut commonality of interests wasn't always so. In fact, formation of the Audit Bureau had a major influence in the development of this relationship.

Chief stock in trade of the early advertising agency was its knowledge of media outside the immediate area in which an advertiser was located. Some advertising agencies maintained lists of specialized publications for which they held exclusive advertising sales contracts—purchasing blocks of space and selling them to advertisers at a profit. Most publishers, however, were satisfied to sell space to any agency who, in turn, resold it to advertisers at whatever price they could get. The agencies' existence relied on their ability to keep their lists and the information on these publications secret—out of the hands of advertisers and their competitors.

Advertising agencies bitterly opposed George Rowell, the Rowell Agency, when he introduced his *American Newspaper Directory* in 1869, which listed publishers' circulation claims and Rowell's estimates, with name, location, and frequency for some 5,000 publications in the United States and Canada. He recognized that he was placing a valuable selling tool in the hands of his competitors. He later wrote, "So far as the success of our advertising agency was concerned, the publication of our directory was probably a mistake. The book placed at everybody's disposal as complete a list of papers as we ourselves possessed. It further caused our space customers to increasingly ask questions on the manner of our business with publishers."

Separation of allegiances, the "special advertising agent" representing the publisher and the "advertising agent" providing creative functions for the advertiser, was under evolution by the time ABC was formed, but not to the stage where either the advertiser or the publisher placed much trust in the agency.

Rowell's mistake, sharing circulation estimates.

Efforts to strengthen the distinction brought about advertising agency organizations in Chicago and New York. Seeing an opportunity of further cementing their relationship with advertisers and ensuring an important position in the industry's future, leaders of the two organizations played a vital part in the establishment of the Audit Bureau and the engineering of its approval.

In return, ABC gave the advertising agencies the opportunity to expand its services to advertisers—the creation of the media selection function with the availability of reliable media evaluation information.

Importance of Advertising Agencies

"All sorts of people claim to have been the father of the Audit Bureau of Circulations," Stanley Clague, the Clague Agency, once wrote a friend, "but I was its only mother." Certainly, Clague's service in conceptualizing and organizing qualified him as "chairman of the one-man committee on insurmountable obstacles." His counterpart in New York, Alfred W. Erickson, the Erickson Agency, quickly adopted Clague's program and effectively steered its acceptance among organizations in the East. Together, they raised the first $5,000 from advertising agency contacts towards ABC's organizing goal.

As the media selection became a more important function of agencies and as the utility of ABC data became more and more important to them, advertising agencies became more vocal in the operation of the Audit Bureau and the standards upon which these data were based.

American Association of Advertising Agencies

The understanding between members of the Eastern and Western Advertising Agents associations that developed during their cooperation in the founding of the Audit Bureau and the opening of branch offices in markets outside headquarters cities helped bring about the formation of the American Association of Advertising Agencies in 1917.

Despite advertiser diffidence, advertising agencies were in "complete support" of ABC publisher participation.

One of the 4A's first acts was to endorse the Audit Bureau and to ensure its "complete support" in encouraging publishers to participate in that organization. When differences between the Audit Bureau and the Association of National Advertisers threatened the future of the audited circulation movement in 1917, it was the 4A's first chairman, William H. Johns, George Batten Co., who successfully mediated the discussions between committees of directors from the two organizations.

To demonstrate their continuing support for the work of the Audit Bureau, the advertising agencies held their annual meetings concurrently with and at the same Chicago hotel as ABC's in 1920 and again in 1924. At the 1920 meeting, 4A's Chairman Harry Dwight Smith, Fuller & Smith, told ABC publishers, "We wanted to show ourselves to the ABC—to let you know that the agents are behind you 100 percent and nothing short of that. A year ago, our association abolished its circulation committee in the national and local councils because they said that they didn't need circulation committees—the Audit Bureau of Circulations did the work for them. The ABC has taken the 'guess' out of circulation, and we can now buy circulation intelligently. ABC has been a constructive force in advertising and the advertising agents are behind you to a man."

Agency criticism, counsel important to the development of standards and services.

The American Association of Advertising Agencies and its media and research committees over the years have prodded ABC when they felt actions were warranted, and freely provided counsel and support when they were requested. Frequently, the 4As has helped to guide and sponsor ABC clinics and media planner educational programs.

Institute of Canadian Advertising and
Canadian Media Directors Council

While Canadian advertising agency people had given substantial service to ABC individually and through advisory committees, it wasn't until 1956 that an advertising agency directorship was specifically designated for a Canadian agency representative. First Canadian agency director was Russell C. Ronalds, Ronalds Advertising Agency, Ltd., then immediate past chairman of the Institute of Canadian Advertising. Ronalds was succeeded in 1961 by C. Warren Reynolds, Ronalds-Reynolds Co. Reynolds, too, was an immediate past chairman of ICA and went on to be elected ABC board chairman in 1968 and 1969. Allan B. Yeates, Comcore/BBDO, Inc., is another ICA chairman who has served on the ABC board. Hugh F. Dow, MacLaren Advertising Ltd. and past president of the Canadian Media Directors Council, served on a number of ABC's advisory committees and was elected to its board in 1987.

Membership

The report of the 1915 ABC annual meeting shows a total of 50 advertising agency and associate advertising agency members. Difference between the two categories of agency membership was the amount of report service to which they subscribed. The "advertising agency" received reports on all publisher members. The "associate advertising agency," with limited or specialized accounts, required the reports on publishers in a single division or reports on a lesser number of publications. Initially, both had an equal voice in ABC affairs, but this was changed in 1916, giving the associate a one-quarter vote for each unit of reports it ordered.

Increasing importance of media selection function and value of reliable circulation data encourages growing participation of both large and small agencies.

Within the next ten years, the combined total had reached 180 advertising agencies, 165 in the United States and 15 in Canada. By this time, however, more and more associates were actually branch offices of full-service agencies, acquired through purchases and mergers and for whom ABC reports were required. The board recognized this in 1935, amending the category to include associate agencies and "duplicate service" offices of existing advertising agency members. The membership total dipped during the depression and Second World War years, returning to the 180 level in 1948.

In 1950, the breakdown of the advertising agency membership included 80 full report service companies and 105 associates and branch offices receiving ABC report services. That year the board eliminated the associate category, with a new dues schedule that incorporated service unit costs. Agency branch offices holding the same name as their parent company were stripped of member-ship, but the member was allowed to purchase report services for these offices.

Fearful that a sudden drop in numbers might send the wrong signal to publishers, the board followed a policy of continuing to count the branch offices in member-ship totals, despite the fact that

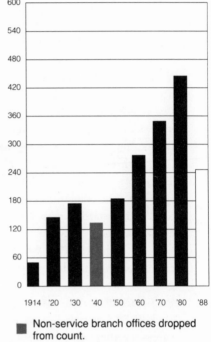

Advertising Agency Membership

■ Non-service branch offices dropped from count.

☐ Reflects new corporate agency membership category.

they did not actually hold membership and vote in ABC affairs. The totals continued to increase through 1985, when a total of 417 members and branch offices, 296 in the United States and 118 in Canada, were reported.

In that year, the board approved a new corporate membership policy for advertising agencies, whereby a single membership, with dues based on combined corporate space billings, covered all branch offices and subsidiaries. The membership total in 1986 dropped to 274, but the number of offices for which ABC report services were requested remained the same as the previous year.

A rash of mergers in the late 1980s has had a negative effect on ABC advertising agency membership totals, but much less a decrease in the number of separate agency offices requiring report services.

Board Representation

One important consideration attracted advertising agencies to support the organizing efforts of the Advertising Audit Association, and the resulting Audit Bureau of Circulations, rather than those of the Association of National Advertising Managers. This consideration was representation on the respective boards. ABC's original board granted two directorships to agency representatives; ANAM's organization proposed only one.

Agency representation remained at two through the board's 1926 expansion. In 1935 and again in 1953, advertisers relinquished a directorship to the advertising agency division, bringing board representation to three and then four. When the board was further expanded to 31 directors in 1956, two additional directorships were given to agency representatives, including one specifically reserved for Canadian members. With further expansion to 33 in 1969, a seventh agency directorship was added. Canadian advertising agency representation was further enhanced in 1987 when advertisers relinquished still another directorship, bringing that constituency's representation to two and overall agency total to eight.

Until 1941, ABC bylaws provided that the chairmanship was to be held only by an advertiser representative. That year the bylaws were changed to allow for the election of either an advertiser or an advertising agency director to this post. First from the agency division to be elected to head the board was Harold H. Kynett, Aitkin-Kynett Co., Inc., who served as chairman in 1951 and 1952.

Postal regulations leave much to the imagination •
Paid and free distribution fight sets long-term policy •
Competition creates bulk discussion • Frequent efforts to
involve ABC in research finally killed • When is a
subscription in arrears • Combination sales rules out of
Hollywood • Interpretation expands association rule
application • Fight over reporting advertising rates •
Request for renewal rates get a big "no" from most
publishers • Litigation brings waiver of damages and
member obligations standards, test of appeals procedure.

Most publishers took the December 1913 announcement of a proposed
"new circulation auditing movement" with less than enthusiasm. They
resented the intrusion of space buyers into what they considered their
business secrets. Actual circulation figures, if they were known at all,
were matters of proprietary interest and subject to varying degrees of
inflation before they were made public. The first law of business ethics
was to question the competitor's circulation integrity. "Circulation liar"
was a popular crosstown charge.

Not all publishers were so disposed. The industry trade press
claimed the new movement "to get out all of the facts about circulation
had considerable support among publishers." A publisher told a group of
Iowa dailies "the day of forced circulations is passing. We must see the
wisdom of a good solid paid subscription list. Only such circulation will
receive the consideration of those placing business. In the future, the
advertising rate will be based on the value, character, and stability of
circulation as determined through unvarnished facts. This new movement will add confidence in our figures and will surely bring about a
suspension in the need for publishers to sow seeds of suspicion on the
circulations of others."

Publisher support grew during the next few months. A start-up
goal of $100,000 was over-subscribed by $18,000 within three months.
All but about $3,000 represented pledges from various publishers. At the

organizational meeting of this new circulation auditing organization on May 20, 1914, were representatives of 338 newspapers, 27 magazines, 52 farm publications, and 55 business publications. Within a year, nearly 1,000 publishers had joined the organization that had become known as the Audit Bureau of Circulations.

ABC certainly owes its existence not only to the demanding needs of advertisers and advertising agencies, but also to the changing attitudes, acceptance, and cooperation of the far-sighted publishers who made it possible.

Standards

Part of the dilemma over adequate circulation facts stems from the lack of uniform standards. In the 1879 United States postal laws, Congress attempted to describe the acceptable paid and free components of publications' distribution in regulations on second and third class mail privileges. The problem was that the regulations didn't work. Vagueness in the language and some 35 years of no enforcement drained most meaning from them. Publishers governed themselves by the laws of competition and the needs of the moment, selecting those interpretations that benefitted themselves the most.

ABC's printed bylaws and rules have grown from 2-page sheet to over 70-page book.

Despite the ambiguities, ABC's initial standards were based directly on these postal laws. Those standards could be covered in less than two pages of type. The current book of bylaws and rules covers 70 pages. Most changes and additions had their bases in publisher competition. Others reflect changing attitudes of buyers or sellers, introduction of new technology, and the desire to address new needs.

Throughout ABC's history, each standard and subsequent evolution has been exposed to the combined influence of advertiser, advertising agency, and publisher member discussion.

Paid Versus Free

No subject has been debated more frequently, nor better reflects the influences of competitive bias, changing attitudes, and lack of decisive buyer leadership than the Audit Bureau's long-time paid publication membership standard.

While paid and free distribution publications were welcomed into membership during the Audit Bureau's first eight years, primary interest centered on correcting the vagueness of regulations relating to paid standards. Perhaps because they represented a very small part of the total ABC membership, little concern was given to rules covering free distribution publications. The resulting disparity in auditing quality would later prove to be a major issue in ABC affairs.

The first quarterly Publisher's Statements issued during the summer of 1914 were based on the postal requirement that a paid publication had to have a "legitimate list of subscribers." A legitimate list of subscribers was deemed to include "persons who have subscribed for the publication for a definite time, either by themselves or by another on their behalf, and have paid, or promised to pay, for it a substantial sum as compared with the advertised subscription price"; "news agents and newsboys purchasing copies for resale"; "purchasers of copies over the publisher's counter"; "receivers of bona fide gift copies, duly accepted, given for their benefit and not to promote the interest of the donor"; "other publishers to whom exchanges were mailed, one copy for another"; and "advertisers receiving one copy each in proof of insertion of their advertisements."

Mapes goes to court and proves even American Motherhood is not above the common practice of fudging on her paid circulation guarantees.

In practice, the Post Office Department permitted publishers to include copies sent to libraries and other public institutions, such as schools, in its legitimate list of subscribers, whether or not they were paid for. The law recognized "the right of publishers to extend good faith credit on subscriptions," but set a limit of one year for serving copies after the expiration of a subscription. It further specified that a legitimate list was not to include "subscriptions obtained at a reduction to the subscriber of more than 50 percent of the regular advertised annual subscription price" or pro rata thereof.

That these regulations were not enforced is exemplified by the 1912 court case brought by Emery Mapes, Cream of Wheat Co., against the Arthur H. Crist Co. and its magazine, *American Motherhood*. Mapes contracted for advertising based on a guaranteed paid circulation of 63,000 copies per issue plus the privilege to have that circulation audited if he so chose. He did, and he learned that only 27,428 recipients had paid for their 1912 subscriptions. In fact, some of the subscribers had paid nothing during the last nine years but were continued in "paid" totals out of an implied contract with the publisher because they had never returned copies. Mapes lost in a lower court judgment based on the custom of the advertising trade but won on an appeal. Unordered copies were considered as free in the higher court's judgment.

As the Audit Bureau began to remove the vagaries from its rules, the affected paid publications began to question the right of lesser-regulated free publications to share in ABC membership. And not the least of their concerns was that they saw free publications as potentially serious competition.

Mason Britton, McGraw-Hill Publishing Co., identified free distribution publication members as a target shortly after his election to the ABC board in 1918. While it was known that some of the publications he represented were in competition with free publications, his suggestions for improving the auditing standards for these publications were quite reasonable. For example, he requested that the board mandate a "verification of at least one-half of the free lists each year. As it is, the Bureau's inspectors have no way of telling whether what the publisher is claiming is in existence."

Some directors sympathized with Britton, but few desired to rock the boat of the yet new organization, and no board action was taken. In early 1920, a business publication member complained to the board that the lack of auditing standard equity between his paid publication and a competing free publication member was causing him to suffer financially. Again, the board took no supportive action.

Between Britton's efforts and those of Ernest R. Shaw, *Power Plant Engineering*, the issue heated up by the middle of 1921. Managing Director Stanley Clague called the board's attention to a "propaganda campaign looking toward the elimination from membership in the Bureau of publications with free distribution."

Britton led the drive to establish paid circulation membership standards.

**Split board sends
free distribution
issue to meeting.**

Since these publications were classified
separately and noted in their ABC reports, he felt
"there is no possibility of error on the part of the
careful space buyer as to the character of these
mediums." After an extended discussion of this
subject and a decided difference of opinion by the directors, the matter
was laid on the table for later discussion.

The advertising and publishing trade press took up the issue and
at the 1921 annual meeting several months later, the business publications passed a resolution to exclude publications with less than 50
percent paid circulation, except for export publications, catalogs, year-
books, and encyclopedias. The general session of the convention passed
a resolution calling on the board to poll the membership.

Four proposals were put to the members. Of the 911 responses,
371 voted for outright expulsion of free publications; 280 voted for
expulsion of some; 133 voted for retention if adequate verification was
provided; and 127 voted for no discrimination.

Not feeling it had a mandate, the board put a clear "yes" or "no"
proposition to the members. This poll produced a vote of 818 against
acceptance of applications from free distribution publications and 267 in
favor. (Of the 818 negative votes, 523 came from newspapers and 133
from business publications. Advertising agencies were almost equally
split on the issue, and advertisers favored retention by almost 2 to 1.)

The intensity of the issue was reflected in the April 1922 vote of
the board. The motion to eliminate free distribution publications from
membership came to a tie and was resolved with the "yes" vote of
Chairman Orlando C. Harn, National Lead Co. The proposed bylaw
change gave existing free distribution members until January 1924 to
qualify as paid or be automatically eliminated from the membership.
The change in the membership eligibility bylaw was confirmed by the
board at its June meeting and passed on to the annual meeting for
review by the members.

In divisional meetings, advertisers, advertising agencies, and
magazines lined up against eliminating free publications; business
publications, newspapers, and farm publications favored the action.

Opposing the action, E.I. Mitchell, Mitchell-Faust Advertising Co.,
warned the general assembly that a vote in favor of the change was
tantamount to willing the creation of "another bureau. Anything you
do today will not stop the free circulation publication. The advertising

agencies believe we ought to have that service of the auditing of free circulation publications."

His position was supported by Stanley R. Latshaw, Butterick Publishing Co., who criticized the change as overkill. Addressing the prevailing majority mood of members (and the trade press) that the efforts of free publications "are iniquitous," he claimed theirs "have been mighty works, because 28 such publications have aroused the desire for complete annihilation on the part of 1,300 publishers." He differed with Mitchell on a possibility of a second audit bureau, saying, "I think the danger is not one that we need to regard with terror."

Louis Wiley, *New York Times*, and C. Lynn Sumner, International Correspondence Schools, spoke in favor of the change. Both spoke to the belief that paid circulation was the measure of reader interest and the conviction that verification standards governing free distribution were seriously lacking.

The question of ratifying the board's proposed change in the bylaws—that no publications should be retained in membership in the Audit Bureau unless it was a publication with paid circulation in accordance with the ABC rules—was put to a vote of the members and approved 772-1/4 to 107-1/4.

ABC's paid circulation membership eligibility standard became a fact and existing free distribution members were given until January 1924 to meet the standard or be excluded. Advertisers and advertising agencies were seemingly unconcerned with the effects of the action until after it was accomplished. And, in later years, some of those who so fiercely fought for the elimination of free distribution publications, newspapers, and business publications, have been called on to reassess their views in the light of changing conditions and attitudes. More on these paid-free discussions in the following chapters.

Latshaw saw the drive as overkill.

Bulk Sales

Another issue that has caused considerable member debate, especially among newspapers and farm publications, arose out of the original standards that permitted copies purchased "by another" on the recipient's behalf to be credited as paid circulation. Before 1914 publishers had refined programs for the sale of copies and subscriptions in quantities. Many of these bulk sales were well within the intent of the rules. For many more, the question of whether such programs were used to "promote the interest of the donor" was a matter of the auditor's judgment. Early ABC audits revealed a substantial number of quantity sales reported solely to enhance paid circulation totals and where the donor was actually the publication itself.

Quantity sales were not detailed in the paid circulation breakdowns. By early 1915, space buyers questioned the composition of these totals and "numerous advertisers" called for a means to specifically identify the amount of circulation sold in quantities. The ABC board responded with a ruling that quantity sales were to be separated from other paid. Both newspapers and periodicals were to report other paid by detail, a total "net paid (excluding bulk)," "total bulk," and "total paid (including bulk)." The ruling provided that all bulk sales shall be explained "in detail in the body of the ABC report."

The following year, publisher members suggested that all bulk sales were not equal in their value to advertisers. As a result of their petition and backed by space buyers, the board ruled that "subscriptions paid for by corporations, institutions or individuals for their employees, subsidiary companies or branch offices" could be excluded from the bulk figure and reported in the paid breakdown as "Mail Subscriptions (Special)." The ruling was clarified in 1919. Thereafter, mail subscriptions (special) sent to the company as a bulk shipment for distribution by the purchaser were to be shown as "Term Subscriptions in Bulk." Single copy sales in quantities were to be shown as "Single Issue Sales in Bulk." Both of the new categories were removed from the bulk total and added to the detail of the paid paragraph.

The years following World War I were highly competitive ones for publishers. With larger budgets to spend, advertisers and advertising agencies openly encouraged these battles with their interest in buying "box car" numbers. The emerging medium of radio and the broad audience potential of "networking" posed still another competitive force. One of the quickest ways to increase circulation was through quantity sales, and publishers took the meaning of bulk sales to carry out a variety of excesses.

The problem had become so serious in 1925 that both space buyers and publishers used the ABC annual meeting to call for new and more restrictive bulk sales rules. After months of discussion and work in crafting a new rule, the board's recommendations were presented to members the following year.

Advertisers and advertising agencies insisted that all bulk sales "be eliminated from paid circulation and shown as a separate total, but not added in to make a new total." Farm publication members voted to exclude quantity sales from paid and report these under unpaid. Magazines unanimously asked the board to "retain the rules regarding bulk sales as they currently exist." Business publications recommended that the rules be left alone except to suggest that they be relieved of the need to segregate bulk sales within geographical breakdowns. Newspaper members were so widely divided on the issue that they didn't even bring it to a vote.

Bulk issue bounces between board and advisory committees.

Faced with a dilemma, the members took the only action practical. After agreeing that members had legitimate reasons for looking at bulk sales differently and that the existing single standard might not apply with equal effectiveness for each of the publication categories, they sent the board's recommendation back to committee for more study. Each division was asked to supply its own advisory committee to counsel the board on the bulk sales issue.

Deprived of the strength of Managing Director Stanley Clague, who died the following January, the board found it difficult to address the problem. Only the magazine division supplied an advisory committee. After hearing this committee reaffirm the position of the division's 1926 annual meeting vote and entertaining the views of individual buyer and publisher members, the directors unanimously voted to "continue to show bulk sales in the paid circulation column" and the "matter of breaking down and analyzing bulk sales be referred to the board committee appointed to consider the rearrangement of information in the Audit Bureau's reports."

In 1930, the board essentially put a cap on the amount of bulk sales a publication member could have by defining a paid circulation publication to be one with at least 50 percent of its total distribution qualifying as paid under ABC rules and of which the total paid plus bulk sales plus advertisers' copies (one only to each advertiser and advertising agency) and correspondents' copies equals or exceeds 70 percent of total distribution.

Resolution leaves each division to set bulk status.

Newspapers, backed by advertisers, petitioned the board in 1935 to remove all "figures except for individual paid from reports for all ABC publications" and to make the definition of paid the same for all members. While few members of the board sympathized with the petition, it did have the affect of setting off another round of bulk sales rule reviews.

Four rule changes for all member publications, becoming effective in 1941, resulted from these studies: (1) Copies or subscriptions sold in quantities of 11 or more and used to promote the professional or business interests of the purchaser were designated as bulk sales; (2) Copies or subscriptions involved in a bulk sale induced or influenced by extraneous considerations (premiums, contests, charitable contributions, special publicity, advertisement, etc.) were designated as unpaid; (3) Limitation on the size of an individual subscription or single issue sale for qualification as bulk; and (4) The total number of copies and subscriptions sold in bulk could not exceed the total of those qualified as paid.

It was in the late 1920s that members in each publisher division accepted differing views concerning bulk sales. The course was set for each division to find its own solution, which was frequently based on the self-interest of the majority of publishers but occasionally tempered by advertiser and advertising agency guidance.

Magazines and business publications have continued bulk sales in paid circulation. Newspapers and farm publications report bulk sales separate of paid and unpaid. The review of how these members sought to find answers to this long-standing and sometimes acrimonious issue is covered in the following chapters.

Readership, Audience Research

With interest heightened by a need to meet first radio and then broadcast listening claims, print media readership and audience research have been proposed both as a service to be considered by the Audit Bureau and a successor to ABC-audited circulation data. The former has been considered frequently; the latter has not happened.

John P. Cunningham, Cunningham and Walsh, Inc. and chairman of the American Association of Advertising Agencies, told the 1952 meeting of ABC members, "Being in the creative end of the advertising business, I live in a world of half-fancy—and I advise the ABC to stay out of it. I note that in the talks here over the last few years, suggestions have been made for the ABC to get into new research fields of audience measurement in terms of audience characteristics, or multiple readership. I say these things are not in the world of fact. They are in my world of fancy, and the ABC should keep strictly out of this world. Its strength lies in its absolute adherence over the years to reporting things that can be counted, things that can be audited."

Buyers vacillate on Audit Bureau's role in making, verifying readership studies.

But buyers have not always been so disposed. In 1938, an industrial advertiser member said, "We feel that the bureau would render a distinct service to its members by washing out all the arbitrary definitions of paid and non-paid circulations and doing a complete job of auditing readers." The advertiser division that year suggested "that some study be made of what is being done in the field of auditing reader interest, with a view toward possibly recommending that it be undertaken by the Audit Bureau of Circulations." While advertisers and the Association of National Advertisers were encouraging this action, the American Association of Advertising Agencies adopted a resolution calling on ABC to make no effort to audit readership.

At the 1942 annual meeting, Gordon E. Cole, Cannon Mills, Inc. and chairman of the Association of National Advertisers, urged the Audit Bureau to "take over readership surveys." A committee under the leadership of Ralph Starr Butler, General Foods Corp., conducted a study and, in January 1943, issued a report unanimously approved by the board. The report said, "We feel that such readership studies are not the proper function of the Audit Bureau of Circulations and that the bureau cannot undertake such supervision without endangering its real function, which is to provide a standardized yardstick for measuring paid circulation as an auditable measure of reader interest and as a basis for fixing advertising rates." It went on to suggest that "steps should be taken by some representative body of advertisers, agencies, and media to develop a survey procedure which may be regarded as standard and uniform," other than ABC.

During 1948 and 1949, a board committee considered readership in connection with a proposed revision in ABC's publicity standards. The revision was not adopted, but the committee recommended and the board adopted, in September 1949, the following statement as a guide: "Because readership claims by bureau members deal always in figures over and beyond the net paid circulation as issued by the bureau in Audit Reports, the board believes the bureau has an interest in these readership claims since the quoting of unaudited figures creates confusion in the minds of buyers."

At its June 1961 meeting, the board's policy committee considered a suggestion from Max Banzhaf, Armstrong Cork Co., that ABC audit readership as well as circulation. The board reaffirmed its position that the auditing of readership falls outside the intent of the Audit Bureau.

But that didn't impress Dr. E.L. Deckinger, Grey Advertising, Inc. The following year, he urged members "to examine the desirability for an ABC-audited survey giving total audience figures of a publication's readership rather than just its audited paid circulation." His views were countered early in 1963 by S. Arthur Dembner, *Newsweek*, who told ABC magazine members that "the Audit Bureau has no business in the mystical world of audience research." While Deckinger's proposal had been debated vigorously over the months since its appearance, the magazines overwhelmingly agreed with Dembner in a divisional meeting vote.

Despite pressure, magazine members agree ABC "has no business in the mystical world of audience research."

The issue surfaced again a year later during two special board studies—on the utilization of ABC data in computers and on the adequacy of ABC services to meet the needs of buyers. According to George C. Dibert, J. Walter Thompson Co., the studies, which were conducted separately, both reached a common question, "Can the Audit Bureau render service to its members by reporting and auditing information on member publications' audiences?"

In an advisory report to the computer study committee, Marty Herbst, Doherty, Clifford, Steers & Shenfield, Inc., suggested that ABC consider "measuring circulation as a total concept. Generally speaking, any measurement of an audience to a medium is circulation—to differentiate it from a measurement of the perceptive audience to specific advertising. The ABC stand on this matter could be that it is organized to audit all measures of circulation. In this way the organization positions itself in a vital and constructive role in the future as opposed to a trend of deleterious attrition—due to the straight jacket concept of the current definition of circulation."

Arthur H. Walsh, American Telephone & Telegraph Co., supported this idea. "To the average advertiser I am sure the ABC stands in the same relationship as a wife of many years to a husband. She is probably cherished in a casual sort of way and, therefore, pretty much taken for granted. If she didn't exist, she would probably have to be invented. We need (and the agencies want it too because clients are demanding it) demographic data. Some media directors describe what we are after in the phrase 'total audience concept.' If ABC could set up to audit demographic data as outlined in a standard established by the 4As for magazines and newspapers, it would be performing a service of very great importance to advertisers. In fact this service will increase in value each year as space costs rise and as advertisers become more and more surly in wanting to know what they are getting for their money."

Walsh: Buyers demand that ABC provide demographic data.

Some magazines were also interested in seeing ABC become involved in the standardization and verification, but not the data gathering, of publication research. Their support was mainly a defensive gesture.

As S.O. Shapiro, *Look Magazine*, put it, "The basic concept of ABC is to protect the advertising industry from the abuses from inaccurate or dishonest measurements of media reach. Advertisers want precise demographic material as to the age, sex, purchasing habits, and so on of the readers of magazines and the viewers and listeners of broadcast. A great deal of this type of material has been provided by individual publications and stations. Much of this information is suspect. The industry needs assurance that the data which it uses to measure the reach are arrived at impartially.

48

Independent research companies are not able to
audit their own research. It is becoming apparent
that only the ABC is in a position to do the auditing
on a large and authoritative scale. I do not antici-
pate that ABC will become a research organization,

**Cooperates in
magazine, business
publication studies.**

but confine its activities to auditing the work of major research companies. Its efforts would not be confined solely to magazines and newspapers, but also encompass the research efforts of television and radio,
where data are especially suspect."

Despite the interest of some publishers, most opposed. At the 1963
annual meeting, Wendell Forbes, *Life Magazine*, noted, "This area of
research is still rather nebulous and there is no one right way of doing it.
For ABC to sanction standards is to imply that they would do it the right
way, and there is no concert of opinion on that particular subject. If the
ABC got into this think of approving research, it would form just one
more organization which we need like we need a hole in the head. It
would by my recommendation that we postpone any serious thought of
ABC getting into auditing audience research." By vote, the magazine
members overwhelmingly agreed with Forbes' position.

As the discussions continued, it became apparent that the Audit
Bureau's existing charter did not authorize the board to go beyond the
auditing and reporting of circulation data. This was corrected at the
1964 meeting when members approved a change in the Audit Bureau's
charter, broadening the circulation data base to additionally include "or
other data" reported by a member.

In late 1964, *Look Magazine*, *McCall's*, *Reader's Digest*, *Redbook*,
and the *Saturday Evening Post* requested ABC's cooperation in that
year's Politz Magazine Study. The effort only involved special breakdowns and verifications of paid and unpaid circulation of the member
magazines. The following spring, ABC agreed to cooperate with Basford,
Inc., the Industrial Advertising Research Institute, and several business
publication members in experimental research designed to determine the
practicality and auditability of measuring, verifying, and reporting pass-
along exposure.

A year later, the board authorized management to proceed with
plans to verify "other data" of requesting business publication members
on an experimental basis. With the verification of a subscriber identification program on *Fortune Magazine*, the experimental service was
opened to magazines and farm publications.

Except for a brief period in the early 1970s when ABC was involved in the exploration of a Newspaper Audience Research Data Bank project, the organization's cooperation in research efforts has been limited to less than 30 studies. Most have been at the request of business publication members, and none have involved the Audit Bureau in the actual data gathering work of survey-based research.

S.O. Shapiro explains the intricacies of the magazine politics to William Weilbacher, Sid Bernstein, Harry Schroeter, and Fred Wittner.

The question of whether ABC should involve itself more deeply in areas of readership and audience research has been close to the surface ever since magazines first introduced, and buyers lauded, such studies. In the early 1980s, pressure for and opposition to an extension of such a service came from newspapers.

At the 1984 meeting of members, Allen H. Neuharth, Gannett Co., Inc., said, "Advertisers need much more than ABC's verified circulation numbers." He stressed the need for ABC to supplement its raw numbers with demographic information, developed through research, on newspaper audiences. In the next speech on the program, Katharine Graham, Washington, D.C., *Post*, agreed that proprietary audience research was important to newspapers, but she voiced the firm conviction that it was not a proper area of concern for the Audit Bureau.

Since August 1982, a special all-industry task force had been studying ways to make ABC's newspaper services more valuable to the buyers and sellers of advertising. One of its agenda items was "the

possible addition of audience information, based on
the results of proprietary research studies, to the
Audit Bureau's services."

*Publishers share
smiles, despite
differences over
ABC's research
role: Edward
Estlow, Allen
Neuharth, David
Kruidenier, and
Katharine Graham.*

After considerable discussion with allied
organizations, surveys of newspaper opinions, and
warnings from buyer members, the task force moved
its discussions from proprietary research to the
potential of census-based demographics.

In a policy statement adopted by the board in
November 1984, the directors strongly reaffirmed
the Audit Bureau's 1943 position. The policy
statement pointed out that there "are a number of viable media research
companies, as well as the Advertising Research Foundation, who appear
to be able to handle industry needs" in the area of readership and
audience research.

Because more expert services already existed, the board informed
the members that:

"ABC does not intend to participate in the establishment of
standards for survey-based audience research. ABC does not intend to
conduct survey-based audience research. ABC will continue to consider
member and industry requests to provide services to audit the auditable
aspects of survey-based research, subject to standards and conditions
ABC may itself impose. ABC intends to continue to expand the types
and quantities of demographic information included in its reports that
may be obtained from generally accepted industry sources."

Arrears

At its inception, the Audit Bureau adopted U.S. postal regulations as the basis for its standards. Depending upon how one read the rules for second class privileges, a publisher was allowed to serve subscriptions up to one year beyond "expiration of the contract term" or for an undetermined term in excess of the one year. Canadian postal regulations placed no restriction on the serving of copies in arrears and still qualifying as paid under second class mail. While publishers debated the law and the post office departments of each country made no efforts to clarify this provision, ABC publishers took their pick and reported their circulations accordingly.

Bramble: Six months plenty of time to secure a renewal.

The first firm ruling came in 1916 when the ABC board voted to permit subscribers retained on active subscription lists up to one year after expiration to be included as paid circulation. This "grace" period was intended as "a reasonable period in which a publisher could solicit and obtain a reorder."

Complaints were registered by Canadian publishers, who pointed out that their postal regulations permitted the service of arrears copies "in perpetuity, if the publisher so desires." The board granted Canadian publishers an exception to the one-year provision but asked the Canadian advisory committee to review the issue. In 1918, B.H. Bramble, Canadian Chewing Gum Co. and chairman of the committee, advised the board that Canadian advertising buyers "and most publishers" opposed the inclusion of arrears over one year in paid circulation and "are of the opinion that half that time is a great plenty to secure an individual's renewal." He said there was "much sentiment among advertisers that since arrears actually represent copies for which no money had been paid, their inclusion in paid totals is seriously questioned." The annual meeting resolved and the board agreed that all publishers must abide by the one-year arrearage provision.

A year later, members petitioned for a further reduction to six months. Recognizing wartime shortages of newsprint and periodical paper and the need for conserving these supplies, the board appealed to the U.S. Post Office Department to specifically change its rules to a six-month limit. In June 1919, ABC adopted the six-month standard. To protect its members from nonmembers reporting on the still-flexible postal regulations, ABC increased efforts to get the post office to follow suit. While postal regulations allowed publishers to report credit subscriptions as paid, ABC allowed "only up to three months" for the recipient to pay or be reported as unpaid.

Even before these ABC rules became effective in June 1920, a board committee was already suggesting that "the Bureau should look forward to the day when subscriptions in arrears would be ineligible as paid. Hope is being voiced that present ABC rules (and those of the government) will be revised to three months."

The six-month arrearage provision continued without issue until the 1928 annual meeting. Members voted by a substantial majority at that meeting to reduce the period during which copies could be served beyond expiration, and still reported as paid circulation, from six months to three. The board voted to change the provision to three months effective January 1930.

In 1931, business publication members appealed to the board for a one-year moratorium on the arrearage rule, citing the effects of depressed economic conditions. A number of newspapers asked that they also be included in the moratorium, but the members voted against this at the annual meeting that year. The next year, business publications asked for a one-year extension on the moratorium. Twenty-nine Canadian newspapers petitioned the board to ask that

Depression leads to relaxation of arrears period.

they be covered by the moratorium. The Canadian advisory committee told the board that this appeal did not represent the will of the majority. In January 1933, the board approved a three-month extension on arrears for all member publications, returning, in essence, to the six-month provision for the duration of the depression. This moratorium ended in December 1936.

Two years later, business publications, feeling the pressure of free distribution competition, asked to be relieved of the three-month arrearage provision but were opposed by both the advertiser and advertising agency divisions.

A request for an exception to the arrearage rule came from a different source in 1939. The Association of Canadian Advertisers was trying to encourage Canadian weekly newspapers to provide audited circulation data. It was particularly interested in a group being organized called the Class A Weeklies. Harry Rimmer, Canadian General Electric Co., informed the board that most of these Class A members did not follow the Audit Bureau's rule on serving arrears. He requested that these weeklies be offered an exception, permitting them to carry arrears up to one year, "until such time as they can get their records in order." A three-year exception was granted.

Rimmer sought exception for Canadian weekly newspapers.

The practice of many publishers of serving arrears out of returns and back copy files was halted in 1940 when the board ruled that copies supplied must be current and distributed at the same time as other copies of each issue. The board approved a 1942 request from business and farm publications for an exception to the three-month rule. Because of wartime conditions, the rule was extended for a period of one year, giving these publishers the three months plus three months for serving arrears and counting them as paid circulation.

During the late 1950s, ABC was involved in an intensive discussion of dwindling business publication membership. Negative industry relations stemmed largely around the Audit Bureau's paid circulation eligibility standard. To offset publicity claiming that ABC was already reporting unpaid arrears as paid circulation, the board's business publication committee recommended in 1960 that the terminology be changed to "subscriptions serviced pending renewal." The suggestion was dropped when the board adopted the paid and free business publication report form. A similar request was made in 1980 but was also dropped when the board approved a plan to more closely align ABC and Business Publication Audit standards.

Over the years, advertising buyers generally expressed little concern over arrears. By the late 1970s, however, some buyers were questioning the possible use of arrears by some publishers to meet circulation guarantees or advertising rate bases.

Arrears become "post expiration copies in paid."

Thomas J. Glynn, Campbell-Ewald Co., wrote the board in 1978 asking for a review of the rules that permit "gracing" for a period of up to three months after magazine expirations with such copies being reported as paid circulation. The board's magazine committee reported that arrears over all for ABC magazine members amounted to 1.4 percent and 1.2 percent of total circulation during the two previous Publisher's Statement periods. It did not feel the problem was such that a revision of the rules was required. The board agreed.

An industry newsletter, *The Gallagher Report*, stimulated buyer interest in arrears in the early 1980s when it introduced a continuing study of magazines showing rate base or guarantee, total paid circulation excluding arrears, and total arrears. The use of arrears became a questionable practice. Many buyers did not understand the time required to process a renewal through a magazine's recordkeeping system. Some buyers suspected magazines of manipulating arrears to meet rate bases.

To offset the negative connotation and confusion over the term "arrears," the board approved the terminology change in 1984 to "post expiration copies included in paid circulation" for use in ABC magazine and farm publication reports. The same change in terminology was adopted by business publications in 1988. Newspapers continue to use the "arrears" term in their reports.

Combination Sales

When the Audit Bureau adopted U.S. Postal Rules and Regulations as its standards in 1914, it agreed to the principle that when two or more publications were sold in combination, if at least 50 percent of the advertised price of each was paid for by the subscriber and met the arrearage rule, they would qualify as paid circulation. The practice was well-entrenched when ABC initially ruled that "to deliver two publications for the price of one; or where the subsidiary publication had a lesser price, to sell the combination at the price of the highest valued publications" met its standards.

No active protest on the part of either publishers or advertisers to this practice of publishers came up until a 1921 competitive situation arose in Hollywood, California. F.W. Kellogg, *Los Angeles Express*, started local daily newspapers in the suburbs of Alhambra, Glendale, Pasadena, Monrovia, San Pedro, and Venice, each with the same single copy and subscription price as the *Express*. He set up a clubbing arrangement for each, initially involving the *Express*.

"Clubbing" offers involved the sale of one publication at full price and the combined distribution of another with no higher price without additional cost to the purchaser. Variations on this practice permitted publishers to offer "clubs," or combinations, of publications at severely reduced prices—in many cases making "five magazines for the price of three" type offers.

When Kellogg started the *Hollywood News* with his usual clubbing arrangement with the *Express*, he ran up against Harlen G. Palmer, *Hollywood Citizen*, a paper long established as a weekly but recently converted to a daily. In 1923, Palmer asked the board to review the practice, pointing out that "the Bureau is crediting as paid copies for which no money has been paid, and encouraging the wasteful double exchange, whereby several publishers arrange to increase each other's circulation by distributing, without additional charge to the customer, copies of each other's publications."

In answer to Palmer's complaint, the board resolved "that as both the *Los Angeles Express* and the local newspapers sold in combination with this publication comply with the fundamental requirement of the Bureau, at least 50 percent of the advertised price of each publication being paid by the recipient, these publications conform to the rules of the Bureau, and the circulation of each publication shall be counted in net paid totals."

Palmer then took his case to the California Newspaper Circulation Managers Association and the daily division of the Southern California Editorial Association. The latter passed a resolution in 1925 stating, "The practice of the Audit Bureau of Circulations in certifying as paid the circulation of newspapers for which the recipient pays nothing is inimical to the maintenance of the highest standards of the Bureau and destructive of the policies to promote the best interests of the advertiser." It went on to request the board to amend the rules and practices so that "the circulation of newspapers given with other papers without additional charge will not be certified as paid."

Participants in many a newspaper debate, E. Roy Hatton and Harlen Palmer.

The International Newspaper Circulation Managers Association, at their meeting that summer, passed the resolution, "that where two newspapers are distributed together, if the circulation of each is to be certified as paid, the price charged for the combination shall be greater than the price at which either may be purchased separately." At this meeting, ABC Managing Director Stanley Clague brought representatives of the two Hollywood newspapers together. He cautioned them that further tinkering with this issue would have ramifications in clubbing or combination sales rules "across the board of the Bureau's publisher membership." Fearing that further action could lead to the disruption of the existing clubbing programs of magazines, farm publications, business publications, and other newspapers, the two Hollywood newspapers volunteered to settle their differences on the basis of the resolution proposed by the ICMA.

Back in Hollywood, Kellogg raised the rates of his newspapers, but Palmer recanted on his representative's earlier agreement. Palmer came to the ABC annual meeting that fall determined to have the rules changed, not "out of local competition, but as a matter of principle. Ask yourself if we are maintaining a standard of which we are proud?"

Palmer recommended and, after lengthy discussion, the division voted for the resolution "that where two daily or Sunday newspapers are distributed together, if the circulation of each is to be certified as paid, the price charged for the combination shall be greater than the price which either may be purchased separately."

At the general session the following day, Clague argued that any rule change that was adopted by one publisher membership division could not differ from fundamental rules applying to all divisions. Members pointed out that while Clague's desire for uniformity was well meaning, nothing in the bylaws prevented separate rules for the different divisions. After being assured that the resolution applied only to newspapers, the members adopted—rather than "merely approving the principle, so that we can return to our home communities knowing that Mr. Clague or the esteemed directors will not alter the wishes of the newspaper members"—the resolution and recommended "quick action" by the board's executive committee.

In February 1926, the board unanimously passed the following newspaper rule:

"Where two or more daily or Sunday newspapers are distributed together, if the circulation of either is to be certified as paid, the price charged for the combination shall be, in the case of single copies of dailies, the highest advertised price of the highest priced paper in the group, plus not less than one cent for each of the additional papers.

"In the case of single copies of Sunday papers the price charged shall be the highest advertised price of the highest priced paper, plus not less than 20 percent of the price of each of the other papers.

"For carrier subscriptions, the price charged shall be the highest advertised price of the highest priced paper for such subscriptions, either in the city of publication or outside of it, plus not less than 10 percent of the advertised price of each of the other papers; for mail subscriptions, the price charged shall be the highest advertised price of the highest priced publication in the respective territories served, plus not less than 10 percent of the advertised price of the other papers."

Combination sales conflict premiered in Hollywood.

Based upon newspaper practice established long before ABC came along, clubbing offers referred to combinations with "outside" publications. In fact, the word "outside" appeared in paragraphs of ABC newspaper reports in which combination sales totals were shown and

explained. This led publishers, the board, and management to a continu-
ation of the policy of excluding combinations involving newspapers
(morning, evening, and Sunday, for example) under the same ownership
from provisions of the rule. This interpretation changed over the years,
but "outside" was not changed to "other" in ABC reports until 1940,
based on a board ruling on an appeal of a management decision by the
owner of the Phoenix, Arizona, *Republic* and *Gazette*.

The wording of the first rule on combination sales was worked out
by a joint newspaper divisional committee and a special committee of the
board. The effective date for the new rule was set as October 1, 1926.

In mid-1926, J.M. Schmid, *Indianapolis News* and chairman of the
ICMA's ABC liaison committee, wrote the board requesting that periodicals that were part of clubbing offers be required to follow standards
similar to the newspapers. "Many newspapers,
Magazine clubbing which do not club with either magazines or farm
offers criticized by papers, are facing competition with other newspa-
newspapers. pers in their respective fields," Schmid wrote, "which
quote ridiculously low clubbing offers, and are under
no obligation to quote the rate at which the club was bought. If these
magazines or farm papers were also required to publish in their ABC
statements the price they receive and the number of subscriptions
secured, it will make at least some of them hesitate before quoting rates
which may be termed at less than nominal, or almost be classed as free."

The board considered Schmid's proposal and, before the end of
1926, the periodical rule was changed to pick up part of the new newspaper standard, adding that "the price for such combination shall be the
price of the highest priced publication, plus not less than 10 percent of
the combined regular subscription prices of the other publications in the
combination, provided that the price shall in no case be less than 50
percent of the combined regular subscription prices." This became
effective as of July 1, 1927.

At the 1928 annual meeting, members approved a magazine
recommendation that the 10 percent be raised to 20 percent for all
publications as a means of controlling "one or two irresponsible agencies
who are putting out a few clubs that are highly objectionable and,
thereby, causing criticisms of the clubbing operations in general." The
members also adopted a magazine recommendation "that the number of
publications offered in combination sales should not exceed six periodicals and one newspaper." Both were approved by the board the following

year. Before the end of 1929, the board amended the latter rule to provide that a limitation of seven publications in a combination offer should exist, whether or not a newspaper was involved.

While most members were in favor of the limitation in principle, few refused to accept subscriptions from agencies that promoted more than seven publications in their offers. Publishers increasingly flaunted the spirit, if not actual disregard, for the rule as economic conditions in the United States and Canada worsened. In fact, publishers and subscription agencies began merging combination and premium plans, citing a "gray area" in the Audit Bureau's standards.

This gray area, along with a concern over what prices were to be considered in the "not less than 20 percent" provision, were clarified in rules amendments adopted by the board in 1932. In writing the new rules, the directors eliminated the embarrassment of many publishers who were violating the combination rule by simply dropping the seven publication limitation.

A number of embarrassing situations arose out of these rules. For example, in 1933, the Manchester, New Hampshire, *Union-Leader* advertised what they called their "Twentieth Annual Bargain Day Offer," in which the newspaper was offered at regular rates in combination with some 30 magazines and farm publications offered at reduced rates. Complicating the offer was the fact that the *Union-Leader*, unaware of the complications, gave each new subscriber a free copy of the 15-cent *Old Farmers' Almanac* as a gesture of goodwill. The board ruled that the newspaper and all 30 publications, including those that disavowed the practice in their advertising promotions, had to report the circulation produced as "sold with a free premium." Several directors, whose publications were included among the 30, were embarrassed. Others threatened to sue ABC and the newspaper or discontinue any further contact with the subscription agency that handled the promotion. Other situations, conditions not authorized by publishers included in the combinations, produced numerous surprises and subsequent requests for board exceptions.

A number of embarrassing situations arise out of new combination rules.

In 1930, F.R. Campbell, Aberdeen, South Dakota, *American and News*, asked ABC, "Are we permitted to offer mail subscribers an opportunity to send magazines in connection with our clubbing offers to a different address other than the subscriber's own?"

Managing Director O.C. Harn answered, "All publications in a specific clubbing offer must be sent to the same address." Some 36 newspapers, which were unlucky enough to query the ABC staff on this subject, were all given Harn's interpretation.

Predicts "storm of protest from magazines" if new rule is approved.

Without clear instructions, ABC field auditors were not uniform in their application of the requirements.

Basil Church, Whitlock and Co., visited ABC headquarters in 1933 on behalf of his client, *Pittsburgh Post-Gazette*. Because the auditors over the previous four annual audits treated a newspaper-sponsored combination gift subscription plan differently, the client was becoming frustrated and needed a consistent application. Magazines, angered over the loss of gift subscription business, one of the primary uses of the combination sales efforts, questioned Harn's decision.

When the opposition reached the "bothersome level," Harn suggested that the board amend the combination sales rule to back up his interpretation. Fred Stone, *Parents' Magazine*, wrote Harn in 1935, "Your 'bothersome level' is nothing compared with the storm of protest this will stir from all of your magazine members once it is generally known. I can't see any useful purpose that the amendment would serve except that it would restrict gift subscriptions, and I am sure that the whole magazine division is ready to fight to a finish on any attack on gift subscriptions. If your practice has been to advise members that combination subscriptions must all be to one address, I am sure that the magazine circulation managers have not been aware of it, nor have most of your own auditors. In fact, the *Hanson-Bennett Magazine Guide* clearly states, as it has for many years, 'Magazines in units and clubs may be sent to different addresses except where otherwise stated.' Your proposition is quite revolutionary."

The issue did come before the board. Harn's interpretation was unanimously "recanted," and management was instructed to write all publishers previously notified otherwise of the board's policy. The board further instructed Harn to institute a "new and improved method of communicating and instructing" the ABC field auditors on the application of the Audit Bureau's standards.

Trade press publicity in 1934 and 1935, relating to questionable combination sales programs used by several subscription agencies, prompted a suggestion from the American Association of Advertising Agencies that ABC tighten and clarify these rules.

Magazines using the questionable agencies relied heavily on the listing "Subscriptions received from intermediary, unable to determine whether sold in combination or not" when reporting channels of subscription sales. The AAAA media committee asked that this listing be eliminated. "It is our feeling that the publisher should be able to determine this fact." They also requested that the channels listing "Known combination sales" provide for a breakdown by magazine combinations and newspaper combinations. "Since individual space buyers place a different interpretation on the value of combination sales, it would be advisable to show this in greater detail," they said.

Magazines opposed the breakdown, contending that it would expose to competitors their subscription promotion policies. They agreed to eliminate the "unable to determine" listing and clarifying language in an amended rule. The "plus not less than" percentage was raised from 20 to 30 percent, and the following paragraph was added to the rule: "In a combination offer the saving effected through the acceptance thereof may be expressed in monetary terms or percentage. In case of an offer of combination of publications at a total price, there shall be no statement indicating that the saving is not spread over the various publications in the combination."

In 1940, a publisher offered two of his business publications in a single sales promotion, both at 50 percent price reductions. When the field auditor sought to eliminate these from paid circulation totals for failing to meet the combination sale rule, the publisher appealed to the board. His sales, he said, were not in combination but "synchronous" sales. After review by the board's circulation rules and methods committee, the directors ruled in favor of the publisher.

The board was faced with another aspect of this in 1949. The directors were asked, "If a publisher or a subscription agency make offers to mail subscribers listing a number of publications, each at a reduced price, with no provision that it is necessary to order more than one publication to obtain the benefit of the reduced prices, and two or more publications are ordered, should the subscriptions be reported as reduced price subscriptions and not be required to qualify under the combination sales rule?" As with the "synchronous" sales, if this plan were acceptable, two or more publications could be sold together for an amount that would be less than required under the combination sales rule.

"Synchronous" sales ruled not combinations.

The combination rule was reviewed and rewritten extensively. In the amendments adopted in 1950, the board ruled that "such sales must be judged in accordance with the rule covering 'Subscriptions to Publications Sold in Combination.'" The alternative, the board said, was for the publisher to report these in the unpaid total.

A new situation arose in 1974 that called for, at least for newspapers, a clarification in the rules. In April, the *San Antonio Sunday Express and News* began including copies of the *National Star*, a magazine applicant for ABC membership owned by the same interests as the newspaper, as a supplement in its issues. While the *Star* was withdrawn from all but a few newsstands in peripheral areas of the San Antonio market, advertising and promotion, with a price reference, was continued.

Can a separate magazine be a supplement?

ABC management interpreted the practice as not meeting the restrictions of the combination rule. Charles O. Kilpatrick, publisher of the newspaper, argued before the board that since the *Star* was not generally available in the market except as a free supplement in the newspaper, the practice did not fall within the purview of the combination rule. The competing *San Antonio Light*, a Hearst newspaper, countered that if this interpretation were approved it might consider including one or more of its company's magazines in Sunday issues as supplements.

The board sustained management and set up conditions for a special audit to cover the period the *Star* was included as a supplement. Kilpatrick agreed, and the *Sunday Express and News* changed the name and editorial and advertising content of its supplement and otherwise met the conditions of the rule.

Recognizing that other newspaper publishers might wish to avoid the restrictions of the combination rule, the board established a glossary definition as to what constitutes a newspaper supplement. In 1975, the board approved a new rule covering the distribution of supplements with newspapers without affecting the qualification as paid circulation provided that: "the supplement is identified as a part or section of the newspaper and is not promoted, offered, or distributed for sale separately; a separate or independent existing newspaper or periodical cannot be considered under the rules pertaining to publications offered or sold in combination; and advertising in the supplement must be contracted for by the advertiser or its agency directly with the publisher of the supplement or its authorized representatives."

While the board has been consistent in denying exceptions in the application of the combination rule to newspapers and magazines, it did approve a 1987 request of a Canadian business publication. Subscriptions to *Finance* were sold in combination with subscriptions to *La Bourse* at a price that did not meet the 100 percent plus at least 30 percent requirement of the rules. Justification for granting the one-time exception was the belief that the publisher did not understand the rule.

A new twist on the subject came up in 1987 by way of Canadian newspapers. Free distribution magazines approached publishers to distribute their publications as an insert in their newspapers. Insert rates were less expensive than mail rates for the magazines; the added source of revenue was welcomed by the newspapers. The magazines carried no price, were not promoted or distributed or offered for sale as a separate entity, and were identified as a supplement to the newspaper, thus meeting the ABC newspaper supplement rule.

The problem for the board arose when publications with separate identities—an established copy and subscription price and offered for sale separately on the newsstands—in both Canada and the United States approached newspaper publishers with paid insert plans to distribute their magazines as supplements or advertising inserts. The quandary for the ABC directors is the abuses the rule has virtually eliminated and its consistent application over the years versus the opportunity of newspapers to exploit additional sources of revenue. It is the question of advertiser (the magazine)-instituted programs versus newspaper-initiated circulation building efforts.

As an advertising agency director said during a recent discussion of this issue, "If ABC were to void its supplement distribution and combination rules in these types of situations, more and more magazines would take advantage of the opportunity.

"I am certainly sensitive to the publishers' interest in cultivating additional sources of revenue, but at what point does the newspaper become simply the envelope in which these other publications are wrapped?"

Association Subscriptions

It wouldn't seem that developing a rule clearly covering association subscriptions would be all that difficult. Yet for most of the Audit Bureau's history, this subject has caused confusion each time it was raised in discussion. Part of the problem arose out of the indefinite postal regulations upon which ABC's initial standards were based. Then there were the variety of association-set membership conditions and recordkeeping practices. Not the least of the confusion was caused by management interpretations, applying the rules to situations that did not involve associations.

In the beginning, it was easy. An association subscription was one received as part of membership in an association, a term that was loosely defined. Whether it was paid for as part of the dues, special assessments, or paid for by the association out of its funds, such subscriptions qualified under the U.S. Post Office Department's definition of "a legitimate list" for second class mailing privileges.

That association subscriptions were "a different breed of cattle" was recognized in 1918. Magazine members called for a special break out of this type of circulation in ABC reports. The following year, the board's executive committee approved a standard practice with association subscriptions to be shown as a separate subtotal in the paid circulation paragraph of the Publisher's Statements and Audit Reports of all the member publications.

In 1921, advertisers and advertising agencies called on the board to further amplify association sales information in ABC reports. "After considerable discussion," the board added the requirement that publication reporting association subscriptions also explain what association it served as an official organ, whether "members' subscriptions were paid for in combination with payment of dues," and whether members "have the privilege of deducting the subscription price of the publication from dues if they did not desire the publication." The board also passed a rule saying that "association subscriptions cannot be classed as paid when carried beyond expiration of the time originally paid for."

It was not unusual for a publisher to provide funds to the association, which, in turn, were used to reimburse that publisher for its members' subscriptions. Several associations had no function other than publishing its official publication, "paying for subscriptions from funds generated by advertising in their magazines." It was not uncommon for the publication to purchase "services" from the association or to compensate the association for the privilege of reporting its publicity and its official proceedings. And it was not uncommon for associations, once affiliation takes place, to carry the member as active many years after dues payments had ceased.

To get around the sometimes embarrassing disclosure requirement, many publishers simply claimed what formerly had been association subscriptions as mail subscriptions-special, gift subscriptions, or bulk sales. At the March 1922 board meeting, Managing Director Stanley Clague cited examples "from 134 audit reports (over one-half of the business publication membership) as typical of existing conditions." Some of these were the same publishers who during that year were calling on the board to disqualify free distribution publications from membership in the Audit Bureau.

From its beginning, justification for not raising ABC standards was the contention that "it has been good enough for the government, why isn't it good enough for the Audit Bureau." In 1922, Clague changed the rules of the game. He worked with the superintendent of mails in Chicago to reassess a number of basic U.S. Post Office second class regulation interpretations. The superintendent issued a series of circulars following each of his and Clague's agreements.

Circular number 4, originally issued in November 1922 and re-issued in January 1923, was nearly pure Stanley Clague. Titled "Subscriptions Made by Members of a Society," it said:

"To meet the requirements of the Act of March 3, 1879, and be properly included in the 'Legitimate list of subscribers' required by that Act, each member or subscriber must express a desire for the publication, and in making remittances, must indicate that he sends a given sum which he wishes applied to a subscription to the publication for a definite time, it being immaterial whether the amount sent forms a separate remittance or is included in a separate remittance of dues, provided the price paid be above what is construed to be nominal when compared with the regular advertised subscription price of the publication. If the application for membership, orders, bill, receipts, etc., used by the society cover both subscriptions and dues, they must show a specific amount for subscriptions; and copies of those forms should be submitted to the office of the superintendent of mails to enable the Department to determine whether or not the above requirement is met." The circular went on to provide a suggested form for associations to use for their applications for membership.

The board "accepted" this interpretation as policy but did nothing to incorporate the change into the ABC rules. Director C.C. Younggreen, J.I. Case Plow Works, suggested that the action "not be extensively publicized, lest we cause disruption among the publishers. Best we let

Younggreen: "Let the government feel the heat."

the government feel the heat." Not only was it not publicized, both the post office and the Audit Bureau appear to have forgotten their respective actions. In fact, the board back-peddled by rescinding the rule that said association subscriptions could not be classed as paid when carried beyond the expiration of time originally paid for. For several years, the directors considered the suggestion that a separate membership category be established for publications with more than 50 percent of their circulation as association subscriptions but gave up that idea in 1925.

The issue of association subscriptions was raised again at the 1928 business publication divisional meeting. Considerable discussion centered on the practices of "association-owned organs." Director E.R. Shaw, Technical Publishing Co., was asked to investigate whether the Audit Bureau's rules were in line with postal regulations.

In a letter to Managing Director O.C. Harn, Shaw pointed out "the post office department's regulation which provides that both the order and the receipt for an association-owned organ must be separate from the bill and the receipt for dues." Harn, who had served as a director of the Audit Bureau and was chairman of the board at the time of the earlier discussions, replied, "I do not believe that I have ever seen these postal regulations before. They have a very definite bearing upon the subject which has been brought up for discussion. Of course, I assume that all our association organ members are conducting their business in a way which satisfies these regulations or they could not get by. The Bureau's procedure, however, has not been quite so severe as the post office regulations if we are to take the latter literally."

Publicity for the 1929 annual meeting reported, "The question has been raised several times as to whether or not the Bureau's present treatment of association subscriptions is correct. Opinions have been expressed which range all the way from the belief that such subscriptions should not be recognized as paid at all, to the belief that they are just the same as any other subscriptions and should not be segregated from other types of subscriptions." In between these extremes, views varied from crediting only those association subscriptions that offered the member the option of refusing to take the publication as paid, to setting up involuntary subscriptions as unpaid, to classifying all association subscriptions as bulk distribution.

The convention recommended that the board revise the association subscription rules to require that "those which are compulsory upon members shall be segregated from those which are voluntary" in the reports of paid circulation, and that complete information with regard to association memberships be reported in the explanatory paragraphs of the publications' reports. A new rule effecting this recommendation was adopted by the board with application date of January 1931.

During the course of an audit in 1932, the ABC auditor was refused access to the records of an association. When he explained his review of these records was essential to the audit of that association's official publication's circulation, he was told the association was not a member of the Audit Bureau and would not "accede to any invasion of its privacy." A management query to other field auditors revealed that such a refusal was not infrequent. When faced with this turn down, the auditor usually accepted the publisher's evidence as accurate and went on from there. Recognizing this auditing deficiency, the board revised the rules the following year, making it incumbent on the publisher to arrange for the association's records to be made available to the ABC auditor if it wished these subscriptions to be credited as paid. Otherwise, these subscriptions would be set up as term subscriptions in bulk. The board then grandfathered existing situations that did not meet the new rule and proceeded to grant exceptions to new members.

Refuse ABC access to membership records for association books.

When publishers complained that many associations simply did not maintain these types of records, Ed Chandler, ABC's chief auditor, queried the Post Office Department as to its requirements as set forward in the 1922 circular. He asked whether these requirements had been changed or were being enforced. C.B. Eilenberger, Third Assistant Postmaster General, responded that there had been no change in the law relating to subscriptions to publications entered as second-class matter by members of societies. He also advised Chandler that the Post Office Department was unable to identify the circular and asked that a copy be sent to him.

Eilenberger subsequently wrote that the circular was not an official statement of the Post Office Department, but had been issued by the Chicago post office. "However," he wrote, "there has been no change in the regulations with respect to subscriptions obtained in this manner, it being necessary, when subscriptions are made in connection with the payment of membership dues to the organization by which the publication is published, for the person applying for membership or transmitting his membership dues to specify that of the amount paid as an application fee or as membership dues a stated sum, not less than 50 percent of the regular advertised subscription price of the publication, is for the express purpose of paying for a subscription to the publication for a definite period. Forms prepared substantially like the ones set forth in the Chicago circular are required when subscriptions are so made." He made no response to Chandler's question as to why this regulation was not being enforced, but this information did serve as background to a later ABC rule change.

Precedent paves way for expanding interpretation of Audit Bureau's association rule.

On Harn's recommendation in 1937, the board approved a precedent that would be expanded on in staff usage and eventually cause problems. The *Daily Iowan*, student newspaper of the University of Iowa, applied for ABC membership. He reported that certain features of the newspaper's operation raised questions as to its eligibility if treated like any other newspaper.

One of these involved 925 copies delivered to residents of dorms and sorority and fraternity houses, which were ordered by the house management based upon the majority vote of the residents and paid for from house funds. The applicant asked that these copies be classed as individual, paid subscriptions. Harn reported to the directors, "It would seem that the best rating that could be assigned to these subscriptions would be 'association subscriptions, non-deductible from dues,' even though these subscribers are not members of an association in the normal sense of the term. This would be my recommendation." The board agreed, and, for the first time, the association subscription rule was applied to a situation outside an association membership "in the normal sense of the term."

In defending his recommendation, Harn provided the opinion on the justification for including nondeductible association subscriptions in paid circulation, an opinion that was later used in a rule amendment discussion. He said: "The thing that

If it met rules "in normal sense" it qualified.

distinguishes and decides the question as to whether those subscriptions are set up in Bureau reports as bulk sales of association subscriptions is the way that the association handles the proposition. If the association sends you a list of members to whom you are to send the publication and makes no announcement to the members that a certain amount of their dues is set aside to pay the subscription price, the publication cannot set those up as association subscriptions.

"The principle underlying association subscription rule is exactly the same as that followed by the U.S. postal department. In other words, inasmuch as the association member does not go down in his pocket and pay for the subscription direct, he cannot be considered as having voluntarily subscribed for the publication.

"If, however, he is properly notified by the association management that he is paying for the paper when he sends in his payment for dues, and told just how much he is paying for the publication, the Bureau allows such subscriptions to be set up as 'Association Subscriptions' rather than 'Bulk Sales.'"

During the ensuing years, ABC management and the board applied Harn's interpretation of being "properly notified" and the *Daily Iowan* precedent to qualify as paid. Subscriptions to publications received as contributing to an organization or charity, or some other type of payment to an organization, likewise not strictly in accord with the rules "in the normal sense," were reported as paid.

The Audit Bureau took a step closer to what was reputed to be the U.S. postal regulations in 1939 when it adopted an amendment to its association subscription rules. To qualify under those reported as "deductible from dues," the option of accepting or rejecting the subscription "must be made known to the member at the time of his joining the association and be clearly stated on each bill for dues in such a way as to make remittance a voluntary subscription to the paper as well as a remittance for membership dues." For those reported as "nondeductible from dues," the board added, "Every person, on becoming a member of the association, must be notified of the subscription price of the paper and that such price is a part of the sum collected as dues. On every bill for dues, the subscription price of the paper must be given and the fact noted that such subscription price is a part of the dues to be paid."

The board's liberal granting of exceptions to the rules for association publications came up for review in the late 1940s. When the *Oregon Grange Bulletin* applied for membership in 1944, it was explained that membership dues were collected by volunteer secretaries of subordinate, local groups. Quarterly reports to the state secretary were in and out membership records, listing only new members and the names of those dropped from membership. No other association records existed for audit examination.

In justifying its recommendation that the application be approved, management pointed out to the directors that the same situation "exists on some association periodicals that are already Bureau members, such for instance as *Columbia, Elks Magazine*, the *Rotarian, Kiwanis Magazine, National Jewish Monthly*, and the *American Legion*, to name a few." The board approved the application, and the initial Audit Report was released.

During each of the succeeding three years, the field auditors questioned the feasibility of making the audit of the *Oregon Grange Bulletin* because it was impossible to verify the individual subscriptions and establish arrears. The audits were based on a count of the mail list, which was simply a list of names and addresses showing no expiration dates or any other identifying marks; this count checked and compared with the figures shown on the quarterly reports sent in by the local Grange secretaries.

Managing Director James N. Shryock and staff had worked with many of the other association publications to bring their operations into compliance with the ABC rules. When the publisher of the *Oregon Grange Bulletin* and companion *Grange Bulletins* in Washington, Idaho, and California was asked to bring the practices of those publications into compliance, he objected.

An exchange of several letters and an offer to personally review the subject with the publisher failed, Shryock brought the situation before the board in 1948. After a lengthy review of the situation, the board unanimously resolved that beginning with the period starting July 1, 1949, it would be necessary for the publications to put their records in such shape that future audits could be made in accordance with the Audit Bureau's standard auditing requirements. Commenting on the action, E. Roy Hatton, *Detroit Free Press* and chairman of the board's

auditing practices committee, congratu-
lated his fellow directors, saying, "We
have just reaffirmed our belief in uniform
standards and hopefully against membership by exceptions. I trust we and other
boards to come will remember the
strength of this day's conviction."

But exceptions to the rules continued to exist. In some parts of western
Canada it is the practice of local municipalities to purchase subscriptions to
weekly newspapers. When several of
these newspapers applied for ABC
membership, Shryock informed Canadian
directors that the "rate payers" arrangement amounted to bulk sales according to
ABC rules, and none was eligible. W.J.J.
Butler, *Toronto Globe and Mail*, and
H.H. Rimmer, Canadian General Electric, convinced Shryock that, based upon
Harn's earlier interpretation, the
weeklies could qualify under the loose
application of the association rule. The
newspapers were elected to membership
without question. The "rate payers"

*Shryock questioned
exceptions to auditing
practices.*

application was reviewed by the board's auditing practices committee
again in 1954, and the interpretation sustained.

Most association publications are business publications. As
membership in this division began to decline during the 1950s, directors
sought ways to stem the trend. A large group of association publications,
especially in the medical field, were not audited and provided a membership promotion target. ABC's rules relating to dues billings and separate
notification of that part of the dues going to the subscription posed a
problem for many of these publications. In 1956, at the request of the
business publication committee, the board amended its rules, exempting
from this provision of the rule for up to two years those applicants
serving associations whose bylaws provided that a subscription was
part of the dues.

A new situation arose in 1974 with the application of the *Chicago Guide*, published by WFMT, Inc. and distributed to subscribers to the public broadcasting station's fund-raising efforts. Here was an association-like magazine, published by a not-for-profit corporation, which appeared to meet the spirit of the Audit Bureau's association subscription rules if not their literal application, and which sought to provide advertisers with verified circulation information. Since the unique operation of the publication did not meet other rules governing paid, management reached into the historical precedent of the loose interpretation of the association rules to justify its recommendation that the application be accepted. The board agreed, and the renamed *Chicago Magazine*'s initial audit was released in 1975. Based on this new precedent, other similar publications became members. This situation brought questions from later boards and, ultimately, a clarification of the rules.

Searching for new marketing strategies, newspapers backed into a controversial interpretation of the association rules in 1985. The *Denver Post* and a local cable company entered an agreement whereby the *Post*'s improved Sunday television section would include the cable company's listings, replacing the company's need to publish its own publication. In return, the cable company would provide the *Post* with its list of subscribers, deduct a qualifying amount from each subscriber's bill, and reimburse the *Post* to supply each cable subscriber with a copy of the Sunday issue. In initial discussions, ABC management agreed that this circulation qualified as individual paid subscriptions. Overnight, the *Post*'s Sunday circulation increased dramatically, and newspapers in Colorado Springs, Las Vegas, and Long Beach began to set up similar arrangements.

Butler argued that "rate payers" met the spirit of the association rule.

Competitors were quick to appeal management's ruling to the board. After an intensive
review, the board adopted a policy statement,
clarifying for newspapers, magazines, and farm
publications the conditions such arrangements had

*Subscriber must
take affirmative
action.*

to meet if the resulting circulation was to be credited as paid. In essence,
the statement, adopted in August 1985 and amended the following year,
provided that for "copies sold in connection with other services, such as
cable television subscriptions, transportation services, hotel or motel
room services, etc., either through subscription or single copy sales"
to qualify: "the subscriber or recipient must take affirmative action in
ordering the publication"; "a separate, clearly identified amount must
be paid by the subscriber" with the amount listed as a separate item on
each service invoice and at least 50 percent of the basic price; "if the
subscriber or recipient chooses not to accept the offer, the amount
charged for the publication" had to be deducted from the invoice and the
invoice amount reduced accordingly; promotion offers must present the
publication as a separate item; terms of the offer must be reported, along
with the quantities involved, in ABC reports; and "auditable records to
support the sale of copies claimed as paid circulation must be available
for Bureau auditors." Qualifying subscriptions and single copy sales
were no longer reported under association sales but within regular
classifications of paid circulation.

In 1986, the board revised the rules, deleting the single rule
applying association subscriptions for all publications, and adopting
separate, but substantially similar, rules for each of the publisher
divisions. The business publication rule allowed for differences in the
paid eligibility rule. The magazine and farm publication rules enlarged
the association scope to include publications directed to public television,
motor clubs, etc., who referred to their subscriptions as "member subscriptions." The board agreed to grandfather existing "rate payer"
weekly and two other newspaper applications that did not comply with
the new rules.

Advertising Rates

Advertising agencies had their beginnings as space representatives.
Publishers refused to openly solicit for advertising, or so they claimed.
At first, individual agencies controlled "exclusive lists" of publications.

As this system broke down, agencies began to sell space to advertisers and then buy from publishers to fill orders. Advertising rates were in a state of confusion and chaos, largely a matter of bargaining. The forte of advertising agents became one of trading. Seldom did the publishers know what price they were actually charging. Even if they had not previously authorized an agent to make rates, the publisher generally accepted the agent's word and gratefully accepted any payments.

Experienced advertisers shopped around for the best deal, submitting a proposed schedule to several agents and accepting the lowest bid. When the Association of National Advertising Managers drafted its Bureau of Verified Circulation in 1913, its proposed forms called not only for circulation data, but also schedules of advertising rates. Most publishers refused to provide information on the rates.

Following the sentiment of the publisher members at the Audit Bureau's first annual meeting, the board's executive committee in 1915 ruled "that the constitution and bylaws cannot be interpreted to cover the auditing of advertising figures or advertising rates."

When ABC was offered the opportunity of acquiring the Balfour Lists in the early 1920s, the board refused, citing the desire of buyers for full information and the publisher members' opposition to the organization becoming involved with advertising rates. Other rate and data digests and directories began to flourish. In 1924, ABC started its "Blue Book" service, bound volumes of Publisher's Statements. Advertisers and advertising agencies were not overly receptive to the new service, claiming they could get circulation and rate data from the directories.

"Constitution and bylaws cannot be interpreted to cover the auditing of advertising figures or rates."

In 1926, the various publisher division advisory committees recommended that ABC include an advertising rate card in the Publisher's Statement so the buyers would have less need to turn elsewhere for essential information. The board approved a rule that "there shall be shown on the fourth page of all statements of publishers, who desire to take advantage of this added service, complete rate cards, preferably the standard adopted by the American Association of Advertising Agencies." This service was to be instituted that year with the September newspaper and December periodical Publisher's Statements. Publicity reported, "From one source, advertisers and agents will now be able to secure not only all circulation information in complete form, but all rate information for ABC publications." It also

*Solomon headed buyers' call
for advertising rate data.*

assured the publishers that while the rate cards information would be edited to exclude "promotional statements," they would not be subject of audit.

By the end of August, staff told the board the response was overwhelming, that rate card information had already been received from more than 700 of the slightly more than 800 newspaper members. Managing Director Stanley Clague also told the board that the New York Publishers Association, representing the major New York City dailies, opposed the plan to publish advertising rates in ABC reports. In fact, the NYPA had already begun to solicit proxies for the 1926 annual meeting for the purpose of defeating this new service. It was generally reported in the trade press that the New York publishers, in a highly competitive market, were not about to have anyone reporting in depth on rates actually charged—especially with their many special and negotiated rates.

On the eve of the annual meeting, the newspaper division advisory committee reversed its support for the service and sided with the New York publishers. At the newspaper divisional meeting the following morning, Fred A. Walker, *New York Telegram*, moved "That no facts or figures relating to any matter other than circulation shall be printed in" an ABC report. Aimed at overruling the board's plan to include the advertising rate information, the motion occupied the full morning session and finally was approved by 477 to 137. Recognizing this overwhelming response, the convention adopted a change in the Audit Bureau's Charter, changing the section that read, "and disseminate data," to "and disseminate circulation data only."

The issue came up again in 1934 as an offshoot to a board study on membership dues. "If we are to improve the value of ABC to publishers and justify a rate increase, we must find ways first to make ABC services more important to advertisers," Marco Morrow, Capper Publications, told his fellow directors. "The suggestion has been made that the Bureau consider the possibility of publishing a directory which would contain advertising rates and other data as well as circulation information."

A special committee was appointed to study the suggestion, but it never got very far. Later that year, the newspaper division passed a resolution asking for a complete review by a special newspaper committee of the Audit Bureau's rules and methods. The ABC rate and data directory discussion went into limbo as the board involved itself with more threatening problems.

While it came close several times during its history to adding advertising rates to its report data, the Audit Bureau, and, more notably, its newspaper members have stood firm to its early decision. Old fears churned slightly in 1967 when an advertising agency member suggested that the board incorporate rate base and circulation guarantee data in ABC magazine reports. It was pointed out that the time lapse during preparation and release of Audit Reports made it difficult for agencies to verify the rate bases and/or circulation guarantees that applied during the period covered by the report. Since the requested data made no reference to the advertising rates themselves, the board approved a new rule the following year making it optional to show this information, if such existed, in the Audit Reports of magazines and farm publications.

At the requests of the magazine committees of the Association of National Advertisers and the American Association of Advertising Agencies in 1983, and an ABC magazine buyers advisory committee headed by Debbi Solomon, Leo Burnett Co., optional rate base and/or circulation guarantee data were also added to the semi-annual Publisher's Statements of ABC magazines and farm publications.

Renewal Percentage

In a recent article on magazines, Ron Lawrence, D'Arcy Masius Benton & Bowles, Los Angeles, wrote, "Trying to even define, let alone measure, a concept as illusive as 'readership vitality' borders on the metaphysical. Yet failure to recognize the unique relationship a magazine has with its audience tends to result in a superficial evaluation process that overemphasizes the importance of boxcar 'readership' numbers as reported by syndicated research.

"There is no single interpretation of any magazine data, on or off the ABC Statement, that provides a definitive answer on reader vitality. And the one piece of information we buyers really crave, 'percent reader renewals,' is a number that most publishers will gladly divulge . . . at gunpoint."

Today, renewal percentages are required for all ABC paid business publications. Some advertising agencies and most publishers of magazines, farm publications, and newspapers believe the value of having renewal percentages does not compensate for the heavy cost of compiling and verifying these data. They also point to the disadvantages of renewal percentages for publications edited to serve relatively short reader interest spans, such as bridal magazines.

Ambiguities in what constituted a renewal causes board to tighten the rules.

The U.S. postal regulations, which served as the basis for early ABC rules, were quite liberal on subscription renewals. On the assumption that an original order represented an interest in a publication, the act could also be interpreted as a desire to receive that publication for as long as the publisher desired to send it. So long as the recipient did not actually cancel the subscription, the interpretation was that a payment could be forthcoming.

The Audit Bureau's initial reports provided for the showing of renewal percentages. The rules "requested" that publishers show this information, "either actual or estimated." The rules were tightened in 1915 when the board voted to eliminate estimates. "Unless percentage is compiled from adequate records supported by original orders kept so as to permit verification by the auditor, the publisher shall state that the actual figures are not available. Any issue within the period covered by this report may be used as the base for percentages used in giving the answer to this question."

The ambiguity of what constituted a renewal was addressed at the 1916 annual meeting when advertiser and agency members requested the board to adopt "as soon as possible a rule limiting the length of time within which an expired subscription shall be considered a renewal." In nearly simultaneous actions, both the board and the Post Office Department adopted a one-year time limit. For ABC members, this renewal period changed to six months when the arrears rules were modified in 1920. The board retained the six-month provision when the arrears rules were changed to three months in 1928.

The board also brought another rule in line with U.S. postal regulations by declaring that reinstatement of service, following a breach after a subscription had expired and without a definite request for a renewal or new order, was to be classed as a sample copy and not shown as a renewal.

During a review of rules in 1919, the board approved the alternate of all issues during the report period (as opposed to just one issue) for use in compiling renewal percentages.

In February 1920, Managing Director Stanley Clague reported to the membership that 35 percent of the business publications, 20 percent of the magazines, and 10 percent of the farm publications were providing renewal percent information in their ABC reports. "There is no question as to the increasing demand of the space buyer to have this question answered, many insisting that a full and complete answer should be made mandatory. The publishers, on the other hand, advance a number of reasons in defense of their using the phrase 'Actual figures not available.' Among the reasons is an apparent failure to not only realize its importance, but also failure to understand the requirements."

The board voted to make the reporting of renewal percentage information mandatory for all magazines, farm publications, and business publications at its March 1920 meeting. A month later, it voted to postpone application of the rule for six months. The advisory committee on magazines reported that "a number of publishers—especially those with large circulations—had made estimates of the cost of complying with this requirement and had found that the extra labor involved would make compliance extremely burdensome, if not entirely prohibitive." Aside from the cost, publishers questioned whether the information had that much value to advertiser. "A new subscriber may be more valuable than an old subscriber; or a new subscriber may, in reality, be an old subscriber, having changed his name or location between subscriptions; or, the subscription may be going to the same family under the name of another member of the family. For the large publication, an even approximate approach to accuracy would be almost impossible, and would cause grave injustice to this class of publisher."

Citing "the opposition to this rule on the part of publishers and, on the other hand, there has been no demand on the part of advertiser members for its enforcement," the board rescinded its action to make renewal percentage information mandatory for ABC periodical reports. The reversal came just six months after it had been adopted. The publisher of the *Farmer's Advocate and Home Magazine*, London, Ontario, offered resolutions at the 1920 annual meeting, seeking to reinstate the mandatory renewal percentage rule. These met with "less than enthusiasm" by the other publisher members, and the convention advised the board to table them.

The question of mandatory renewal percentages came up again in the 1923 business publication divisional meeting. More than 50 percent of the business publication members were reporting the optional data. Recognizing that publishers in other divisions might have difficulty in compiling these data and that questions existed on a standard method for computing these percentages, the business publications voted to make mandatory for members of this division the reporting of the "percentage of mail subscriptions renewed." Following the annual meeting, the board adopted this requirement, applying only to business publications. (Efforts to develop a uniform method for computing their renewal percentages is covered in Chapter 7.) The *National Geographic Magazine*, which provided renewal percentage data on its member subscribers, was one of the few in either the magazine or farm publication divisions to exercise this option.

Several magazines brought up the issue again in 1936. Some publishers were making renewal claims, independent of ABC, in their promotion and selling. Competitors complained to the board. "They are not attributing these to the Bureau, but they also are not dissuading those who understand the renewal claims have been verified or even computed under Bureau standards." The subject was brought before several membership divisions at the 1937 annual meeting, along with the suggestion that the reporting of renewal percentages be mandatory for magazines and farm publications "who claim a certain number of renewals or percentage of renewals, either direct to advertisers or through advertising matter," reported in the Publisher's Statements and be subjected to audit.

Magazines fight buyers' request for mandatory renewal figures.

While this was being debated the following spring, magazines were almost as opposed to the suggested amendment as buyers were in support of it. N.L. Wallace, Time, Inc., told the board that magazines did not oppose the reporting of renewal percentages, which, in fact, they were doing outside of ABC reports anyway. Their opposition was to complexity and expense of the method of compiling that percentage in accordance with the Audit Bureau's practices. A committee of member publishers offered to work with the board to develop a simpler and less expensive method.

After two months of study and negotiation, the circulation rules and methods committee of the board reported that "no practicable method had been developed," and, in June 1938, the board unanimously adopted the requirement that member publishers who claim a renewal percentage outside of ABC must also report a percentage in their Publisher's Statements and submit this to audit.

In its February 1939 issue, *Fortune Magazine* declared that its "renewal rate is higher than any other monthly magazine, except one geographic membership periodical." Competitors jumped on the statement and demanded that the Audit Bureau test its new rule. Time, Inc.'s Wallace told the board, "The whole thing is a little wacky—a slip on the part of a newly employed copywriter who did not understand his instructions. Obviously, the statement that *Fortune* has a higher renewal rate than any other magazine is one which cannot be proved, because all magazines do not report their renewal percentage and there is no way to check it. To hold us to the letter of the rule is unrealistic. It would be impossible to audit records which have not been maintained and do not exist. Under the Bureau's 'exact' method of determining renewal percentages, records would have to cover 18 months. Even if we were to agree to provide renewal information for some future period, it would have no bearing on the conditions that existed prior to the time of the publication of this unfortunate statement."

Errant promotional copy forces opponent to bear audit of renewal rate boast.

Fortune agreed to a retraction of this claim, and it was published in its June 1939 ABC Publisher's Statement. Embarrassed by the publicity given to this, Time, Inc. immediately initiated necessary records for compiling renewal percentage data. Two years later, the publisher announced that, "at a cost of $20,000 plus an intricate bookkeeping job," the ABC Statements for *Time*, *Life*, and *Fortune* would include their respective subscription renewal percentage information. The publisher characterized the data as offering "a tangible fact, never before available, in judging any magazine's value to an advertiser; a direct index of the interest with which a magazine is read by its subscribers after they have bought it."

Members of the board and staff spent many hours in search of new and simpler methods for calculating renewal percentages, frequently with ABC's New York office and Chicago headquarters personnel in disagreement. In fact, business publication members debated back and forth on methods, which led to a questionnaire in 1952 on the suggestion that the division attempt to overturn the mandatory showing of renewal percentages all together.

Advertising agency members requested the board consider it be made mandatory for all publications at their 1940 meeting, but the issue was quiet during the World War II years. Buyers picked up on the renewal percentage issue as the economy turned to peacetime production. Edward G. Gerbic, Johnson & Johnson and chairman of the Association of National Advertisers, brought the issue to the fore during a 1955 ABC annual meeting speech. One of the "ways in which advertisers believe ABC reports would fulfill their basic function to better

advantage," he said, was by making it "mandatory to report the renewal rates of publications." Gerbic's suggestion was discussed at several divisional meetings. Advertisers adopted a resolution requesting the board to make renewal percentages mandatory for all publications. Farm publications went on record as being opposed to it. Magazines went on record "as being definitely opposed to being required to furnish any information in addition to that already furnished on the present Publisher's Statement." The board's policy and auditing practices committees discussed the resolutions and passed them along to management for study of possible alternative methods of compiling renewal percentage data. The study produced no new methods.

Advertisers and advertising agencies continued to seek these data from magazines and farm publications. A resolution in 1962 resulted in a survey

Gerbic suggested mandatory renewal percentages.

Simko: Looking for "insights into a magazine's value to its readers."

of periodical publishers on the question of mandatory renewal percentages. Managing Director Alan T. Wolcott reported that "the response to the survey was almost unanimous that the reporting of a renewal percentage should continue to be optional, not mandatory, for magazines and farm publication members. The objection which was voiced most strongly was that it would involve excessive recordkeeping costs."

It was raised again in 1964 and in 1969. In 1972, George J. Simko, Benton & Bowles, Inc., told the magazine division one of the best ways to improve their ABC reports would be to "provide us with detailed data relating to the extent to which a magazine's buyers renew their subscriptions and for what term. Subscription renewal rates can provide interesting insights into a magazine's value to its readers. Perhaps we can liken the renewal rate in publishing to the repeat rate in product marketing. In the marketing of a grocery product, for example, trial is critical and we use many devices to induce trial, such as price reduction, couponing, trial sizes, and many others. But once we acquire a customer, we want to keep him and this is where repeat purchase analysis comes in. The vitality or worth of a product to the consumer is partially measurable by its ability to attract repeat customers. In line with this, we believe renewal rates of magazines is an indicator of reader satisfaction with the magazine."

A pragmatist, Simko recognized in making the recommendation "that similar comments have been made by buyers periodically over the past 50 years with notable lack of success. But it also occurred to me that the frequency with which these important issues were being raised was declining."

A special magazine ad hoc committee of the board reviewed Simko's recommendation but reached no positive conclusions. At their 1976 meeting, magazines voted to keep the reporting of renewal percentages optional. The board agreed but made another unsuccessful attempt to develop simplified procedures for compiling auditable renewal data.

Expanding its efforts to improve ABC reports the board, in 1983, invited input from the magazine committees of the Association of National Advertisers and the American Association of Advertising Agencies. Robert Bolte, The Clorox Co., and Art Edelstein, Campbell-Mithun, Inc., responded with a joint recommendation. One of their recommendations called for the mandatory reporting of subscription renewal rates. Following extensive discussion of this proposal, the board's magazine/farm committee recommended that no action be taken. "The rules for renewal rates are optional and magazines can provide this information if buyers make it necessary." At the committee's request, a board task force was established to work to resolve this with the advertiser and agency organizations.

Campbell: Option currently exists.

In 1984, the task force gave way to the establishment of a magazine buyer advisory committee to provide for broader discussion with and input from advertiser and advertising agency members. Following its first meeting, the committee reported it "felt renewal rate information, after first taking into consideration the publication's editorial thrust and marketing strategy, would be valuable to planners in determining a publication's vitality."

During an annual meeting panel discussion that year, William S. Campbell, Hearst Magazines, responded to a question on renewal percentages by agreeing with the buyers advisory committee position. The option for reporting this information currently exists in ABC reports, he said, and magazines have historically responded to the requests of buyers when their needs were made known and where the additional data would add to better print media evaluations.

The resoluteness of publishers and the lack of unanimity of buyers on the issue were demonstrated at the 1986 annual meeting.

Panelist Wilma Jordan, *Esquire Magazine*, called renewal rates "proprietary information. Adding another very controversial and very easily misunderstood piece of information to the pink sheet (magazine Publisher's Statement) would be disastrous as far as both publishers and advertisers are concerned." She said that magazine publishers do not want to give competitors information on the types of renewal promotions they are doing. "Once you release that to the buying community, you have given it to your competitors."

Leo E. Scullin, Young & Rubicam, Inc., agreed that renewal rate informa-

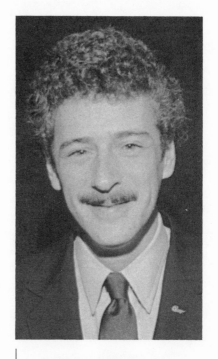

Scullin: Data "very hard to understand."

tion is "very hard to understand. Rates vary by type of publication." His fellow panelist and buyer, Allan R. Linderman, HBM/Creamer, said it was "totally wrong" to assume that the buying community would have difficulty in understanding the data. "I think it is both the responsibility of the buying and selling community to understand what is there, and I think withholding the data just because it might cause a problem is the wrong way to go about it."

The subject of renewal rates was a "very important" request when it was introduced for discussion by the magazine buyers advisory committee. But it quickly lost a lot of its steam and was ultimately dropped from the committee's active agenda. The turnaround came after several meetings between representatives of the buyers committee and key magazine publishers. The publishers' refusal to consider reporting renewal information, citing cost and confidentiality, convinced the buyers that further efforts would prove no more successful than had past attempts.

Waiver of Damages

Throughout its history, the Audit Bureau has frequently been called upon to provide expert testimony in cases tried in the courts of the United States and Canada. It wasn't until 1964, ABC's 50th anniversary year, that the organization was cited as a defendant in a court case. The suit, brought by a Montreal, Quebec, magazine publisher, dragged through court agendas and continuances for eight years before the suit was dropped.

In his report to the board, President Alan Wolcott said that "although the Bureau has incurred expense in successfully defending this litigation, such expense should be considered as a cost of doing business. ABC can take justified satisfaction that the suit has been finally dismissed without any liability to ABC, and the accuracy and integrity of the Bureau audits has once again been upheld."

A decade later, during a period popularly referred to in the United States as the "age of litigation" (and dramatically increasing liability insurance costs), ABC was again involved as a defendant in four suits. Legal actions evolving from competitive newspaper practices in Trenton, New Jersey, and Sacramento, California (1983), Cookeville, Tennessee (1985), and Dallas, Texas (1986), each named the Audit Bureau as a party in the suit. Again, each of the actions against the Audit Bureau was settled, and the integrity of ABC audits and auditing practices upheld.

With the filing of the Trenton case, the ABC board and management began a process of re-examining its "cost of doing business position." In announcing several actions resulting from this review in 1986, ABC Chairman David K. Braun, General Foods Corp., told members "the process began with the deep concern of

Braun was concerned with increasing cost of litigation.

86

the ABC board over the increasing expense of litigation involving ABC and its members, as well as the escalating expense for even the very limited amount of coverage available in professional liability insurance. Increases in both types of expenses, of course, must ultimately be borne by ABC members.

"Central to the board's consideration was the need to assure the continued ability of the Bureau to provide its vital and necessary auditing services, and to do so at a realistic cost."

The first action, adopted in 1986 after lengthy discussions with members in each publication division, was a new waiver of damages and indemnification bylaw. As a condition of membership, the bylaw says, "each member waives any right to assert claims for money damages against the Bureau for any action, negligence or breach relating to its performance or nonperformance of its activities or services, except that this waiver shall not apply to damages that are determined by final adjudication to have arisen from intentional misconduct on the part of the Bureau in verifying and disseminating erroneous circulation data."

> *"There is no assurance that ABC will be 100 percent perfect."*

The bylaw further provides that each member may assert claims or actions for nonmonetary relief against the Audit Bureau, but the "member shall not make or bring any claim, suit, or proceeding against the Bureau until after the member has exhausted all rights and remedies provided under the bylaws and rules." All costs and expenses to ABC must be reimbursed by the member unless the member's action is successful in establishing a right to the relief sought.

Another point of the bylaw went directly to the heart of part of ABC's recent litigation. As pointed out by President M. David Keil, "There is no assurance that ABC will be 100 percent perfect. The comparable situation might be that of financial auditing, now under legal scrutiny, except that these firms may choose their clients. ABC does not have the privilege of refusing to audit a member publication and must accept the conditions that exist. If there is an organized and managed attempt to deceive by the creation of fictitious audit trails, it is not a certainty that any auditor will uncover this carefully planned fraud. ABC completes over 2,500 audits a year in a highly competitive publishing climate with individual publishers making use of a variety of competitive devices to maintain and build circulations."

In answer, the bylaw says, "if the Bureau is subjected to any claim, action, or proceeding arising from inaccurate information supplied by a publisher member, then the member shall fully reimburse and indemnify the Bureau for all costs and expenses (including reasonable attorneys' fees) incurred in the defense and for all sums paid by way of settlement, judgment or other disposition."

No suits involving ABC as a litigant have been filed since the adoption of this waiver of damages and indemnification bylaw at the board's November 1986 meeting.

Publisher Appeals Procedure

Shortly after the Audit Bureau was organized and on several subsequent occasions, members of the newspaper division called for the establishment of an appeals panel that would sit in review not only of management decisions, but board actions as well. In each instance the proposal was rejected as an intrusion of responsibilities vested by members in the board of directors.

During the discussions concerning the litigation problem, representatives of the American Newspaper Publishers Association and the Newspaper Advertising Bureau again raised the subject of an appeals panel to adjudicate problems arising out of management decisions.

The board did agree in 1986 to establish an experimental appeals procedure to be tested during an 18-month period. It was intended to provide all publisher members with an optional additional forum, "prior to their right to appeal to the board of directors from any decision of the managing director interpreting and enforcing the bylaws and rules of the Bureau." The procedures provided for the creation of an appellate panel to review any challenged decision of the managing director, the makeup of the panel, the submission of the review results to the board, and the financing of each appeal review.

Publisher appeals procedure passes test period without a trial.

During the period of the experimental appeals procedure was in effect, no member chose to avail itself of this option and, in accord with the agreement, the program was abandoned in 1988 after the conclusion of the test.

Member Obligations

Another result of the litigation experience was an intensive review of bylaws and rules relating to member responsibilities that led to important clarifications and strengthening of these standards in 1988. In all, nine bylaws and rules were amended and a new rule added.

In essence, the changes for the first time bound members to abide by all of the published standards, policies, and practices of the Audit Bureau and amendments that are subsequently made to them; made it incumbent upon publisher members to ensure the accuracy, completeness, and accessibility not only of their own records but also those required of independent persons or organizations that sell and/or distribute the publication; and that claimed circulation that cannot be substantiated because of the absence or unavailability of adequate records are subject to deduction in the Audit Report.

A key to the changes was the new rule covering member obligations and specifying the intent of the ABC rules by defining the purpose of the audit, the publisher's responsibility for information in Publisher's Statements, and the requirement that publishers fully cooperate with the ABC auditors.

Newspapers: Big, Complex, Blustery, and Deeply Supportive

5

ICMA helps, ANPA considers alternative auditing service • Membership and board representation grows • Question value of bulk sales • Support free publication ouster • Debate market definitions, maps, and population updates • The long road to postal code breakdowns • Include census-based demographics • Newspaper audience research experiments • When is "morning" not "evening" frequency?

The selection of Russell R. Whitman to coordinate the organization of the Audit Bureau and then as the association's first managing director recognized the importance of newspaper support to ABC's success. His experience spanned newspaper editorial, circulation, advertising sales, and management functions; he had established widespread contacts in the industry.

While many rallied to support the Audit Bureau, seeing Whitman as their friend in court, he counseled the board's first standard forms and audits committee that newspaper publishers were "as independent, stubborn, and contentious a lot as one can find."

Once initial standards were accepted, diversity of operating conditions and personalities favored the comfort of tried, existing rules and a reluctance to change. Failure to develop a consensus frequently stymied progressive leadership. The signals publishers received from local and national advertisers were often confusing and sometimes in opposition. In membership numbers, there was a perceived protection from advertiser buyer pressures. Change, when it did come, was more frequently the result of competition within the industry or from new media forms.

Despite the on-again, off-again controversies that have marked ABC newspaper relations over the years, the overwhelming sentiment of these members has been one of support. In 1986, during one of those controversies, more than 50 newspaper executives issued a joint statement addressed to "the continuing need of an organization to do precisely what ABC is doing." Donald Graham, *Washington Post*, described the statement as a pro-ABC move. "We issued the statement because a few newspapers have withdrawn, and we wanted to say to everyone, particularly advertisers and agencies, there is strong support for ABC in the industry." About the statement, Richard J.V. Johnson, *Houston Chronicle* and chairman and president of the American Newspaper Publishers Association, said, "It's a reaffirmation of our feeling as an industry that there should be a strong ABC."

The Newspaper Associations

Today's generally excellent relations between the Audit Bureau and the associations that represent the collective views of newspapers have been molded from a checkered past—most times supportive but frequently critical of ABC's efforts.

Whitman: Publishers "independent, stubborn, and contentious."

One of the first actions of the ABC board following the organizational meeting in May 1914 was to create a standard forms and audits committee. To assist this committee, the International Circulation Managers Association created its own "committee to cooperate with the ABC," headed by J.M. Schmid, *Indianapolis News*. Members of the two committees met together 11 times during June and the middle of July when ABC's initial newspaper statements and standards of practice received the ICMA's blessings. The ICMA's committee on ABC has been a standing feature of that association and newspaper activities ever since.

The ICMA committee cooperated further with ABC by encouraging newspapers to complete and return the statements after they were sent out in late July and by carrying out educational efforts on recordkeeping practices. When the Audit Bureau's staff initiated audit work on September 21, all five were on newspapers.

By the end of its first year, 643 newspapers had signed up for ABC membership. Of these, only 85 had circulations in excess of 50,000. Part of the wait-and-see attitude of many larger newspapers was conditioned by the reluctance of the American Newspaper Publishers Association to endorse the new organization's work. While daily newspaper membership grew at a moderate rate during the World War I years, reluctance turned to open criticism on the parts of some ANPA members. They resented the fact that advertisers, and not publishers, controlled circulation auditing standards. Several publishers of large newspapers were embarrassed when ABC auditor's findings did not confirm their claims.

Graham: "Need organization to do precisely what ABC is doing."

In 1918 and again in 1920, the Canadian Daily Newspaper Publishers Association requested that the board consider a position on the directorate for a Canadian newspaper representative in addition to the existing newspaper directors. The ICMA also asked for circulator representation on the ABC board. Out of concern that such additions would diminish advertiser control, the board took no action on these requests.

At their convention in April 1919, ANPA members directed Frank P. Glass, *Birmingham News* and ANPA chairman, "to appoint a committee to investigate the advisability of the association establishing a circulation auditing bureau of its own." Jason Rogers, *New York Globe*, visited various regional press associations to fight against the ANPA plan. When advertisers indicated their unwillingness to accept data produced by a publisher-controlled auditing service, the ANPA's plans appeared to evaporate.

Ill feeling towards the ABC continued, however. In 1920, newspaper members complained to the board that unaudited publications used required U.S. postal statement circulation figures in competing against

ABC-audited data. Since these figures were actually unaudited publishers' claims, given a degree of authority by the Post Office Department acceptance, they felt nonmembers had an advantage.

With the support of most members, the ABC board, and newspaper representatives associations, Managing Director Stanley Clague called for the abolition of the post office's sworn statement. Members of Congress reported the move would be favorably received, since the continuance of the sworn statement had caused the government "no little embarrassment." At a critical time, both the International Circulation Managers Association and the American Newspaper Publishers Association entered their opposition to ABC's bid to abolish the post office statement, effectively killing the effort.

During their 1923 convention, ANPA members heard a vigorous condemnation of the Audit Bureau and its auditing practices by E.H. Butler, *Buffalo News*. Not telling his audience that his newspaper had run afoul of ABC rules and that he had been personally embarrassed by certain revelations, Butler claimed newspapers lacked adequate representation on the ABC board and urged ANPA to reconsider the possibility of setting up its own auditing organization.

ANPA members voted that the question of circulation audits be referred to their board. A committee was appointed to "secure a better plane of relations between publishers and the Audit Bureau." That the views of ANPA members and those of the publishers who served on the committee were not in agreement with the action is evident from a letter from committee member John Stewart Bryan, *Richmond News-Leader*, to L.B. Palmer, ANPA manager. "Since the matter was originally discussed," he wrote, "I have given it considerable thought, and made some investigation, with the result that I am impressed with the magnitude of building such an organization as we now have in the Audit Bureau of Circulations. Frankly, I am not convinced that an auditing bureau, under the guidance of the ANPA, would be an improvement over the ABC.

ANPA chairman urges newspapers to consider own auditing service.

"It is practically impossible to invest as much authority and power in an organization as the ABC has without creating opposition and discord from some individuals. We know the ABC is endeavoring to function in a way that will satisfy and please the greatest number, and it is conducted on the basis of what they have encountered over a period of many years, with the result that they are well qualified to intelligently audit circulation of publications of all kinds.

"Unless there are some serious charges against the ABC with which I am not familiar, I would not be in favor of the ANPA going to the expense, work, and worry which such an effort would require."

The committee reported, generally crediting Butler for its conclusions, at the 1924 ANPA convention. The report suggested that ANPA not "sever relations with the Audit Bureau" but correct "abuses." While "the wretched condition in which some publishers present their circulation books explains in part the friction," the committee said it was able to cite what appeared to be cases of "rank injustice." Most important of the five committee "demands" approved by ANPA members were one calling for additional representation for newspapers on the ABC board and one calling for the creation of a "board of review" to which publishers not agreeing with ABC board could appeal.

Newspapers' demand for "super-censorship body" rejected by ABC board.

While the ANPA action was taken in April and was heavily covered in the trade press, it was not communicated to the Audit Bureau until two months later. A committee of the ABC board expressed regret that the ANPA committee inspired criticism of ABC without having facts to support charges and without making any effort to consult with the ABC concerning the allegations on which the report was based. The board said the demand that "a super-censorship body be established, which could be swerved or controlled by any of the various publishers' associations . . . would automatically, to preserve their self-respect, dissolve the board of directors of ABC, thereby disintegrating the ABC, undoing all the work of the circulation verification that has been accomplished during the last decade."

After a discussion with representatives of the ANPA committee, the board reported that it could not accept the committee's recommendations, simply because they would destroy the fundamental principles upon which ABC was founded. They did approve the creation of advisory committees for each of the membership divisions, "whose duty it shall be to bring before the board any suggestions which they may consider desirable for the welfare of their division of any member thereof."

At the 1924 ABC annual meeting, members of the ANPA committee called for a rewording of the newspaper advisory committees charge, to empower it to "hear complaints and protests, to make investigations, to review all bylaws and standards of practice affecting the newspaper members, and to report their findings" for ABC board action. After spirited discussion, the motion was tabled, and an advisory committee, as proposed by the board, was elected. The ABC newspaper members did not discuss a change in the numerical makeup of the board as had been suggested by the ANPA committee.

The only overt act by a minority group representing another association to take over and change the fundamental principles of the Audit Bureau failed.

In the years since, ABC has worked out a close working relationship with its allied newspaper associations. Occasional meetings between directors of ANPA to discuss questions of mutual interest gave way in 1984 to regularly scheduled meetings between ABC directors and members of an ANPA/Newspaper Advertising Bureau liaison committee. ICMA's ABC committee meets regularly in conjunction with the Audit Bureau's annual meeting.

These organizations, along with the Canadian Daily Newspaper Publishers Association; the International Newspaper Advertising and Marketing Executives; the International Newspaper Financial Executives; and the weekly newspaper organizations, the National Newspaper Association and the Canadian Community Newspaper Association; maintain close liaison on both the director and staff levels. ABC has encouraged input from these organizations and, in turn, has turned to these organizations to discuss problems and various proposed actions.

Membership

From the founding of the Audit Bureau, newspaper division has been the largest membership group. At its organizational meeting, officers reported that 338

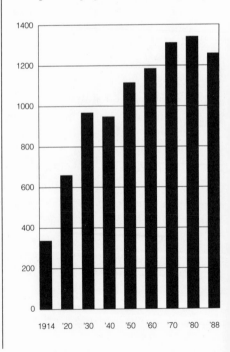

Daily Newspaper Membership

out of the charter membership of 595 were newspapers. A year later, the number doubled to a total of 643. By 1920, the total was 723 daily newspapers—660 in the United States and 63 in Canada, and 24 weekly newspapers—17 in the United States and 7 in Canada.

Daily newspaper membership dropped off slightly during the depression years, grew to a record high of 1,325 in 1971, and again tapered off during the period of consolidations and mergers in the 1980s. Today's count also reflects a 1987 change in the bylaws, which eliminated newspapers with morning and evening frequencies to hold separate memberships.

Weekly newspapers were represented in the Audit Bureau's charter membership, reached a high of 827 in 1961, and have since declined despite ABC efforts to minimize costs and recordkeeping requirements. Lack of advertiser demand for audited circulation facts from weeklies, the competition of increasing numbers of free distribution publications, and the availability of alternative, less disciplined circulation verification services have contributed variously over the years to this group's general reluctance to support ABC.

Throughout the Audit Bureau's 75-year history, newspapers have been the largest of the organization's membership divisions, rivaled, in recent years, only by advertisers. Besides the strength of its support of the audited circulation movement, the newspaper division has, throughout the years, supplied approximately half of ABC's total annual revenue. The importance of ABC to daily newspapers is reflected in the fact that more than 94 percent of all paid circulation in the United States and over 97 percent of that in Canada is audited and reported in accordance with ABC standards.

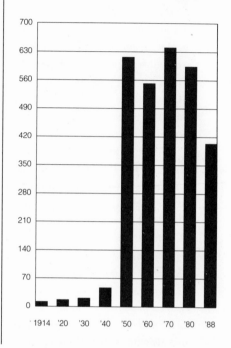

Weekly Newspaper Membership

Board Representation

The sheer numbers, the variety of circulation sizes, and the geographical dispersion of newspaper members early on caused board representation problems for ABC. Two directors, they reasoned, could not adequately present the views of the division. While bylaw and rule changes were subject to approval of annual meetings, newspapers did muster a number of controlling votes. When this condition was eliminated, the pressure to enlarge the board to provide for more newspaper directors became an ongoing issue.

The question was raised in 1919 and 1920 but rejected out of the fear that the addition of newspaper directors and a compensating addition to ensure advertiser control of the board would establish an unwieldy body. A key demand by the ANPA in its efforts to modify the Audit Bureau in 1924 was the addition of two newspaper directors. While the board rejected this demand, it did approve a revision in 1926, which increased newspaper representation to four directors.

During an emotional divisional meeting in 1935, the newspaper majority threatened to secede ("taxation without adequate representation") if additional directors were not provided for. While newspapers adjourned to give the board an opportunity to consider their challenge, leaders from the various divisions worked out a plan to add two more newspaper directors.

Threaten to secede if request for extra directors is denied.

In 1956, the board expanded its membership from 27 to 31 and added a seventh newspaper director to represent weeklies. An eighth newspaper director was added in 1969 when the board was enlarged to its current 33.

While the Canadian Daily Newspaper Publishers Association first requested consideration of direct representation for Canadian newspaper members in 1918, it did not come to pass until the 1935 reorganization of the ABC board. That bylaw amendment established classes of representation: newspapers published in Canada, newspapers published in the eastern standard time zone, newspapers published in the central standard time zone, newspapers in the mountain and Pacific time zones, newspapers having less than 15,000 paid circulation, and newspapers having more than 100,000 paid circulation, with the latter director "actively engaged in or experienced in newspaper circulation work."

The 1969 change added a newspaper director to represent members in the 15,000 to 100,000 paid circulation size and went on to restructure qualifications for these representatives. Under the new system, the three daily newspaper directors representing members in the time zones must have experience in advertising or general business and were to be voted on only by member newspapers within the particular time zone. The three representing newspapers by circulation size must be experienced in circulation work and were to be voted on by all U.S. daily newspaper members. The remaining two directors, representing Canadian dailies and all weekly newspapers, were to be nominated and voted on by their own respective constituent members. The newspaper members informally agreed to impose a limit of five consecutive two-year terms for their representatives' board service.

Bulk Sales

Donald B. Abert, Milwaukee, Wisconsin, Journal Co., once cautioned his fellow ABC directors that "the mere mention of the words 'bulk sales' is enough to start an argument among newspapers." This was true before his time and has been true since. Few subjects have been so thoroughly debated than bulk sales. Few ABC newspaper subjects better demonstrate differences in member attitudes—both advertisers and publishers—and the resulting dilemma for those who were charged with finding equitable solutions.

In the years after World War I, national advertisers increased their advertising expenditures dramatically. Circulation dominance was the overriding factor in the selection of newspapers to carry their advertising. So long as a newspaper could maintain a lead, even only a few hundred copies, over its

Abert: Mentioning bulk sales a good way to start newspaper argument.

competitors, it was assured a place on the advertisers' lists. Pressures on circulation managers to produce in some metropolitan centers resulted in incidents of violence; but for most, it demanded ingenuity. Quantity sales produced the quickest positive results and were the easiest to manipulate.

In New York, copies of daily newspapers were sold in bulk "to every hotel, to ice cream shops, the Chevrolet Motor Company of Broadway, the Brunswick Radio Company, to motion picture theaters, to theater ticket agencies, steamships, taxicab companies, department stores, and the like, to give away free."

In Chicago, 25,000 copies of a newspaper were sold to the suburban Aurora Downs Jockey Club for free distribution to race track patrons. Another newspaper sold copies in bulk to "newsdealers at $5 to $27.50 with each distributing copies free ranging in number from 600 to 3,000."

The problem wasn't limited to the larger cities. In Clinton, Iowa, a publisher's brother-in-law, an employee of the newspaper, purchased more than 8,000 copies to blanket the market (and many farms beyond) for local advertisers. A publisher in Reading, Pennsylvania, sold copies to the chamber of commerce; a publisher in Logansport, Indiana, promised to "completely cover all homes" in the market with copies financed through advertising accommodations; and in Jackson, Michigan, a publisher sold bulk to merchants "at whatever return he could get, and making up the rest through advertising accommodations," usually by special discounts of rates.

Popularity contests were also a popular circulation promotion practice. Many publishers openly encouraged contestants and friends to purchase copies in quantities to secure an adequate supply of in-paper official ballots.

The rules gave the Audit Bureau no justification for disqualifying these sales as "bulk sales" and, therefore, paid circulation. By 1925, advertisers, advertising agencies, and publishers were beginning to question the adequacy of the ABC's bulk sales rule. The subject was debated at that year's annual meeting, and the board was asked to revise it "to protect this industry from its own excesses." A new rule was written, but, at the following annual meeting, members sent it back to committee.

S.E. Thomason, *Chicago Tribune* and a past president of the American Newspaper Publishers Association, took the occasion of that group's fall convention to urge ANPA to "go on the record as requesting

ABC to change its bulk sales rules. Bulk sales are bad business and this fooling the advertiser should not be allowed to continue."

Several months after his 1927 appointment as ABC managing director, Orlando C. Harn lectured to the Detroit meeting of the Association of National Advertisers, an organization that he had helped to found and had served as its president while he was advertising manager of the National Lead Co. "Advertisers are misguided," he said, "when they are encouraged to buy space according to circulation numbers alone. Hundreds of thousands of the funds of manufacturers are being entirely wasted by not looking behind these numbers and discovering what commodity they are buying." He cited the bulk sales excesses and told the advertisers this was a problem created in answer to their own pressures for circulation growth.

The board's committees struggled with their dilemma for three years without resolution. By the 1929 annual meeting, newspaper positions had polarized, and a number of members across the United States and Canada requested that issue be listed for discussion. Petitions merely suggested that "since recipients of bulk sales had neither ordered nor paid for these copies, nor expressed any desire for the publication, such sales did not measure up to the fundamental standard by which in other cases subscriptions are judged as paid."

Hotel competition starts fight on bulk circulation rules.

Max Annenberg, *New York Daily News*, came to the newspaper divisional meeting with a carefully prepared statement and an ample supply of supporters. He was roundly applauded when he said, "Bulk sales are not part of paid circulation and to permit the continued printing of bulk sales circulation figures with the net paid circulation figures on the first page of publishers' ABC statements is to continue to permit advertising buyers to be fooled. In justice to all, the present practice of this Bureau in regard to bulk sales should at once be changed."

In a reply, Hugh A. O'Donnell, *New York Times*, said the issue was largely one of competition. "The *Times* circulation in hotels is legitimate and superior to much circulation. The *Times* will continue its bulk sales to hotels regardless of what action the ABC might take. Bulk sales simply need classification to let advertisers know what they are getting."

The newspaper membership overwhelmingly voted to ask that the ABC board remove bulk sales from paid circulation. The resolution adopted at the following day's general meeting of members read: "That

the members of the Audit Bureau of Circulations in
convention assembled request the board of directors
to revise the rules and definitions of the Bureau in
such a way as not to include any bulk circulation
under the heading of 'net paid' circulation in the
newspaper and farm paper [these members also
voted to eliminate bulk from paid] forms, and that
the figures and explanation of bulk sales shall be set
forth in Audit Bureau reports separate and apart
from the net paid circulation and separate and apart
from free distribution."

ABC's annual business and divisional meeting discussions sometimes produce more controversy than consensus.

Following the meeting, the board approved a newspaper rule that
provided: (1) bulk sales were quantity sales, for which the purchaser had
paid no less than 50 percent of the regularly advertised price, and for
free distribution to recipients; (2) bulk sales did not include copies sold
to public libraries or as gift subscriptions; (3) bulk sales included copies
bought by hotels and restaurants for free distribution to their guests;

(4) copies bought in bulk for term periods and mailed in single wrappers were designated "term subscriptions in bulk," and such copies served after expiration were classed as free samples; (5) single copies delivered in bulk were to be reported as "single issues in bulk"; quantity sales made to an individual, group of individuals, or corporation having a financial interest in the publication were to be set up as free samples unless it could be proved the sale was made to benefit the purchaser and not the publication; (7) all bulk sales were to be explained in the body of the report; and (8) bulk sales would be set up on the second page of newspaper reports in a separate paragraph.

Louis Wiley, *New York Times*, immediately appealed to the board. He said that his newspaper "offered no argument that all so-called bulk sales are of worth to the advertiser and supported most of the new rule. It is absurd to throw all bulk sales out of paid circulation, however, and hotel copies in particular, because of the high caliber of individuals who patronize such establishments." He pointed out that his newspaper sold an average of 10,115 copies daily as bulk, 9,835 of which represented sales "to the better hotels and restaurants in New York City and to steamship lines."

After listening to presentations on both sides of the issue, the directors voted to reaffirm the changes in the new rule and to make them effective with the Publisher's Statement period beginning April 1, 1930.

But the discussions continued at newspaper meetings in the United States and Canada. E. Lansing Ray, *St. Louis Globe-Democrat*, accused the board of buckling under "in what is really a competitive battle between morning and afternoon papers. We know hotels don't buy afternoon papers and are using ABC to serve their purposes. It is a classic case of the more numerous have-nots ganging up on the haves." In calling for hotel copies being returned to paid, he was supported by, among others, the Fuller and Smith Agency and one of its clients, the Statler Hotels.

Fred A. Walker, *New York Sun*, presented a brief signed by "500 persons or organizations whose joint opinion is that bulk sales in any form should not be included in net paid circulation." C.J. Palmer, *Houston Chronicle*, accused his fellow afternoon papers of attempting to "force others to do what they do and not out of an interest for the space buyer. I sympathize with those who feel bulk sales are an important part of their circulation, even those who have threatened to withdraw from ABC membership."

At their 1930 divisional meeting, newspapers voted 180 to 150 to move hotel, restaurant, and transportation bulk sales to the first page of ABC reports, separate of paid and of other bulk. A group of advertisers headed by Ralph Starr Butler, General Foods Corp., and S.E. Conybeare, Armstrong Cork Co., fought the move to separate types of bulk sales.

A center road for the board was to reaffirm the separation of all bulk sales from paid but to revise ABC newspaper report forms to include a breakdown of bulk sales at the bottom of page one. It was approved at the 1931 annual meeting with "virtually all individual newspaper publishers and groups of such publishers" supporting the board's action.

During the early depression years, space buyers criticized newspaper publishers who had "pushed circulations and accompanying advertising rates up too far and too fast." Publishers were turning to heavy promotions to offset circulation losses. The spirit of the bulk sale separation rule was being tested through the use of premiums, contests, charitable contributions, special publicity, and other inducements, many not specifically covered by the rule. The ABC board issued a "friendly warning to those publishers who, under the stress of circumstances, might be allowing questionable methods to creep into their circulation departments, to check up and avoid trouble later."

A 1935 newspaper division request that all ABC publications be forced to follow its lead in eliminating bulk from paid eventually led to changes in 1940. Quantity sales of 11 or more and used to promote business interests were to be reported as bulk; quantity sales induced or influenced by extraneous considerations were to be reported as unpaid; and total bulk sales could not exceed the total of those qualifying as paid.

While advertisers and advertising agencies called for more detailed paid circulation breakdowns, the effect of the new rules and the influence of World War II newsprint shortages pushed bulk sales off newspaper meeting agendas. Revision of Audit Report and Publisher's Statement formats, reflecting more detailed paid breakdowns by market areas and the descriptions of these areas, forced newspaper bulk reports to a single total and, in the mid-1950s, to the inside pages of the forms.

Depression brings changes in publishers' views.

During a 1955 board campaign to simplify ABC rules (one of many such efforts), members of the Mid-Atlantic Circulation Managers Association requested a study of the bulk sales rules, "with a view to bringing them into conformity with the present national economy and on a basis that will prove more satisfactory to publishers and advertisers; that will more accurately describe the circulation of daily newspapers furnished to hotels, motels, restaurants, hospitals, and similar demands for the product of publishers." This was also raised at the ABC newspaper divisional meeting but failed to produce a consensus.

The proposal to move hotel, restaurant, and transportation company sales back into paid circulation came up again at the 1959 meeting of newspaper members. The discussion concluded with a request for "an intensive study of the bulk sale rule." The study was conducted by a special committee of newspaper directors. At the 1960 annual meeting, newspaper members concurred with the committee's recommendation that no changes be made in the rule.

Ask board to return bulk sales to paid total.

In 1973, the same proposal regarding these types of bulk sales was raised. The board sent a mail ballot on the subject to each newspaper member, with 55 percent of the respondents in favor of returning these sales back into paid circulation. A proposed rule to affect this change was offered to the 1974 divisional meeting. Advisory committees, both within the Audit Bureau and reflecting the interests of allied newspaper associations, had debated this issue long and hard. When it came time for a vote in the newspaper division, John Kauffmann, Washington, D.C., *Star-News*, suggested that "no matter which way the action might be voted, there would be a large losing minority, and this would have a rending effect on the division." He strongly urged members "to postpone a decision on the liberalization resolution to allow another year of education and understanding." The membership concurred, and the proposed rule was laid on the table.

It was raised from the table at the following year's meeting. After a bitter debate, the newspapers voted 692 to 227 to make no changes in the bulk sales rule. The board then agreed to remove the subject from its agenda.

Newspapers distributed nationally were always recognized as facing conditions different from locally distributed newspapers. Not serving local markets, they were permitted under board policy to provide paid circulation breakdowns according to a periodical state/province and regional format. They were also permitted to eliminate the required one-day breakdown of distribution by towns and counties receiving 25 or more copies.

In 1981, the board had launched into a study of national and business newspapers, particularly with an interest in assuring that reports of these publications met the needs of media buyers. The question of bulk sales was an important part of this study. It

Conditions different on some newspapers?

was also on the mind of E. Roy Megarry, *Globe and Mail*, who expressed his paper's differences with a number of ABC rules and services. As he pointed out, under ABC rules such quantity sales as those for approved school programs and copies supplied to employees of the newspaper were credited as paid, while copies sold to companies for free distribution to their executives and branch offices were reported as bulk.

In the fall of 1982, the board adopted a new rule aimed at clarifying and expanding upon previous policies governing the reporting of national and business newspapers. Significant here is the fact that the new rule permitted national (and large regional) newspapers to report "group (mail subscriptions special)"—subscriptions sold in quantities to corporations, institutions, or individuals for employees, subsidiary companies, and branch offices in their paid circulation breakdowns and totals.

The announcement of this new rule for national newspapers brought another discussion of whether or not bulk sales should be returned to ABC's newspaper paid totals. The study, which included input from allied newspaper associations, was summed up in a "white paper," and members were queried for their views. The board received 717 daily and 151 weekly newspaper responses from the United States and Canada. In the U.S., the vote favored a return of bulk to paid circulation by a better than 2 to 1. In Canada, members voted 1.5 to 1 against the proposal.

The subject was brought before the 1982 divisional meeting. The sentiment was almost evenly divided, and the members voted to continue study of the proposal and expand efforts to obtain the input of all newspaper members. After endless hours of discussion and concern that a clear member consensus was not developing, the board gave preliminary approval, which would allow newspapers to include bulk sales up to 5 percent of their paid circulation (excluding bulk) in paid circulation totals. Those sales in excess of the 5 percent would continue to be reported separately of paid and unpaid. This served to increase member debate. Delegations of those opposing and those favoring the proposed rule change appeared before the board with their presentations.

Still no newspaper consensus appeared.

be called on to find a way to verify handbill and advertising shopper distribution. These were nettlesome but tolerable competition for local market advertising revenues.

Free distribution competition was a different situation for weekly newspapers. Like most other publications, new weeklies start out with free distribution and then convert to paid. In some areas, especially in Southern California, this conversion was difficult, and publishers found the only way they could stay in business was to provide copies to every home in their markets without charging the recipients. Even the small weekly newspaper markets were not immune to the seemingly ever-present shopper competition. A few newspapers bought out their shopper competition or were bought out by them; some folded; some fought back with shoppers of their own; and many, planned or unplanned, gave up the paid standard to fight free with free.

Retail advertisers openly abetted the growth of free distribution weeklies by demanding distribution of their advertising to every home. Those ABC weekly newspaper members who tried to maintain a substantially paid circulation but were forced to add supplemental free coverage increasingly found themselves in violation with the Audit Bureau's first 50 percent and then 70 percent paid eligibility requirement. This has been a major factor in the decline in ABC weekly newspaper membership since the middle 1950s. Frequently during this period, weeklies and their national associations petitioned the board to ask ABC to extend its auditing services to newspapers that did not qualify under the Audit Bureau's eligibility rules.

By the middle 1970s, several factors combined to cause daily newspapers to change their attitudes on free distribution shoppers. National retailers defined their store trading markets through the use of postal code area building blocks. In pressing newspapers to report circulation by these same geographic areas, they learned some parts of their markets were not being covered by the paid circulation to the household ratios their marketing plans called for. When these advertisers looked to alternate services to distribute their advertising supplements, daily newspapers added free distribution to supplement their paid in these areas—first through increased sampling and then through separate advertising publications.

While advertisers indicated a desire to have the distribution of these free supplemental market coverage publications verified, they did not insist on it. Most newspaper publishers were not anxious for ABC to open its membership to free distribution publications, nor were they anxious to add the cost of verification to their own free publications.

In 1978, during an ongoing discussion of the audit of unpaid publications stemming from a request by Canadian magazine advertisers, the board approved experimental audits of a daily newspaper, a weekly newspaper, and two supplemental market coverage publications of daily newspaper members.

Just prior to the 1978 annual meeting, members of the ABC newspaper research and development committee (an independent advisory committee of the newspaper division made up principally of representatives of the International Circulation Managers Association) voted 16 to 6 to "indicate their desire that ABC not become involved in further audit of unpaid distribution." The annual meeting discussion was divided on the issue. Harold Schwartz, Milwaukee, Wisconsin, Journal Co., said "the future of ABC hangs on our keeping up with the times and auditing all forms of print media. The issue isn't going to go away because we don't like it. It's here. It's viable. It's real. We've heard the reports today, and I suggest that we do it." Leon Reed, Little Rock, Arkansas, *Gazette*, countered with "I can see absolutely no value to the auditing of nonpaid circulation, call it a shopper if you don't happen to have one. It seems to me a tremendous competitive disadvantage. It's going to force a lot of people who aren't in it to get in it because you are now going to give the throwaway some respectability through ABC."

An admitted long-time paid purist, Bryon C. Vedder, Lindsay-Schaub Newspapers, said his attitude had changed and that he favored "further study, at least, of the auditing of unpaid distribution or supplementary shopper distribution of ABC members. Such an audit would add credibility for sales for our supplementary coverage to retailers."

Schwartz: "The future of ABC hangs on our keeping up with the times and auditing all forms of print media."

At one point, Steven Ryder, Medford, Oregon, *Mail Tribune*, suggested the possibility of an ABC-affiliated service (he even suggested a name for the service—LAND, for Limited Audit of Newspaper Distribution) to verify free distribution newspaper publications. The discussion closed with the approval of a resolution that recognized the need for continued study of the audit of unpaid issue, but requested that the board take no formal action to implement such a program prior to the next annual meeting.

Many newspapers use supplemental free distribution, but publishers and buyers aren't sure ABC or subsidiary should be involved in auditing these vehicles.

Managing Director Alan Wolcott reported to the board that during the following year ABC had received correspondence from only two newspapers opposed to the audit of unpaid publications. At the 1979 annual meeting, the newspapers, while less enthusiastic than the advertiser and advertising agency members over such a possible ABC service, voted to ask for more information and time to study these data.

Survey was made of daily and weekly newspaper members to determine the extent supplemental free distribution was being used. In early 1980, almost 47 percent of the daily newspapers were using some form of free extended market coverage and another 25 percent indicated that they would be adding free within the next year. Among weeklies, 33 percent were using supplementary free, and another 10 percent planned to add it. Wolcott distributed to all newspaper members a "white paper" on the issue, making no case for or against the audit of unpaid. The "white paper" was also reviewed by the board and marketing committee of the International Newspaper Advertising Executives association. The INAE board announced its support of an extension of ABC auditing services to unpaid coverage publications of member newspapers "as an option for those publishers who wish it." The "white paper" mailing produced virtually no reaction. Only two newspapers had written to the Audit Bureau, both from multiple newspaper publishing companies and both threatening to withdraw their papers if ABC offered a service to unpaid publications.

At the 1980 meeting, the newspapers requested that the board drop the subject of auditing of unpaid from its agenda. At its next meeting and citing "a widespread lack of advertiser, agency, and publisher support," the board voted to table further discussion of the audit of free publications.

It was off the board's agenda but not so that of the board's Canadian committee. Concerned by the declining weekly newspaper membership in that country and in response to a weekly group's request that ABC consider verifying its free extended market publication, the committee asked that it be reviewed by the board's newspaper committee. An ad hoc subcommittee studied the request during much of 1982 and 1983 and recommended that management continue to research the subject as it applied to the decline of weekly newspaper members.

In the spring of 1984, the ABC liaison committee of the American Newspaper Publishers Association and the Newspaper Advertising Bureau conducted a survey of 78 of their members on a number of issues. One of the questions asked whether ABC should audit free distribution, with special reference to the total market coverage of member newspapers. The survey reported that over 65 percent of the responses opposed such a service. Once again, the board voted to table the subject of the audit of unpaid circulation publications published by ABC members.

Markets

Reporting for a 1933 committee studying ABC newspaper market area rules, Managing Director Harn opined, "Probably no one question has been so continuously the subject of controversy, since the beginning of the Bureau, as that of the establishment of city and retail trading zones for the various cities where our member newspapers are published." His assessment was at least partially correct. Several other issues generated continuing debate, but the Audit Bureau's efforts to find a universally acceptable standard for defining newspaper markets, within which circulation could be reported, was only then becoming complicated.

Prior to the formation of the Audit Bureau, publishers generally provided a total circulation figure, allowing their advertising salesmen to "break down that figure in a way that best befits the needs of the company he is calling on." The advisory committee that developed ABC's first newspaper report forms during the summer of 1914 agreed that circulation should be shown by "City," "Suburban (trading territory)," and "Country" designations. City referred to the corporate limits of the city of publication. The Suburban territory was an agreed area surrounding the city limits, defined in miles radius. The eight largest towns within each were identified in the report. Circulation not sold in these two areas was reported as Country.

Rule mandates city, state breaks of distribution.

An option was the reporting of separate gross distribution figures, first for the eight largest towns in the Suburban territory, then any town outside the City receiving 25 or more copies of a typical issue.

Early on, competing publishers disagreed on boundaries for the segments of their markets. In 1915, the board ruled that "the Bureau shall send an auditor as soon as possible to effect a settlement and define such limits in order that all statements of newspapers in dispute in that city may be rendered on a uniform basis." The following year, ABC clarified existing practice by giving publishers the option of reporting circulation within each market segment by distribution methods (carriers, dealers, street sales, counter sales, and mail subscriptions), the "Classified Plan," or supplying a single total, called the "Metropolitan Plan."

During these early years, the board was deluged with requests for exceptions from boundaries agreed to by other publishers in the market or from the findings of the auditor. By 1919, the board constituted a special committee to deal exclusively with newspaper members who refused to accept ABC recognized market areas. This experience later produced a number of changes and clarifications in the rules.

In 1922, the newspaper members voted two changes. The first was to make the gross distribution breakdown in Audit Reports of a typical issue by all cities and towns outside the City receiving 25 copies or more mandatory for all newspapers, and for these data to be verified by ABC. This requirement was adopted by the board at its next meeting, along with the qualifying comment to appear in the report, "Includes spoiled in distribution, free copies, unsold, and allowances." The second was to make the "Classified Plan" of breaking down paid circulation in market areas by distribution methods mandatory for all newspapers in cities of 500,000 population or less. While it was supported by the newspaper directors, the more numerous buyers on the board refused to accept one standard for the larger papers and another for those serving medium and smaller markets.

At the 1923 annual meeting, Charles M. Morgan, Burlington, Iowa, *Gazette*, raised several questions that led to later rule study and changes. "The manner in which ABC sets boundaries has caused controversy ever since the standards were put in place and the board has recognized their inadequacy by granting numerous exceptions. Consider, if you will, the situation at Troy, New York, where the publisher cannot claim Albany in its suburban territory, even though it is only six miles away, yet it can claim another town 50 miles in the other direction—this, only because there happens to be another newspaper located in Albany. I ask you why ABC cannot recognize that natural markets aren't bound by political lines, and that the markets of two newspapers can overlap.

"Secondly, the ABC terms are misleading. One of the farm papers in our state is advertising that it has 22 percent more country circulation than all of the dailies put together. Most of the circulation we must report under the 'Country' designation isn't rural at all, but goes to such places as Chicago, New York, or other heavily populated places."

At the board's next meeting, it adopted a rule change that recognized that "City" boundaries "may include more territory than the exact corporate limits." It also changed the responsibility of the committee to investigate market area differences to reviewing current standards and recommending new rules. The first recommendation of the committee, adopted by the board, was to permit publishers "to report figures showing the population of markets as estimated by local authorities" along with and as a means of updating census figures.

During 1924, the committee queried newspaper members on a series of 14 "specialized, definite problems." One of the questions was, "How can suburban or trading territories be adjusted to meet the divergent claims of morning and evening papers as to its limits?" Of the 177 responding publishers, 63 had no specific answers to offer, 41 thought it was a job for ABC to make an arbitrary decision, 17 thought this was a task for the local merchants in the market, and the remaining 56 were scattered between almost as many observations, including one who simply suggested that "it can't be done." Since the board and management were currently adjudicating these controversies, the vote was hardly a mandate to action. Another board committee was

Do morning and evening papers serve the same geographical market areas?

constituted in 1927 to study the subject of market areas served by newspaper members, searching for a uniform standard for defining these areas. Morgan's question on misleading terminology for marketing areas took four years to get around to action. The board approved the committee's recommendation to make these changes. "In order to eliminate the ambiguity and misapprehension, the word 'Country' is now abolished and the term 'All Other' is substituted." The term "Suburban" was also changed to "Trading Territory."

After a year of study, S.E. Conybeare, Armstrong Cork Co., reported the committee's recommendations. "First, it should be recognized that determining trading areas is not the function of the Audit Bureau. Second, advertising buyers are interested in density of circulations, which means that relation between circulation and population. It is suggested, therefore, that three or more zones be established for each newspaper city. The first zone be that which is now considered as city circulation. The second zone shall be an area determined by the density of coverage of the total combined daily circulation of the newspapers published in the city for which the zone is established. From this study the percentage of density of coverage, yet to be determined, shall be included in zone two. Zone three is to include all other circulation. Should the newspapers in a given city wish, additional zones outside of zone two may be set up on a percentage of density yet to be determined and to which the various publishers and the Audit Bureau agree."

Determining trading areas not ABC function.

At the January 1933 meeting, after hearing zone boundary appeals from newspapers in Harrisburg, Pennsylvania, and Charlotte, North Carolina, the board concluded that "the whole theory of the traditional ABC trading areas was wrong" and appointed a committee to study the question. Under the leadership of T.F. Driscoll, Armour and Co., the new committee was charged with "finding, if possible, a formula that would be uniformly applicable, without guesswork, and thus put an end to these bitter controversies." The board further declared a moratorium on trading area changes in markets where competitive differences between publishers existed.

After a six-month review of the subject with advertiser and advertising agency members "to see how they use the information and what particular segregation they most wanted," Driscoll's committee reported two discoveries. "Buyers do not make any distinction between actual residents within the corporate limits and those living so close as to be city-minded. Secondly, they are not interested in what this person or that might consider the 'trading area' of a city, but very much interested in overlaying circulation coverage by units on what the advertiser considers to be his market."

Simplicity in itself, the committee recommended that newspaper circulations be broken down by corporate city of publication, county of publications, and then by counties within which total circulation of the newspapers in the market was at least 5 percent of the population and radiating out from the central city to a limit of 100 miles. The plan was submitted to the divisional meetings at the annual meeting. Advertiser and advertising agency members strongly supported the Driscoll committee's recommendations; newspapers asked that it be sent to all members of the division "for further consideration and study." The plan was sent to the members and after a review of some 100 responses, the committee reported its feeling "that it would be difficult, if not impossible, to develop any method or formula which would be acceptable to the majority of newspaper members." At the committee's recommendation, the board lifted the moratorium on trading area changes. This the board did at its April 1934 meeting, along with assigning the committee the responsibility of adjudicating such disputes as were appealed from management decisions.

With that issue temporarily put aside for later boards to grapple with, the directors turned to another long-simmering controversy. Years earlier the board ruled that newspapers having distributions outside their city zones in the cities of other ABC newspapers had to report this if it amounted to 25 copies or more. Publishers in the smaller cities complained that this rule, which was intended to protect them from unfair claims of metropolitan papers, actually didn't work. Comparisons were made on the basis of average net paid *Efforts to protect smaller papers called unfair.* circulation of the local newspaper versus actual issue gross distribution (including unsold, unpaid, and copies reshipped elsewhere) of the nonlocal newspaper. When the board ruled that city zones could expand beyond the corporate limits of the city of publication, the extensions were into suburbs and nearby municipalities, many of which were served by local newspapers. In Los Angeles, for example, 22 separate communities were absorbed into the city zone of the newspapers in that city. The Los Angeles newspapers' circulation in those communities became part of the total they reported in the city zone, for which no separate breakdown was required.

The issue had been on the board's agenda for several years when it became a point of bitter debate at the 1934 annual meeting between representatives of small city and metropolitan newspapers. A proposal was submitted to the advertiser, advertising agency, and newspaper meetings in 1935 suggesting a special net paid break out in any city where claimed distribution represented 5 percent or more of the local newspaper's circulation. Advertisers favored the resolution, but a break out at a 15 percent level; agencies favored it with a 25 percent level. Newspapers generally agreed with the 15 percent level, only in the retail trading zone and only at the request of the local paper. A committee representing both small and large newspapers was established to resolve the differences.

Zones to recognize census tracts wherever feasible.

The committee's recommendation, following the newspaper division's resolution, was unanimously approved by the division at its 1936 meeting. In crafting a rule at its next meeting, however, the board included two changes. First, cities "inside and outside" the city zone of the outside newspaper were included. Second, if the circulation of one newspaper was broken down, each other newspaper in the market would also show a breakdown.

In 1940, the board turned down a request by the St. Louis newspapers to realign its city zone in accordance with the Bureau of the Census "metropolitan area" designation, but did establish the policy "that in delineation of future ABC city zone districts, it be basic and fundamental for the Bureau to follow and recognize definitely delineated census tracts, wherever feasible and possible, within management's discretion."

The issue of reporting newspaper circulation in the city of another member came up again in 1941. It had been "solved" nearly a decade earlier with a rule requiring newspapers claiming distribution in the city of another member totaling 15 percent or more of the local newspaper's circulation, to report an average net paid circulation breakdown for that city. The rule, as adopted, referred to cities "inside or outside" of the incoming newspaper's city zone. The Ohio Select List of newspapers called the board's attention to the fact that ABC was not requiring such breakdowns for distribution within city zones and asked that the rule be enforced. The board reviewed the subject with buyers, determined the cost and effort involved in showing circulation in communities adjacent to metropolitan cities far outweighed the benefits to advertisers, and made the breakdown inside city zones optional for newspaper members. None exercised this option.

As the 1940 U.S. and 1941 Canadian census data became available, ABC approved the optional use of "occupied dwelling unit" figures along with population data. Because of dramatic wartime shifts in population subsequent to the census taking, the board approved update estimates based on other than federal data.

At its September 1944 meeting, the board heard a request from members of the Pacific Northwest Circulation Managers Association asking that a then under consideration new map plan, "as it might affect city and trading zone boundaries, be held in abeyance for the duration of the war." The newspapers cited the shortage of competent help and the drastic restrictions on the use of newsprint as already complicating publishing life. "We do not need the added problems that ABC action might give us." A moratorium on boundary changes was approved. It remained in effect until December 1946. During the moratorium, a "summary of procedures relative to establishing and changing ABC city and retail trading zones" was developed and approved as a future guide for management. The document was less a "summary" than a complete and complicated textbook; Ben Duffy, Batten, Barton, Durstine & Osborn, commented on the document that he hoped "management understands this because no one else does, but that seems to have been part of our problem all along."

The summary didn't solve any significant controversies. Population relocations, which continued after the war ended, made earlier census data virtually useless. Arguments grew out of types of alternate data that could be used. Adoption of the summary contents did establish several lasting policies, however. It gave the managing director responsibility for establishing and realigning zone boundaries. It also attempted to establish that market definitions were to be based on "accessibility, transportation possibilities, highways, and other factors influencing the flow of trade either in personal shopping or by mail," rather than density of coverage. "Circulation coverage and markets are related, but not deemed to be identical." It further recognized census tracts as a possible building block for delineating zones that included part-county areas.

Moratorium on zone changes until census is set.

The board's committees began a study of government plans for 1950 and 1951 census takings. Proposed new urban and metropolitan county areas were considered as possible alternatives to city and retail trading zones. At its 1949 meeting, the newspapers advised the board "that inasmuch as there has developed confusion and misunderstanding in connection with changes of city and retail trading zones; and inasmuch as an entirely new set of figures, information, and other pertinent, helpful, related facts will be available as guiding factors from the census bureaus of the United States and Canada, the directors should put into

effect a moratorium with respect to any contested
changes in city and retail trading zones for a period
of 18 months." The board again agreed.

     The board's committee on city and retail
trading zones reported in June 1950 that Bureau of
the Census "Urbanized Areas" were not generally an
alternative for ABC city zones. It concluded that the

*Verne Joy
congratulates
Gene Robb on his
committee's
advice.*

census "Metropolitan Areas" would provide "little help with regard to
establishing combined ABC city and retail trading zones." In its recommendations, the committee asked the board to "reaffirm the practices
and procedure of the management" set forth in the 1946 summary. At
the 1950 annual meeting, advertisers and advertising agencies applauded the committee's efforts. Newspapers, however, citing continued
confusion and misunderstanding, voted to create a "central committee of
interested newspaper members to make a further study and recommendations with respect to retail trading zones."

     Under the direction of Gene Robb, Hearst Newspapers, the "cen-
tral" committee of the newspaper division met frequently during early
1951 and made its report to the board in June. In essence, the report
clarified but made no substantial changes in provisions of existing ABC
policies and recommended that these policies be made a part of the rules.

These were approved at the board's October meeting. In his report to the general convention the next day, Chairman H.H. Kynett, Aitkin-Kynett Co., said, "To summarize, the work of the central committee resulted in virtually the same recommendations as those developed by the retail trading zones committee of the board. The recommendations represent no major change in present or recent rules and definitions. It is very encouraging to note that when understanding is developed by all parties concerned, there seems to be little room for argument. The outcome of the retail trading zone study represents definite progress in general comprehension of the fundamental philosophy of the ABC, which is to meet changing times with practices that fit the times."

The following year, the newspaper committee of the American Association of Advertising Agencies requested that the board establish rules to make it mandatory for newspapers servicing Bureau of the Census-defined Standard Metropolitan Areas to report a special circulation breakdown for these areas. This issue was debated during many meetings, and, in 1954, the newspaper division voted to "reaffirm our continued opposition to any rule which would require newspapers to make or show a separate compilation of their circulations in Standard Metropolitan Areas," and asked that a committee be appointed to study the matter. In 1956, the board approved a rule that would identify with an asterisk counties included in the Standard Metropolitan Area in their Audit Report listings of cities and counties receiving 25 or more copies of an actual issue. At the publisher's option, a summary of total circulation within SMA counties could also be shown in the explanatory paragraph of the newspaper's report.

Agencies call for circulation breakdowns by census-defined metropolitan areas.

As had been true so often in the Audit Bureau's relations with its newspaper members, the second time around was less troubling than the first. By the mid-1950s, the impact of television on advertising revenues was making itself felt. Newspapers were seeking ways to offset this diversion. Audited paid circulation was a strong plus for newspapers, and members turned to ABC to find ways of making its reports more useful to media buyers.

Like radio, television brought with it new market area designations. Most were simply a circle defining the effective strength of the broadcast signal. ABC city and retail trading zones, on the other hand, were more complicated. Buyers were calling on publishers to provide circulation data in breakdowns that could be compared with television. The concept of showing maps of newspaper market areas, which had been suggested and discarded a generation earlier, was again raised. The board approved an optional map plan, and, when it was introduced with the September 1959 Audit Reports, more than 200 newspapers had requested the option. Within six months, nearly half of Audit Bureau-defined city and retail trading zones were scheduled for visualization.

The board further liberalized provisions for reporting circulation by Metropolitan Areas, "as established by the U.S. Bureau of the Budget and/or the Dominion Bureau of Statistics." Pushed by Sidney W. Dean, McCann-Erickson, Inc., the board continued its efforts to improve its reports, often at the displeasure of the newspaper directors. The question of updating population and dwelling figures between census takings had long been a concern of the board.

The practice was optional, and, in some cases, the sources of data were questionable. Dean suggested that the "Bureau develop a formula for annually updating these figures with an eye to offering a single authoritative source for these data in ABC newspaper reports." The action was approved with the plan to test the accuracy of a formula "with census figures forthcoming in 1960." The test was conducted, but the updating process was not implemented.

With the inclusion of market area maps locating independent municipalities within the city and retail trading zones, the requirement for newspapers to list the eight largest towns in their retail trading zones was discarded. Occupied dwelling unit figures were added to the typical day breakdown of distribution in towns, counties, zones, and areas for those listings with 2,500 dwellings or more.

Pleased by the newspapers' new spirit of accommodation, advertising agency members at their 1960 meeting suggested that "in view of the new information on city markets that will be made available in the various divisions of the 1960 census, the board is asked to restudy the present city zone and retail trading zone definitions, with a view toward aligning them, for circulation analysis, to the greatest degree possible with other geographic areas employed for the reporting of population and marketing information."

ABC's first reaction was to offer newspapers an optional series of breakdowns of one day's distribution by states and provinces, counties, and cities within counties receiving 25 or more copies. The alternative to the existing breakdown further offered the publishers the option of showing separate total gross distribution figures and figures adjusted to the net paid for the period of the report, approximating a paid circulation figure, for each listing. This, the board explained, brought county figures into more prominence and allowed buyers to use them more easily in constructing marketing areas of their own choosing.

Seven years after it was first proposed by media buyers, ABC approved a rule to let newspapers report average paid circulation by "county of publication and/or Standard Metropolitan Statistical Area (U.S.) and/or Census Metropolitan Area (Canada)." This was subsequently amended to include other geographic areas used by advertisers.

Members celebrated the Audit Bureau's 50th anniversary in 1964 by voting a change to the association's charter. To the charter mission statement's reference to ABC's concern for "circulation data," the members added the words "or other data." The intent was to give the board more freedom in exploring ways of broadening ABC services to the advertising industry.

Newspaper members immediately called on the board to create a special task force to make "a comprehensive, in-depth evaluation of all data currently reported by newspapers, as well as the manner in which these data are reported." The study was to include a review of market area definitions and the possibility of including demographic data in ABC reports. At its next meeting, the board agreed to the study and declared a suspension of all city and retail trading zone changes until the study could be completed.

A committee, headed by Lester A. Walker, Fremont, Nebraska, *Tribune*, went to work to explore "modernizing ABC reporting procedures; inclusion of market demographic data and other pertinent basic market characteristics in newspaper Audit Reports; making newspaper audience studies and reporting them; and any and all ways in which ABC might assist the newspaper publisher by providing a better tool for selling advertising." Early in 1965, the committee took its questions directly to advertisers, advertising agency media buyers, and representatives "of virtually all facets of the newspaper publishing business."

The initial proposals of Walker's committee were dramatically different from existing standards and generated controversy. The concept of city and retail trading zones would be dropped, substituting Standard Metropolitan Statistical Areas (U.S.) or Census Metropolitan

Areas (Canada) for newspapers located in the central
cities of such areas or the county of publications for
newspapers outside such areas. Optional variations
would permit a break out of circulation in the city
of publication. An optional additional breakdown
would allow publishers to designate and report
circulation within its own "Primary Market Area."
In practice, the primary market area would encompass substantially the same territory currently

*Lester Walker,
center, with
Richard Babcock
and William
Steers: Report
generated
controversy.*

covered by the city and retail trading zones but would be composed of
whole counties and/or selected abutting portions (census units) in which
the newspaper had at least 20 percent coverage. Elimination of the city
zone would make it mandatory for the breakdown of one-day gross distribution to include all separate municipalities receiving 25 copies or more,
inside and outside the central market.

In answer to publisher criticism of the proposed elimination of
zones, Walker asked "what value do they have? Most buyers tell us ABC
zones have little value since they are established by opinion, not fact,
and that as economic units they have been or are being replaced by
counties. Modern marketing research is basically on a county level,
and it is on that basis that marketing data is fed into computers.

"The marketing man cannot normally compare these zones with any standardized and accepted available marketing data. Nor can he accurately relate them to claims of other media competing for the same advertising dollars we all profess to be seeking. By eliminating zones and using counties we would be giving the buyer what he says he wants, not what we publishers think we want him to have."

A major concern at the time was the difference in philosophies between the zonal and primary market concepts. ABC's zonal definitions followed lines of urban development, trading habit, or political boundary. The primary market area, defined by the publisher with ABC approval, could be any combination of abutting counties or smaller census units in which the newspaper had at least 20 percent coverage. Zones were uniform for all newspapers in the market, while the primary market areas could differ from one newspaper to the other. Zones were intended to define the market, and the primary market area was intended to define the newspapers' circulation penetration within the market.

The back-up of zonal alignment requests forced the board to lift the moratorium on changes in September 1965 despite the fact that the task force's study was far from complete.

After a year and a half of discussion, the board finally approved the reporting of paid circulation by primary market areas as an optional breakdown and in addition to the existing city and retail trading zone breakdown. The provision that newspapers had to have at least 20 percent coverage in the component units of the primary market was eliminated. Determining factors in establishing the boundaries included "evidence that the newspaper provides primary editorial and advertising service to the area; that the area consists of abutting census units, none larger than a county; and that the ratio of paid circulation to households could be considered, but not as a determining factor." In approving this option, the board agreed to the reporting of distribution in all cities receiving 25 or more copies in all marketing areas. The provision for including municipalities within the city zones was withdrawn after considerable objection was voiced at the newspaper divisional meeting.

"Old gray lady" begins moving too fast for some.

Over the years, the Audit Bureau had gained the reputation among newspaper members as "the old gray lady of Wacker Drive," a disdainful reference to the meticulous care and long time it took the board in reaching decisions. However, at the 1966 meeting, the newspapers complained that the board "was moving too fast in too many directions." They requested that the newspaper directors appoint an advisory committee of nominees from national and regional associations through-out the United States and Canada. This formalized

Review Committee created to study new ABC services.

an informal committee that assisted the task force working on recent changes. Largely influenced by members of the International Circulation Managers Association, the newspapers also created a divisional review committee "to study all of the new activities undertaken by ABC or its newly created affiliate, the Audit Bureau of Marketing Services."

All of the March 1967 Publisher's Statements included the new population and occupied housing unit updates. More than 40 news-papers had opted to report the supplementary primary market area breakdown, with another 60 primary market areas being developed.

Later that year, the board queried members of seven industry committees on a number of related issues. Approximately 75 percent of those polled favored the optional replacement of city and retail trading zones with a primary market breakdown. They also favored the contin-ued optional use of maps by those reporting by zones but the mandatory use of maps for those electing the primary market option. These new rules were approved and became effective with the audit period begin-ning April 1, 1968.

Buyer response to the primary market area concept was encourag-ing. To wean newspapers away from zonal breakdowns, the board simplified recordkeeping procedures for those who used the PMA option. In 1969, it approved a single paid circulation figure in reports of PMA, rather than requiring separate totals for each county or county part within the market. Separate break outs were still required for all municipalities outside the central city receiving 25 or more copies daily. By 1970, 51 papers had adopted the PMA reporting in place of zones, and another 56 were reporting by both breakdowns.

The use of PMA reporting grew over the years but did not become the universal standard. Many newspapers continued with their zonal breakdowns. Some publishers held onto what they considered the best of two worlds, reporting by a city zone within a primary market area.

In 1982, the board's newspaper committee, under the chairmanship of Grover Friend, Levittown, Pennsylvania, *Bucks County Courier Times*, established a task force of directors and members, "to consider ways of making ABC's reports and services more valuable to buyers and sellers of newspaper advertising." First item on the task force's agenda was "the reporting of circulation data by marketing areas commonly used and generally accepted in the industry."

Historically, by the time the market definition needs of buyers were identified, discussions held, consensus determined, and board actions taken, the industry was already moving on to new standards. Friend's task force already knew that city and retail trading zone and primary market area definitions did not match market definitions used in developing marketing plans by other media nor those used by advertisers and advertising agencies.

After two years of study and discussions with allied advertiser, advertising agency, and newspaper associations, the task force proposed new terminology and a new concept to replace the primary market area designation. Where the PMA was based on areas

Friend's task: Make newspaper reports more valuable.

where newspapers were considered to have primary editorial and advertising influence, the new "Newspaper Designated Market" permitted the newspaper to define the market as it considered it was serving.

Factors set for determining areas to be included in the NDM included "evidence that the area is that geographical area in which the newspaper is marketed; the area consists of abutting census units"; and, while not a determining factor, "the ratio between the average paid circulation and current estimate of households within each county or portion thereof." Publishers reporting circulation by the new definition were required to report a complete breakdown of distribution for each town, city, or recognized community within the newspaper designated market receiving 25 or more copies, according to their county of location. As in the case of the primary market area, publishers reporting by the newspaper-designated market were required to include a map of the NDM breakdown.

Representatives of the American Newspaper Publishers Association and the Newspaper Advertising Bureau "were enthusiastic about the changes." Response from the American Association of Advertising Agencies and the Association of National Advertisers strongly supported the move. At its August 1984 meeting, the board approved the changes, and set their effective date for Publisher's Statements for the period ending March 31 the following year.

Currently, daily newspaper members have the option of reporting average paid circulation in their ABC reports either according to the Newspaper Designated Market, by city and retail trading zones, or a combination of these designations, plus the circulation outside the market boundaries. In addition to either of these, newspaper publishers may elect to show their average paid circulation by county of publication (for newspapers not published in the central city of a metropolitan area), or by Metropolitan Statistical Area, Consolidated Metropolitan Statistical Area (U.S.), or Census Metropolitan Area (Canada). A further supplementary option allows publishers to show average paid circulation in the Area of Dominant Influence, a market area definition established by The Arbitron Ratings Co.

Maps

The initial concept that newspaper market areas be based on census tract boundaries had long since given way to the many exceptions and new agreements. Buyers complained to ABC that these areas bore little resemblance to generally recognized marketing areas. "To try to make sense out of the verbal descriptions of these zones, as reported by the Bureau, is generally more a problem than the fact that a uniform standard does not exist," S.E. Conybeare, Armstrong Cork Co., told the board.

ABC market areas bear little resemblance to generally used definitions.

The newspapers sought a solution at the 1930 annual meeting by unanimously moving "that the Bureau adopt an outline map as a method of showing trading areas in place of the verbal description now provided." This action was adopted by the board, and management was instructed to begin developing such maps for all daily newspaper members. Managing Director Harn pointed out to the board that many of the city and retail trading zone boundaries defied accurate mapping "without incurring huge expenses of on-site inspections. The use of boundaries such as power lines, private property lines, and parochial terms are common but cannot be located on available maps. We doubt that these publishers will accept such increased costs."

Never a constituency to steer clear of controversy, newspapers resurrected the market area map issue even before the separate breakdown issue was resolved. Maps as an alternative to verbal descriptions of the market areas had been discussed in 1930 and approved the following year. Because of the controversy over standards for establishing the market segments, the map provision was never implemented. In a 1936 review of how ABC newspaper Publisher's Statements and Audit Reports could be made more useful to advertising buyers, the question of market area maps was once again raised.

Two proposals emerged and were submitted to the newspaper division for vote. One, showing a map with circulation totals in each county, received 55 percent of the vote. The other, showing the map without circulation totals, received 43 percent of the vote. Two percent didn't want any map at all. Because of the divergence of opinion, the visualization proposals went back to committee for more study and an eventual vote of the membership. As happens from time to time, not only do newspapers differ on issues, people within newspapers also disagree. The issue of maps in ABC reports was debated at the meetings of allied associations during 1937. Interestingly, members of the Newspaper Advertising Executives Association voted overwhelmingly to support a map plan. Members of the International Newspaper Circulation Managers voted in just as large a proportion in opposition to any map plan.

Visualization plan vote indecisive, returned for more study.

Part of the confusion was the result of missed communications between ABC management and members of the committee charged with developing a plan for visualizing the market areas. Managing Director Harn, in addressing national and regional newspaper associations, offered his version of the probable map plan to be offered. The committee, headed by Howard Stodghill, Hearst Newspapers, was discussing different proposals in their discussions with newspaper representatives.

One of the proposals under review by the committee at the time, but not finalized for presentation to the members despite Harn's assurances, called for use of a map showing the individual newspaper's circulation in counties surrounding the city zone where the paper's coverage was 20 percent or more of the households. Under another plan,

Doubt and hostility cause confusion, open opposition.

the trading territory would be described in terms of a circle surrounding the central city. Projected examples for Denver and Billings would be roughly 300 miles across; New York, Charlotte, and Chicago, 200 miles in diameter; and Peoria, 50 miles. In September, Stodghill's committee asked that any vote on the issue be withdrawn from the agenda of the 1937 annual meeting.

"As you know, some divisional allied newspaper groups other than the ABC newspaper members, themselves, have received the benefit of verbal explanations of a plan, and what was proposed has, to a degree, been given official presentation. Doubt and hostility over this has caused increased wrangling over long-continued territorial alignment controversies, for which no remedy has yet been found. The information the committee has secured from various geographical centers indicates confusion, skepticism, and pronounced opposition to the plan or plans under consideration. We recommend the study continue but emphasize the futility of a yes-or-no vote at this time."

The board agreed, and, while no vote was taken, the subject was discussed at the divisional meeting. Major concerns were expressed by evening metropolitan newspapers whose reach, based on point of sale, frequently did not extend as far into the trading territory as their morning competition. This "weakness," they felt, was offset by purchases made in the city zone and carried out into the trading territory by commuters, a condition that the county penetration map plan would not demonstrate. Other publishers were concerned that any plan to show density by counties would expose absurdities in alignments generously granted by ABC under not-so-scientific standards.

The discussion continued through 1938. In June, ABC newspaper directors met with a special committee of the International Circulation Managers Association and secured partial agreement. The representatives of the ICMA were about equally divided between the 20 percent county coverage standard and a plan that would show circulation, "without reference to families," within successive circles with 50-, 100-, and 150-mile radii definitions.

The committee proposed a trading territory alignment formula that would establish the most distant counties (or townships for smaller newspapers) having 20 percent coverage as the outer limits. All counties within this ring would be included. This was presented to the advertiser, advertising agency, and newspaper members in September for their

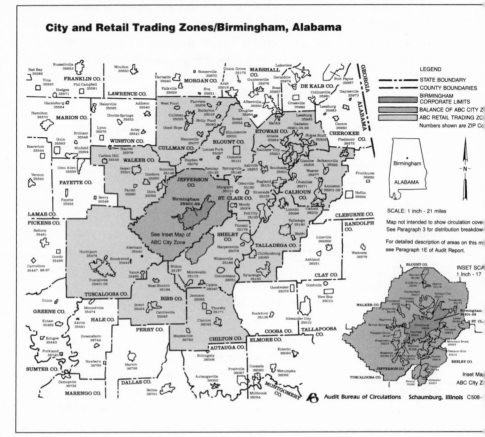

City and Retail Trading Zones/Birmingham, Alabama

After several yeas and nays, the newspaper market area map became an important part of the Audit Report.

reaction. The buyers approved by a response of 116 to 3; newspapers opposed by a response of 246 to 131. At the annual convention a month later, the buyer divisions again favored "some plan of visualization," while newspapers voted 580 to 125 to recommend "the abandonment of the idea of the addition of maps to reports."

In speaking to the issue, E.R. Chapman, Flint, Michigan, *Journal*, said, "The proposals will not result in an accurate visualization of the newspaper's distribution. Individual newspapers can better and more efficiently present to advertisers all the information which a map plan is intended to convey. The preparation and auditing of the maps would increase Bureau costs. The compilation of data would add greatly to the expense of publishers."

The issue came up again "for considerable discussion" at the advertiser, agency, and newspaper divisional meetings in 1939, with a resolution by the convention to create a newspaper member advisory committee "to study and consider the so-called visualization plan in an endeavor to reconcile divergent views and to report a constructive plan as expeditiously as possible."

With publishers in 651 markets (out of 1,079) electing to show maps in their ABC Audit Reports in 1971, the board voted to make the visualization mandatory, first for newspapers with 25,000 or more paid circulation and, later that year, for those above 15,000 paid circulation. Below that level, the map plan was optional.

Population and Housing Updates

During the spring of 1966, management undertook pilot studies in Galesburg, Illinois; Philadelphia, Pennsylvania; and Akron, Ohio, to test a formula for updating population and occupied housing figures. Based on the success of this research, the board approved annual updates, along with latest census figures, to be prepared and reported in all newspaper reports. The new service was initially hailed, later criticized, and ultimately dropped in favor of using updates from other sources.

When the board approved staff-prepared annual updates, or ABC "estimates," of population and household figures for the market areas and cities included in the mandatory breakdown of a typical day's gross distribution of its newspaper members in 1966, the procedure called for a straight line projection. Objections, and there were a number of situations where ABC's estimates were questioned by publishers, were resolved with the help of supplemental data supplied by the newspaper from non-federal census sources.

ABC's efforts were not authoritatively tested until 1970 and 1971 census data became generally available in 1974, and the revelation of a significant decline in both family size and the number of persons per household. To reflect this information, ABC's procedures were modified in 1975, using additional housing statistics obtained from federal sources and those available from local government agencies. Each year, ABC estimates were compared to the projections of other recognized sources such as *Sales and Marketing Management, Editor & Publisher,* and *Standard Rate and Data Service.* If significant differences were apparent, the ABC figures were reviewed again.

Responding to continuing criticisms of its estimates, ABC, with the help of outside consultants, revised its procedures in 1977. The complicated formula used population data from the latest two censuses and current estimates of the U.S. Bureau of the Census and Statistics Canada. These were calculated in terms of ratios. A comparison of these ratios provided a basis for calculating an annual change increment. These increments were then added or subtracted from the federal government's current estimate to arrive at the ABC estimate for the succeeding year.

ABC's efforts to update population and household figures continued to raise complaints. Few people outside of staff members directly involved in the calculations understood ABC's complicated formula. However accurate, ABC's figures differed from those supplied by other industry sources, and both buyers and publishers found these differences confusing. Early in his tenure, Managing Director M. David Keil identified this service as a point of continuing conflict between the Audit Bureau and its members and urged staff and board studies to find an alternative to these efforts.

The board's newspaper committee, under the chairmanship of Grover Friend, Bucks County, Pennsylvania, *Courier Times*, established a task force of directors and members in 1982 "to consider ways of making ABC's reports and services more valuable to buyers and sellers of newspaper advertising." One of its initial concerns was the possible use of population and household information from sources other than ABC and generally accepted in the industry.

ABC's efforts to update population and household figures continues to raise member complaints.

After a two-year review of population and household data used by members, the task force recommended and the board approved the use of county data from Market Statistics, a service owned by Bill Communications, Inc., for U.S. newspaper reports. ABC would continue to calculate estimates based on these county updates for cities and areas smaller than counties. Canadian publishers requested that ABC continue to compile its own county data in that country, considering it more accurate than that provided by services there.

By requiring that differences between publishers and Market Statistics be negotiated with the service and, to a major degree, getting itself out of the updating process, the Audit Bureau was able to close out a major source of controversy.

Analysis by Postal Code

The Audit Bureau had barely announced plans to include newspaper
circulation figures in its county-unit based Data Bank Services computer
library when advertisers broached a new reporting subject.

For many years, major retailers grappled with the problem of identifying and defining markets and measuring advertising coverage to
these markets. Circles around store locations had given way to county
building blocks. While population and demographic data were available
for counties, these were too large to define segments of metropolitan
multi-store trading areas. Census tracts were too small, and demographic data were available for only a limited number.

When the U.S. Post Office created the Zoning Improvement Plan
in 1963, the retailers recognized ZIP Code areas as a potential as a sub-
county measure for defining store trading territories. They began to
compile store customer and sales data by ZIP Code areas. With the 1970
census, census tract demographic information was reassembled to
approximate the postal areas in metropolitan markets. Because ZIP
Codes were so easy to use, because people tend to live near people of
similar habits, and because ZIP Codes reflected mailing and transportation patterns, advertisers began to see them as ideal marketing units in
which consumer behavior could not only be measured but predicted.
Major problems by the mid 1970s were that full five-digit ZIP census
data were only available in metropolitan centers; three-digit ZIP, areas
too large to be useful, were available outside metropolitan centers; ZIP
Code areas were altered at the discretion of the local postmaster (over
43,000 changes were made in 1976 to the boundaries of 39,500 ZIPs);
and ZIP Code area maps were generally unavailable.

Major retailers had already begun to evaluate newspaper advertising coverage against ZIP Code areas by converting city and county
breakdowns and reassembling this information to areas approximating
their store trading areas. Sears, Roebuck and Co., JCPenney Co., and
the Montgomery Ward Co. each appealed to the Audit Bureau to provide
supplemental circulation breakdowns by ZIPs in each newspaper's
Audit Report.

"We generally believe," John D. Flakne, Montgomery Ward Co.,
wrote ABC, "the retail trading zone concept is nearly valueless, and
that the city zone is a device used as often to disguise market coverage
weaknesses as to provide useful information to the advertiser. Since

retailers know quite accurately where their customers are coming from, they find it equally important to know how well the local newspaper reaches the areas in which those customers live. The present way of reporting circulation does not adequately meet our needs."

Early in 1976, the board initiated a study to determine the feasibility of reporting newspaper circulation by these U.S. postal code areas.

Gerald M. Byrne, Sears, Roebuck and Co., told the newspaper members that fall, "Perhaps the lack of comparable circulation didn't matter way back in 1960, but this is 1976, and the retailer now has a wealth of useful customer demographics and retail marketing facts at his disposal. He is likely to have far more sophisticated data in the future. Much of this data, both generated internally by the retailer and that available from other sources is organized by ZIP Code. It is obvious that a compatible unit of newspaper measurement is needed so that this new-found information can be put to work effectively. The use of a standardized unit, such as ZIP Code, can also permit the retailer to measure circulation by almost any definition of the market.

"We have examined the use of the ZIP Code to analyze circulation in several of our markets. It is not perfect, but it works better than anything we have used before. We ask you to think hard about, and begin working with, the ZIP Code as a basic newspaper circulation measurement tool. We ask ABC to consider adding these numbers into its Data Bank. The ability to retrieve circulation data for each ZIP Code singly, or in selective groups, by whatever market definition the advertiser chooses, is vital to both you and us."

At the same meeting, David Thomas, Louisville, Kentucky, *Courier Journal* and *Times*, said ZIP Code breakdowns were not only possible, but offered many management benefits beyond serving the needs of advertisers. He said his papers got into the ZIP analysis

Byrne pushed reporting by postal codes.

several years earlier "to compete with pre-prints and doorknob delivery people, and now use it to eliminate duplications, carrier route identification, improved complaint delivery, and determination of distribution costs. We have only begun to tap the potential of this method of circulation reporting. I urge you to consider it in your future."

The presentations were "exceptionally well received," and the board was asked to move ahead with its feasibility study. Pilot test audits of newspapers promoting ZIP Code breakdowns were not completed because publishers lacked sufficient records. The project languished. Five-digit ZIPs existed only in metropolitan areas. Postal officials were unclear as to the exact areas covered by individual ZIPs. Publishers interested in cooperating needed time to revise their systems and construct auditable records.

At the 1979 annual meeting, Robert Kissel, Sears, Roebuck and Co., told the newspaper publishers that 80 percent of the 30 largest retailers in the U.S. favored the ZIP Code breakdowns. "Let's keep the dialogue going. For our mutual benefit, let's not just keep on talking— let's get some action. Let's do something."

The board announced in mid-1980 that, as new U.S. census data became available, ABC would offer an optional plan for newspapers wishing to report a one-day breakdown of distribution by ZIP Code areas. "Initially, ZIP-coded circulation data will be available on the basis of information provided in the mandatory Paragraph 3 and will consist of one figure for multiple ZIP cities and towns. Plans for the future include the making of available circulation data for individual ZIP Codes within multiple ZIP Code cities and towns."

The first postal code breakdown appeared in 1980 Audit Report of the Levittown, Pennsylvania, *Bucks County Courier*. James Boynton, JCPenney Co., encouraged publishers to adopt the ZIP Code breakdown at their meeting that year. "I think I can speak for the major chains and say the implementation of such an audit can be of tremendous value to each of us, you and the retailers."

In June 1982, the board extended the option to include a Canadian newspaper breakdown by Area Code Designators, the first three characters of the Postal Code. Despite the obvious enthusiasm of advertisers for this breakdown, newspapers were less than enthusiastic in exercising this ABC service option. In the first three years of its availability, only 19 newspapers were reporting circulation by ZIP Codes in their Audit Reports.

Concerned by their reluctance to join the service, ABC surveyed its daily and weekly newspaper members to learn why the service was progressing so slowly. Of the nearly 650 respondents, 72 percent said they favored the service. Interestingly, 118 dailies and 32 weeklies reported that their circulations were currently analyzed by ZIP or Postal Code and that this information was being made available to advertisers on a selective basis. Major reasons reported for not opting for the ABC program were the concern of increased recordkeeping, the added costs of auditing, and the continuing requirement to show a typical day analysis by cities receiving 25 or more copies.

As more buyers spoke out on the postal code option, more newspapers added the data in their reports.

Zip Code Town	State	MORNING	SUNDAY
45505 Springfield	OH	43	40
45601 Chillicothe	OH	2,565	4,747
45620 Cheshire	OH	23	37
45628 Frankfort	OH	51	61
45631 Gallipolis	OH	378	559
45634 Hamden	OH	40	78
45638 Ironton	OH	22	178
45640 Jackson	OH	936	1,411
45644 Kingston	OH	190	591

Backed by a strong appeal from the 1982 joint advertiser and advertising agency meeting and the recommendations of the newspaper information task force and its own newspaper committee, the board "affirmed its intent to make the analysis of circulation by ZIP Code areas a mandatory requirement for U.S. member newspapers within the next three years."

Continuing discussions revealed additional, perhaps deeper, newspaper concerns. The requirement for publishers to report circulation by more finite market units would expose coverage patterns, especially within the central city. For those newspapers still reporting on the city zone basis, the exposure would cover an even larger market area. While they were generally agreeable to providing these data to selected advertisers, some publishers felt that to have this information published in the readily available ABC Audit Report was an open invitation to exploitation by broadcast, alternate delivery, and other newspaper competition. The difficulty in major markets to align carrier routes to ZIP Code boundaries was also pointed out as a concern.

Further, some publishers contended, the necessity of crediting circulation to the point of sale seriously distorted ZIP Code coverages. One publisher pointed out that following the Audit Bureau's formula, it would have over 400 percent coverage in one ZIP Code area where there was a concentration of single copy sales, but would show up weak in several abutting areas.

These concerns were addressed by the board in 1984. Publishers were granted the further option of controlling the distribution of their ABC-audited ZIP Code analyses, separate of their Audit Reports. The board decided not to develop an alternative to solve the newsstand allocation of copies and retained the point of sale formula after being assured by advertisers that perceived distortions could be properly evaluated. In addressing the members, Sonja Larsen, Target Stores, said the use of ZIP marketing units is growing and there is a "very real need for this information to be audited." On the publishers' concern over the allocation of single copy sales, she said, "I don't think this is a very big hangup. It is an easily understood concept."

Representatives of the American Newspaper Publishers Association and the Newspaper Advertising Bureau advised that they were receiving objections to the mandatory ZIP Code reporting and asked the board to delay the effective date until the matter was further discussed with their members. At ABC's 1984 meeting, newspapers detailed their opposition to this proposed requirement, and, at its next meeting, the board voted to rescind its 1982 action, in effect continuing the ZIP and Postal Code plan as an optional service

Advertisers continue to seek ABC-audited circulation data by these postal units. In the nine years since the service was first made available, some 800 daily and weekly newspaper publishers have chosen to use this optional reporting breakdown. Retail marketing analysis is increasingly relying on high-speed computers and the electronic dissemination of data. As the availability of accurate related market data improves, and as newspapers find a way around potentially negative competitive situations, many more publishers, even in noncompetitive markets, will yield to these buyer interests.

Census-Based Demographics

The promise of the Bureau of the Census to make available sample demographic data for ZIP Code areas following the 1960 U.S. census, along with the efforts of some magazines to merchandise their circulation in "high class" ZIPs, whetted the interest of newspapers. For some of them, the government data offered an inexpensive alternative to survey-based research and a possible answers to buyers' complaints that newspapers were deficient in providing useful audience information.

At the 1965 newspaper divisional meeting, Felix Tomei, Jr., *Chicago Tribune* and chairman of the research committee of the International Newspaper Advertising Executives association, told the members, "The provision of demographic market data by newspapers is a key factor in their acceptance as a medium for national advertising. Many now request much more detailed information than is provided by ABC circulation reports. Attempts to compile demographics from various sources in reference form make it evident that to furnish this information in uniform standardized format, it could best be developed and reported by an authoritative central agency, such as ABC." The meeting was informed that the inclusion of demographics was on a task force's agenda and would receive consideration by the board.

The following spring, the board approved an optional supplemental market demographic data report service for member newspapers. The census-based data, following the uniform format recommended by the American Association of Advertising Agencies, was to be shown in a supplemental report issued at the same time as the newspaper's Audit

Report with data updated annually through ABC "estimates." The data were obsolete before they became generally available. Though staff had little previous data on which to base update calculations, a pilot census-based demographic report was developed for review with members in 1967. The project did not prove feasible.

The subject of adding census-based audience information surfaced again in 1982 through a special task force studying ways to improve the data and formats of ABC newspaper reports. A ZIP Code/Demographic data report format, developed and submitted for review by allied newspaper and buyer associations in 1983, was approved the following year by the board. The demographic data were for each ZIP Code area in the newspaper's market to total households, owner-occupied households, renter-occupied households, median household income, total population, population in the 18 to 34 age group, and population in the 35 to 64 age group.

Postal code demographic data on hold pending reliable source.

By this time, the data gathered in the 1980 U.S. census were obsolete, and ABC studied update estimates from outside sources. A comparison of supposedly comparable data supplied by the five most used services showed serious discrepancies, each to the others. The project has been on hold since, pending an advertiser and advertising agency membership consensus as to an authoritative data source.

Readership, Audience Research

Buyers had long been recommending to newspapers the development of standardized research procedures. Their desire was to have uniform reader demographic data from compatible research techniques regardless of the particular research company doing the work. There was nothing really new to the idea of standardized research techniques for newspapers. Both Nielsen and Standard Rate and Data Service unsuccessfully tried to sign up a sufficient number of newspapers throughout the United States to make this an economically feasible project.

It was in this context, the needs expressed by buyers and less-than-enthusiastic response from publishers, that the Audit Bureau of Marketing Services, an affiliated organization controlled by the ABC board, entered into a 1968 pilot project to verify research on the demographic characteristics of subscriber households of the Burlington, Vermont, *Free Press*. This was a survey-based study carried out by a private research

141

company. The ABMS involvement was limited to auditable parts of the study, not with the actual data gathering or interpretation. This study, carried out under guidelines established by the technical committee of the Advertising Research Foundation, was the first newspaper effort on the part of an industry-sponsored association to verify not only that the interviews were conducted, but that the overall research project was carried out according to a predesigned operational plan.

While members of the International Newspaper Advertising Executives supported the pilot study, Frank Orenstein, Newspaper Advertising Bureau, warned ABC of three "undesirable results which could evolve from ABC's entry into the field of verifying audience research. The great prestige of the ABC would appear to give authenticity to one particular set of procedures, and this to the detriment of other, equally valid, approaches. The second objection is that ABC audit figures must remain above the area of controversy. There is a feeling that the new projected service, being tested at Burlington, in so difficult an area would tend to cut into the prestige and total acceptability that the ABC has developed for its operation. Finally, there are doubts about the propriety of the ABC taking on a role in setting standards which would be more properly filled by a research authority."

Those on the ABC board who supported offering the service exemplified by the Burlington experiment did so out of a conviction of the need for the Audit Bureau to seek out new ways to serve buyer and newspaper members. Those who opposed such a continuing service questioned whether the Burlington-type study would produce any useful information; whether ABC had the research expertise necessary; and the even more basic policy of whether or not ABC, even through a subsidiary, could or should get into audience measurement.

The Burlington project was successfully completed, but controversy, lack of enthusiastic interest by buyers and publishers, and the announcement later that year of the planned dissolution of ABMS saw further activities in this area wither.

A meeting between ABC directors and ten members of the American Newspaper Publishers Association board of directors was held during the spring of 1969. The discussion led to general agreement that ABC should continue to explore the feasibility of utilizing census data analyses in connection with circulation reports. The ANPA directors also urged the Audit Bureau to extend its verification services to include other publication data similar to the Burlington experiment.

Outcome of the meeting was a proposal, worked out between ABC Managing Director Alan Wolcott and Leo Bogart, general manager of the Newspaper Advertising Bureau, for the Audit Bureau to become the central source for newspaper market and circulation information. As explained to a Newspaper Advertising Research Workshop sponsored in January 1970 by the International Newspaper Advertising Executives,

Plan for audience data bank dies for lack of newpaper participation.

ABC would add 1970 U.S. census data and members' county circulation figures to its existing Data Bank. A second portion of the Data Bank would serve as a central storage facility for market data collected, processed, or estimated by the Newspaper Advertising Bureau. The proposal envisioned NAB collecting audience data on individual newspapers from existing research and new studies. Bogart also agreed to work with the newspapers and their research firms to translate existing information into terms compatible with the American Association of Advertising Agencies demographic classifications within county or Standard Metropolitan Statistical Area boundaries. The proposal suggested that for newspapers in non-competitive markets where no audience data existed, NAB would develop a statistical simulation procedure, which the ABC computer could use to estimate audience data. Participation would be optional, with individual publishers approving any research data that included their newspapers.

At one point in the planning, Bogart announced that "82 newspapers, as of this moment, have either conducted surveys within the last year or two, that could be incorporated into the Data Bank, or have definitely announced plans to conduct studies in accordance with this program, or told us that they would conduct such research." ABC moved ahead, acquiring the census tapes and loading newspaper county circulation figures into the Data Bank. It insisted that all survey data result from studies reviewed by the technical committee of the Advertising Research Foundation. To meet the limitations of computerization and a primary reason for the Data Bank, data from the various studies had to fit a standard format.

Despite extensive promotional efforts by both organizations, plus repeated support from buyer groups, participation in the ABC Newspaper Audience Research Data Bank languished. At its high point, the Data Bank included 72 studies, very few of which included all of the information required for the standardized format, and many for which acceptability rules were waived. Buyers were reluctant to request reports because of insufficient data; publishers were reluctant to commit money to new studies without a demonstrated interest by buyers.

Publishers and buyers continued to encourage newspapers to provide audience data. Long antagonistic to ABC board actions, John H. Kauffmann, Washington, D.C., *Star*, commented, "We do not want to lose the concept of net paid circulation for print media, but the need to correlate net paid circulation with audience demographics appears to merit experimental study." Kauffmann's guarded support later turned sour, however, when a survey he had commissioned failed to meet Advertising Research Foundation standards and the Audit Bureau's standardization requirements.

Donald B. Abert, Milwaukee, Wisconsin, Journal Co., said, "We newspaper people have for years asked national advertisers and agencies to tell us specifically what tools they needed from us to help them understand and use our medium more efficiently. The concept that there is a definite need for better print media audience data is incontrovertible."

In an effort to stimulate publishers towards participation in the Newspaper Audience Research Data Bank in 1971, the board developed an experimental study of standardized audience research data. ABC Chairman Fred W. Heckel, United Air Lines, assured members that ABC-audited circulation data would continue as an essential foundation for print media evaluations, but "the Audit Bureau must seek additionally to meet the need for reliable, standardized print media audience data." He went on to assure that the study was not intended to substitute for or replace existing or planned individual newspaper research, but to complement other data developed independently.

Author of the experimental study, James J. Tommaney, LaRoche, McCaffrey & McCall, said the plan "is designed to provide limited basic standardized data on newspaper readership and market demographics, the lack of which has undoubtedly contributed to the long-term trend in the decline of national advertising in newspapers. Availability of this data could give us a national profile of the newspaper audience which we do not now have."

After extensive review of the plan by interested newspaper groups and professional researchers, experimental studies were conducted by ABC in Denver, Colorado; Rochester, New York; and Marion, Indiana. The telephone survey work was conducted by a private contractor, with ABC auditors monitoring all aspects of the plan and survey operations. Results were submitted to the Advertising Research Foundation for

Tommaney's plan for newspaper readership and market demographics politically unstable.

review. Calling the studies "a forward step in newspaper audience research," the ARF technical committee confirmed that the results conformed to the objectives set and to ARF's standards.

Meanwhile ABC and the Newspaper Advertising Bureau continued to find ways of making a viable central newspaper data facility a reality. Problems with data collected by NAB, besides a drought thereof, stemmed from the lack of comparability and timeliness.

Despite Bogart's earlier predictions, three years after the joint program was introduced, the NAB was only able to provide 43 studies covering 47 newspapers. No data were presented for 15 of the top 50 markets; no data for 60 of the total 120 newspaper markets. In 11 of the top 25 competitive markets, only one paper was involved, giving a less than adequate picture of the total audience.

At their 1972 meeting, newspapers voted enthusiastically in support of the Audit Bureau's separate study of audience research. The Association of National Advertisers, the American Association of Advertising Agencies, American Newspaper Publishers Association, NAB, and the International Newspaper Advertising Executives voiced their support for the plan. The following spring the ABC board agreed to offer the survey and Newspaper Audience Research Data Bank as a regular newspaper service. By summer of 1974, 99 newspapers had signed "letters of intent," signifying their plan to participate, including 63 in the top 100 markets and 45 in the top 50 markets. The survey plan was revised for use in Canada and offered to newspapers there.

Intentions and expectations were much stronger than actual data input to the data bank, but ABC announced that its Newspaper Audience Research program would be ready for business by January 1976. The ABC computer held data on only 37 studies; it held 103 a year later.

The ABC board's marketing services committee agonized over the lack of publisher participation and buyer interest. Only one newspaper, the Norristown, Pennsylvania, *Times Herald*, had a survey done and verified under the Audit Bureau's program. Publishers refused to allow ABC to include the mention of their papers contained in competitor's research. For the majority of newspaper publishers, surveys, if conducted at all, were promotional investments intended to prove a competitive point or points, rather than supply comprehensive research. Many publishers in small and non-competitive markets were not convinced audience research was necessary.

Frustrated by the lack of cooperation by newspapers in providing standardized data and by ABC's reluctance to lower its acceptability standards, the Newspaper Advertising Bureau established its own library of available newspaper audience data and gradually withdrew, expressing criticism of the "ABC effort."

During its existence, the ABC Newspaper Audience Research Data Bank service provided buyers with three editions of edit listings, printed recaps of available data. While more than 150 of each were distributed, not one request for a computerized report was requested. In 1977, Tommaney reported to the board that he "was neither unduly optimistic nor unduly pessimistic" over the future of the service. A decision by the board in the summer of 1978 to drop all study data over three years old pretty well decided the fate of the research data bank.

At its February 1979 meeting, the board voted to put the Newspaper Audience Research Data Bank project in a hold position. The possible addition of audience information, based on the results of proprietary research studies, was again raised in 1982 but was on the board's agenda only briefly. Despite requests from newspaper publishers since, the board has refused to reactivate the service.

Daily Frequency of Issue

Newspapers of daily frequency are designated in ABC reports as either morning, evening, or all-day. The selection of the designation used is solely the prerogative of the publisher. That, in essence, was the Audit Bureau's newspaper frequency rule in 1914, and has been since 1979. The intervening 65 years provide an interesting example of publishers complicating the lives of their competition. And at the end of this period, when in-market competition had dwindled to a bare few, publishers

Morning, evening designations cause confusion.

criticized the Audit Bureau, not themselves, for preventing them from exploring the same marketing methods their rules sought to stifle.

The question of when a newspaper's frequency was not what the publisher claimed and reported in the running dateline was discussed at the division's first meeting in 1915. The issue was over the popular practice of publishing predated editions essentially to meet delivery and distribution schedules to outlying areas. Frequently copies of these predated editions were put on sale in the central market in competition with an opposing morning or evening newspaper.

The ABC board thought they had an answer to the question early in 1916 when it ruled that the circulation of predated editions of evening newspapers carrying the caption of a morning newspaper or a morning dateline, and that of predated editions of morning newspapers under an evening designation, must be shown separately, along with a combined total, in Publisher's Statements and Audit Reports.

This action served to galvanize the predate publishers. The newspapers voted against enactment of the board's ruling at their 1916 meeting. The board reversed itself by resolving that "evening newspapers carrying the following morning dateline or morning newspapers carrying an evening dateline shall not be segregated, but shall be shown under the morning or evening totals in ABC reports." As a proviso, however, the board also ruled that each newspaper must report its editions and the presstime, approximate area of distribution, and copy carried in each.

The question of reporting the circulation of morning and afternoon editions of the same newspaper came up at the 1917 annual meeting. These were usually identified as separate publications by the addition of "Morning" and "Evening" to their respective name plates, with subscriptions sold either separately or in forced combination. Following directions from the newspaper divisional meeting, the board voted to require that the circulation of such editions were to be segregated in ABC reports, along with a combined total, but that "the amount of duplicate circulation between morning and evening editions of daily publications shall not be shown, either on request or voluntarily, in audit reports."

A snag in the enforcement of the segregation part of the rule arose almost immediately after its enactment. William R. Perkins, Sioux City, Iowa, *Journal*, objected to reporting morning and evening editions separately. He explained to the board that the five editions of the *Journal* published between the hours of 3:30 AM and 4:30 PM were not distinguished by morning and evening labels. Except for updates in news content, each edition was substantially the same as the earlier edition carrying the same dateline.

After six months of debating this unique situation, the board established a new category of newspaper frequency of issue for the *Journal*, simply called "Daily." The 1918 divisional meeting confirmed the board's action. In 1928, after many more newspapers adopted the publishing practice in the hopes of increasing single copy sales, the term was changed to "All Day."

In 1919, four Philadelphia newspapers, the *Inquirer*, *North American*, *Press*, and *Record*, requested that the board require the competing *Daily Public Ledger* and *Evening Public Ledger* to segregate their morning and evening totals. "Combined totals are not only unfair to the other newspapers that are members of the Audit Bureau of Circulations, but are misleading to many advertisers and advertising agencies," they wrote.

The board agreed, ruling that "Morning"- and "Evening"-identified editions of a newspaper were, in fact, separate entities. "Membership must be taken out for each publication and its circulation reported separately, except when all advertising in all such publications is sold only as a unit," the board ruled. The *Public Ledger* appealed, but the board refused to deviate from what was now recognized as standard ABC procedure.

Should AM edition circulation be included in PM newspaper's total paid figure?

The board established another procedural precedent later in 1919. The Portland, Oregon, *Journal*, an evening newspaper, published two late editions, both carrying the following day's dateline. The later of the two, the 11:30 PM edition, was labeled the "Morning Edition." The publisher requested that the circulation for all editions be included in the evening total, the same as a predate but not identified as a predate.

The board held that "a paper marked 'Morning Edition' could not even be called an 'Evening Predate,' but must be segregated as a 'Morning Edition,' as the publisher himself had so determined by labeling it 'Morning Edition.'"

During the next few years, publishers worked hard to get around the specifics of this board ruling. The evening *Milwaukee Journal* called its morning issue the "Sunrise Edition." The morning *St. Louis Globe-Democrat* had its "Night Edition," and the morning *New York Daily News* had its "Afternoon Edition." The board saw these labels as subterfuges and insisted that either the newspapers remove them from the display of the front page nameplate or report their circulation separately within the ABC reports. The board did, however, give permission for these new designations to be carried in the front page datelines of the editions.

Responding to the ABC decision regarding his newspaper's request to continue the use of "Night Edition," E. Lansing Ray, *Globe-Democrat*, angrily accused the board of "branching out into the field of paternal control, which is outside the primary functions of the Bureau and the ideas of the membership when organized. We do not print an evening edition. We go on the street not earlier than 9 PM, which is the beginning of what has been recognized by the Associated Press for many years as the morning paper publication hour." Ray finally conceded, renaming his predate the "First Edition."

At least 15 rules were proposed, advocated, and abandoned for serious causes.

Meanwhile, back in Sioux City, Iowa, a competitive battle between the *Ledger* and the *Tribune* involved the Audit Bureau. The "Daily" designation gave the *Ledger* permission to print editions anytime during the 24-hour cycle. The *Tribune* followed suit, expanding its presstimes to include three morning editions and reporting this circulation in its evening total. The *Tribune*'s Eugene Kelly objected to management's decision in following standard practice, requiring that morning and evening circulation had to be segregated. The board agreed with management's decision, but Kelly continued to protest—to the directors and to the trade press.

Under pressure from the Sioux City stalemate and other similar problems in other markets in the United States and Canada, the board turned to the newspaper divisional advisory committee for a solution in 1926. The committee recommended that "when an evening newspaper publishes an edition for circulation the following morning which precludes it from using its regular afternoon news service, such edition shall be classified as a morning newspaper."

The board settled the Sioux City issue on this basis, saying that "all editions of the *Tribune* printed after 9 PM, and until 9 AM the following morning, shall be set up under the morning caption in Audit Bureau reports."

The new precedent had hardly been announced when P.L. Jackson, Portland, Oregon, *Journal*, asked the board to consider rescinding its actions. "We are not members of the Associated Press and use our regular news service in all editions without restriction of any kind, so on this ground we do not come within the rule. For many years the ABC has been giving advertisers information about what the publication does: editions, presstimes, pressruns, distribution, etc. We maintain that you are going beyond 'facts without opinion' and are actually expressing opinions in endeavoring to define what is 'morning' circulation and what is 'evening' circulation."

The board backed Managing Director Stanley Clague's enforcement of ABC rules in the *Portland Journal* case at its September 1927 meeting. A month later it reconsidered its action and challenged the newspaper and buyer divisions to come up with a standard for distinguishing between morning and evening newspapers. The newspapers couldn't agree on a resolution. A joint meeting of the advertiser and agency members tossed the subject back to the board.

Substantial portions of the next five board meetings were devoted to discussing "the proper set-up of morning and evening circulation." Ralph Starr Butler, General Foods Corp. and chairman of the board's special committee, reported in April 1928 that "at least 15 various tentative rules have been proposed, advocated, and finally abandoned for serious causes. There is a fair chance that a rule considered worthy to be submitted to the membership for consideration may come from this effort within the next few months."

It was. The new proposed rule identified that circulation for "newspapers, 98 percent of whose total production is printed between the hours of 6 AM and 9 PM," was to be set up as "Evening." Those with 98 percent of their production printed between 9 PM and 6 AM were to report their circulation as "Morning." Those with more than 2 percent of their total production outside these hours were to segregate the circulation of these editions. Circulation totals that included predated editions were noted and the report reader's attention drawn to the section on presstimes, press runs, and distribution information.

Submitted to the membership in the advertiser, advertising agency, and newspaper divisions for an advisory vote, the new rule was approved by a 442 to 89 margin. With what Board Chairman Philip L. Thompson, Western Electric Co., said was "a huge sigh of relief," the new rule was adopted at the September meeting of the directors.

The general membership ratified
the action at its meeting a month later.
It also ratified a bylaw change providing
"a morning and evening newspaper, even
though published by the same company,
must without exception hold separate
memberships, and an all day newspaper
must hold two memberships."

By and large, the new "Morning"
and "Evening" rules adopted in 1928
provided more than 40 years of relative
newspaper division peace on the subject
of daily frequency of issue. There were
problems, but nothing that stirred
controversy among the members outside
individual markets. The board simplified
the language of the rules in 1947. Only
significant changes were to include a
long-time ABC practice to designate
Sunday editions published after noon
on Saturday as regular editions of that
issue and not predates (these Saturday
evening editions of Sunday newspapers
were generally referred to as "Bulldogs");

*Thomson: "A huge sigh
of relief."*

and that the use of "Morning" or "Evening" or any other connotation
implying same "in the ears or elsewhere" to describe an edition (differently from the newspaper's regular designation) was cause to require
that the circulation from such editions to be reported separately.

A serious controversy broke out in 1949. What started out as
purely local competitive situations in Portland, Oregon, and San Francisco, California, expanded to a general evening versus morning newspaper argument. Evening newspapers proposed rule revisions that would
change morning publishing hours. Instead of starting at 6 PM the day
before, it was proposed to limit the morning cycle to from 9 PM to 9 AM
of the issue date. No change was proposed in the evening 6 AM to 9 PM
cycle. The chief complaint was that "more and more morning papers are
backing their editions into the evening sales period and the situation is
getting out of bounds" (a complaint that would have its reversed application 30 years later).

Ivan M. Annenberg, *New York News*, accused proponents of the change of "admitting that the enterprising abilities of their morning competitors have made it necessary for them to seek means other than selling newspapers as a way of balancing the circulation scales." P.H. Burgdorf, *Philadelphia Inquirer*, called the proposal "an unfortunate attempt to convert the ABC into a vehicle for regulating or suppressing newspaper competition."

Controversy evaporates, at least for present.

Matthew G. Sullivan, Gannett Newspapers, had the right idea about this effort to limit the publishing hours of the morning newspapers. "Forthright discussion by any dissatisfied publisher with the managing director or newspaper board members either would resolve the differences or point up presently undisclosed inequities. No good reason has been presented to my knowledge to justify any consideration of changing publication hours in effect satisfactorily for many years. I am confident wise heads will prevent this flurry from appearing as a tempest."

Following the recommendation of its newspaper committee, the board refused to make the proposed rule changes. The local situations that prompted the proposal in the first place continued in board discussions, but the general controversy quickly evaporated.

In 1949, morning newspapers were accused of "backing editions into evening sales periods." The situation was just the opposite in the mid-1970s. Increasingly, television was competing for evening readers' attention. Home delivery, especially to suburban markets, posed increasingly more difficult distribution problems for evening newspapers. In many markets, afternoon dailies closed or were merged into their morning counterparts.

In an effort to meet the pressures, many evening newspapers chose to introduce editions during the early morning hours, well within the 9 AM until 6 AM hours set by the ABC rules. It was the promotion of these editions, which led the board in 1979 to divest the rules from any reference to "Morning" and "Evening" publishing hours and to impose restrictions on the terminology used in identifying editions.

As early as 1919, the board had ruled that while the publisher had the sole prerogative of identifying the daily frequency of a newspaper, an edition of an evening newspaper identified as a morning edition had to be reported separately.

The reverse was also true for morning newspapers identifying an edition as evening. As the 1970s progressed and more and more evening newspapers introduced next morning editions, efforts to promote these editions came closer and closer to conflicting with ABC rules. In 1975, the *Detroit News* received ABC management's approval to call its morning run the "Early Edition." The *Oakland Tribune* got permission to call its edition the "6 AM Edition" "because it is a fact that it is put on sale at that time." The *Dallas Times Herald* and the *Sacramento Bee* were refused permission to call theirs simply the "AM Edition" because "it identifies too closely with Morning."

Evening publishers were smarting under the ABC rules, saying they were "archaic, obsolete, and impeded publisher's rights to market their newspapers." The whole issue of the daily frequency of issue rules was a continuing discussion on the board's agenda.

The tug-of-war over how to identify a morning edition without implying it was a "Morning" edition even confused management.

Fine: When is an "Evening" not a "Morning" paper?

When the *Detroit News* asked a ruling to do the same as the *Oakland Tribune* in renaming its "Early Edition" and continue to report its circulation in the evening total, management agreed. The renamed edition appeared early in 1978 carrying the words "AM Edition" in the front page ear. This apparent contradiction of the rule and previous management decisions brought an outraged response from the *News* morning competition and from a wide representation of morning newspapers from across the United States and Canada.

A board ad hoc committee, headed by Jules P. Fine, Ogilvie & Mather, was established to review the rule in the light of the swirling controversy and to offer a recommendation. At the board's November meeting, the committee proposed, and the directors gave preliminary approval to, a rule change that would eliminate restrictions on what a publisher could call editions of a news-paper published outside designated "Morning" and "Evening" newspaper hours, and still include these within regular circulation totals. Publicity on the proposed change brought a strong response—mostly favorable from evening newspapers; mostly unfavorable from morning newspapers.

At the request of the committee, Managing Director Alan Wolcott wrote all daily newspaper members in May 1979 telling them that it was the "feeling of the ad hoc committee that because of current and antici-pated changes in newspaper marketing practices and needs, it would be in the best interests of the majority of daily newspapers, advertisers, and advertising agencies if ABC modified its requirements relating to the identification of editions."

The alternatives considered by the committee, he wrote, were "to continue the rules as written without amendment; amend the rules by deleting portions dealing with time periods for 'Morning' and 'Evening' newspapers; and add a new section to ABC newspaper reports to show the circulation of 'Morning'- or 'Evening'-identified editions published outside normal hours separately."

Actually, the committee offered an expanded version of one of these alternatives. It recommended that ABC return to publishers the sole and full prerogative of identifying its daily frequency of publication, including all issues, by completely eliminating any rule reference to normal publishing hours for "Morning" and "Evening" newspapers. To ensure that buyers were apprised of the publisher's practices, it offered an expanded report section showing presstime, date printed, issue date, net press run, sales release area, total paid, and a paid circulation figure (adjusted to approximate the average paid reported for the report period) by market areas for each edition. The recommendation was adopted unanimously by the board at its June 1979 meeting and became effective with newspaper reports later that year.

With the elimination of "Morning" and "Evening" hours, members began to question the requirement that "All Day" newspapers hold two memberships. The board completed the return to 1914 frequency of issue standards in 1987 when it voted unanimously to eliminate this provision from the rules.

Consumer Magazines: ABC Helps in Transition from Uneconomic Practices to Today's Sophistication

6

Gentle art of publishing before ABC • Membership grows, a director added • Paid versus free eligibility issue settled once, but still rumbles • Magazines keep bulk in paid totals • Debate demographic edition full disclosure • Channels of subscription sales, clear or confusing?

"You hear of strange circulation practices which were in style up to the birth of the Audit Bureau in 1914," Fred W. Stone, *Parents' Magazine,* once reminisced about the early magazine business. "These stories are usually not exaggerated. It is difficult for those who did not practice the gentle art of publishing before the ABC came into the picture to fully realize the strangely uneconomic conditions that prevailed—conditions that were considered normal and reasonable under the circumstances.

"A circulation manager was commonly called a 'circulation liar,' and, to be a good and effective circulation manager, you needed to be a skillful liar with an imagination developed to the nth degree. The publisher wanted to believe what the circulation man claimed and did not ask too many searching questions, provided the figures were good. The advertising salesman, if he was a top-notcher, was insulted if his customer expressed curiosity about circulation.

"Publishers whose integrity had never been questioned, who considered themselves in the class with big businessmen respected for their honesty, were shocked and hurt when the first auditors asked to see all the records, expense sheets, control accounts, etc. To them it was preposterous to think that an expense account had anything to do with circulation records! They had declared for auditing and thought they believed in it, which to them meant answering a few questions and examining print orders, postage expenditures, and paper bills. The sort of thing that the new ABC proposed to do was a distinct shock to many old-fashioned publishers."

Rounding out 28 years as an ABC director in 1948, Fred Stone congratulates his successor, Benjamin Allen.

Stimulated by real and assumed threats from advertisers and advertising agencies and the pressure of competition among themselves, magazine publishers reluctantly took to the audited circulation movement.

The sophistication of both magazine circulation management and distribution systems has grown dramatically over the years. With growth of circulation size, and more involved practices to maintain that growth, came the cost of accounting for this distribution. ABC changes, whether driven by media buyers' needs for additional or new information or as a result of competitive pressures between magazines, added to publishing costs. Early on, magazine publishers became sensitive to proposed changes.

While magazines have sought to comply with advertiser and advertising agency requests for additional data, complexity of recordkeeping systems and costs have caused a reluctance to satisfy such buyer desires as renewal percentages and analysis of subscription sales by subscriber costs.

Membership

While Frank A. Munsey led the way for circulation audits by the Association of American Advertisers by offering his four magazines for the initial test audits of that organization in 1899, magazine publishers were not generally anxious to join the movement. Only 27 were represented at the organizational meeting of the Audit Bureau in 1914. Twenty magazine audits were completed by the first annual meeting, and 41 the second year. Magazine membership began to grow following World War I as advertisers increased their expenditures and, not incidentally, increased their insistence on publishers to prove their circulation claims. In 1920, for example, 104 magazines were members of the ABC.

Despite the depressed economic conditions of the 1930s, membership growth continued steadily upward. At the end of World War II, ABC magazines totalled 228. Again, postwar advertising expenditures led to the expansion in the number of magazines. By the mid-1950s, television entered the scene in sufficient force to become a major competitor for advertising dollars. It wasn't for a decade that the magazine industry began recovering, and ABC's magazine membership reached more than 300 members.

During the mid-1970s, many advertisers changed their approach to marketing, from investments in broad market coverage to the attempt to isolate coverage to target audiences, high probability customers based upon specialized interests. Magazines responded to this desire for fragmentation with new demographic and regional editions but, more especially, with new publications editorially directed to specific audiences. By 1978, ABC magazine membership totalled 412. The dramatic membership growth continues,

Magazine Membership

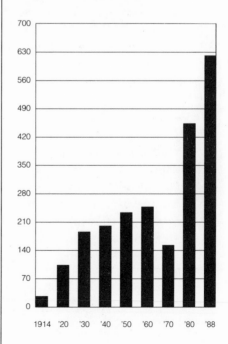

with 505 in 1983 and 622 (551 in the U.S., 65 in Canada, and 6 outside these countries) in 1988.

Board Representation

Throughout the history of the Audit Bureau, magazine members have maintained an effective communications network, partially because of the large number of publications published by a relatively few publishing companies, but mainly because of situations that enabled directors to be in contact with large numbers of members, either directly or through advisory committees. Magazines were the first to respond to the suggestion of divisional advisory committees, the first to establish their own newsletter dealing with ABC issues, and the first to develop their own ABC recordkeeping guides and rules primers.

Consequently, the division made no requests for added board representation. The original allocation of two directors satisfied the members' needs. When the board analyzed the growth and different conditions faced by Canadian periodical publications, a director was added in 1956 to represent magazines, business publications, and farm publications in that country.

Recognizing the similarity in ABC issues and discussions and the disparity of U.S. board representation (two directors for 292 magazines versus two directors for 37 farm publications), the farm publications, in 1973, suggested that one of their directorships be given to magazines. Approved, this gave the magazine division a third directorship.

Paid Versus Free

Free distribution consumer magazines have been around since the beginning. While limited in numbers, they were usually the house publications of transportation companies or a large manufacturer. The economics of publishing eventually forced some to fold. Others sought new revenues through advertising sales. The "wantedness" image of paid circulation, along with their audited data, generally kept advertising buyers from questioning the Audit Bureau's paid membership eligibility standard as it applied to magazines. And, whenever the subject of lowering that standard was raised, magazine members steadfastly insisted that they not be made a party to such an action.

During his term as ABC chairman, Fred Heckel, United Air Lines, posed the possibility of ABC providing a service for the then emerging airline magazines distributed free to passengers. ABC's bulk rule and the fact that none of the publications maintained records adequate for a detailed audit precluded any serious consideration.

The situation in Canada changed significantly during the middle 1970s when several controlled circulation consumer magazines were established. While not sizable in numbers, the free distribution magazines became a competitive concern to the paid ABC members. By 1977, they were claiming distributions of over eight million copies per issue and buyers were calling on the Audit Bureau to consider extending its services to these magazines.

Hodgkinson: Let's explore.

In an unexpected position, since it seemed to run counter to the consensus of his constituents and to the long expressed wishes of U.S. magazine members, Lloyd Hodgkinson, Maclean Hunter Publishing Co. and the Canadian periodical director, urged the board to explore the auditing of unpaid circulation magazines in Canada "to the standards of ABC." Doubtless Hodgkinson wanted the paid versus free competition put on a more equitable level, but he was keen enough to understand that the distribution practices of these controlled magazines could make it impractical for them to meet ABC auditing standards, and that the board would never permit those standards to be compromised.

While others were beginning to understand these realities, the Canadian Circulation Audit Board moved in to provide a verification service. Industry representatives in Canada then turned their attention to the differences in audit standards for paid and free publications and the need to strengthen those covering controlled distribution. The exploration of ABC service to free consumer magazines in Canada was eventually dropped from the board's agenda.

Bulk Sales

From the time they voted to remove bulk sales from their paid circulation totals at the 1929 annual meeting, newspaper publishers resented the fact that magazines had not chosen to do likewise, and that the Audit Bureau allowed them to be credited as paid for members of that division. When the newspaper division cited this difference in its 1934 investigation of ABC, Fred W. Stone, *Parents' Magazine,* took the stump on behalf of his constituency.

In a brief to advertisers and publishers, Stone explained the "bulk circulation situation for each of the 198 magazine members of the Bureau." After his lengthy discussion of how many and how they were sold, he said, "Out of a total paid circulation of about 62,000,000, magazines sell 242,000 subscriptions and single copies in bulk, representing only one-half of one percent of the total. Does that appear to be a device for inflated circulation that should be reckoned with? Out of this bulk total, some 40 percent is reported by three publications, *The National Parent-Teacher Magazine, Our Sunday Visitor,* and the *Elks Magazine.* I don't think that fact frightens anyone.

"As I remember the earliest reports of the Bureau, all divisions reported bulk circulation in the same manner. No one found any fault with it, until a small group of newspapers developed a strong sentiment in that division to put it into a secondary place. It was the newspapers, themselves, citing improper selling practices and unfair competition. It was they, not magazines, who chose to make their bulk sales standards different.

"I submit that there is a great difference between the solicited newspaper bulk circulation and the unsolicited magazine bulk circulation. In spite of that, the magazines have no objection to the newspapers counting their bulk or not counting their bulk, as they so choose. But to accede to their wishes that all member publications follow the newspapers' direction would be an error.

"It seems to me that the Bureau would stray far from the purpose for which it was founded if it attempts to grade circulation that is bought and paid for, and disqualify these legitimate sales because the publisher cannot show by whom it was read, although he is able to show by whom it was purchased. If we go so far as to ask a publisher to guarantee the quality and volume of reader interest, I think we would be obliged to be consistent and disqualify all subscriptions in arrears, all contest subscriptions, all subscriptions sold at no net to the agent or wholesaler, and all subscriptions influenced by over-generous prize offers to agents and distributors. This, you will admit, would be very radical and unnecessary for a safe and orderly conduct of this Bureau."

"On the basis of new information," the newspapers withdrew their request that magazines and business publications exclude bulk sales from their paid circulation in ABC reports.

Demographic Editions

Consumer magazines that sell advertising on the basis of coverage of industrial audiences have long been a problem for business publications. They saw these magazines as competition for their advertising share without being required by ABC to supply an audited breakdown of their business or occupational coverage claims, as were business publications.

When magazines began to expand their efforts to cash in on the post-World War II surge of industrial advertising, ABC agreed to permit the circulations of special demographic editions in which advertising was sold separately in their reports, along with the breakdowns of regional editions.

It was the advertising agency division, capping off a lengthy discussion of the issue, that formally requested at the 1957 annual meeting "that publications which have editorial content regarding business and industry, and which sell advertising on the basis of coverage similar to business publications, be required to include a business analysis of subscription circulation."

Chairman of the board's policy committee, George C. Dibert, J. Walter Thompson Co., identified the "publications" as consumer magazines—*Fortune, Business Week, Newsweek, Time,* and *U.S. News and World Report.* He

Dibert's committee found the idea of a business break down for certain magazines was not practical.

reported that the committee had discussed this issue and agreed that it "would not be practical or feasible, and would be too costly for these magazines to show such an analysis." Where most business publications were required to provide such an analysis on circulations "of under 50,000, most of the demographic editions are over the half-million subscription level."

The Audit Bureau's desire to seek new and improved services for member publications following the 1964 Charter change put the board in a receptive mood for *Fortune Magazine*'s 1966 request that ABC audit and report its Subscriber Identification Program. This verification of the basic data and procedures used by *Fortune* to accumulate data on the company position and occupation of subscribers was not only approved, but the board requested ABC management and the magazine directors to encourage other publishers to take advantage of this new service. Procedures closely followed standards set for business publications, except that the occupational breakdown was reported in a Supplemental Data Report, rather than as part of *Fortune*'s regular Publisher's Statement.

Member calls for full audits of all demo editions.

In 1969, *Harper's Bazaar, Town & Country*, and *House Beautiful* received board approval for audited Supplemental Data Reports providing an analysis of subscribers by title and function. *Time*'s request to provide this information for its *Time* B edition followed in 1970.

A magazine member requested that the board eliminate Supplemental Data Reports on demographic editions in 1971, pointing out that the audits of these editions did not extend to the subscription production information. A special board committee reviewed the Audit Bureau's procedures. Because recipients of demographic editions were part of the magazine's total circulation and served with the special edition only after the subscription order was processed, and since this production was already audited during the course of the magazine's regular audit, the committee recommended the board reaffirm existing procedures.

Business Week applied for and was granted separate business publication membership for its Industrial edition in 1973. This action had the effect of providing buyers with full information on the demographic edition. But it also set a precedent of the publication holding membership in two divisions at the same time, reporting its full circulation as a magazine and part of that circulation as a business publication and subject to rules covering business publications.

Shortly after *Newsweek*'s request in 1974 for a Supplemental Data Report covering subscribers' titles, industry, and income was approved, *Forbes* and *Business Week* registered a complaint against *Time* for its efforts in promoting its ABC report on the *Time* B edition. *Time* was promoting subscribers as "heads of households," which competitors claimed they might or might not be. *Time* agreed to change its subscriber questionnaire to provide "head of household" or "major wage earner" evidence. Added to its ABC report was the qualification, "The title and type of business specifications for qualification to receive the edition are based on the publisher's designation and interpretation."

Competing magazines were never happy with the Audit Bureau's decision to allow publishers to report on the special subscriber characteristics without subjecting this circulation to a separate audit. Rumblings on the issue were heard at the 1975 annual meeting, and a divisional ad hoc committee was selected to review the subject. The issue gained momentum in the advertising and publishing business press later. Both information and misinformation were exchanged as to the extent of ABC's verification procedures.

Early in 1976, an agency member raised the concern that publishers might be using arrears and cut-rate subscriptions to hype the circulations of demographic editions and that the reports of these editions did nothing to ease this concern. The *New Yorker* and *Scientific American* contacted the board requesting that rate, term, source, and arrears information be mandatory in Supplemental Data Reports on demographic editions. When the subject came up for discussion at the magazine divisional meeting that fall, the issue was somewhat defused when *Time* and *Newsweek* volunteered to a one-time breakdown and audit of the source, rate, and term data on their *Time* B and *Newsweek* Executive editions.

The division did ask the board to study the need and feasibility of making such separate reporting of production information mandatory in these reports. The breakdowns and audits were completed and a special board committee, consisting of ABC advertising agency directors, made their study and recommended in 1977 that these analyses should not be made mandatory.

Despite the fact that *Time* requested and submitted to another more extensive audit of data on prices, duration, channels of subscription sales, premiums, arrears, and collection stimulants on *Time* B in 1980, the issue wouldn't go away. Competitors used advertisements in the

Keil: No advocacy position.

trade press to solicit industry support for requiring the additional data on demographic editions. The expressed support was minimal, and the board decided not to take any action. Continued public statements by magazine members and editorial comments relating to these statements did prompt the board's magazine and farm publication committee to initiate a continuing review—not only of the issue, but of ABC policies and practices at they relate to members' comments. In 1982, the board reaffirmed existing standards and its confidence in management reporting and auditing practices. Because of the confusion in the industry, ABC carried out an extensive educational program on its handling of demographic edition audits and report services.

In a statement to members and the press, President and Managing Director M. David Keil said, "The issue of the possible need for additional information is properly a function of the competitive media marketplace and the interaction of publishers, advertisers, and advertising agencies. The option to provide additional audited data is available to publishers who believe sufficient advertiser and advertising agency interest warrants their additional investment in providing these data.

"ABC is not an arbiter of the competitive marketplace. As such, ABC cannot, does not, and will not assume an advocacy position in support of members' competitive marketing positions in regard to the interpretation and evaluation of the information it provides."

Channels of Subscription Sales

As stated in its initial bylaws, the Audit Bureau's purpose was "to ascertain all of the facts with regard to the circulation of any and all" member publications. With the development of report forms and initial rules, it was evident that members early on considered "all of the facts" to include quality as well as quantity. Governed by specific standards, quantity is susceptible to verification. Quality is susceptible to individual interpretation. The positive sales strategy of one publication is usually the negative advertising sales argument of its competitor.

Business publication members were the first to propose a series of questions in ABC reports aimed at supplying buyers information upon which circulation quality might be determined. These were adopted for all periodical members as the "analysis of circulation methods." Answers to most questions were optional, but publishers were "requested to provide their best estimates." The questions covered a wide variety of "quality factors"—from prices, returns policy, inducements, sales methods, arrears, uniformity of contents, and quality of paper stock between issues. Most questions were answered either "yes" or "no"—"Were canvassers employed on salary?"—or through the use of percentages—"What percentage of subscriptions were received through canvassers?"

While the circulation methods analysis surfaced as an issue for members in each division over the years, it has been a major continuing problem for magazines and their advertisers. In 1919, when the board made its first attempt to revise ABC report formats, a "collect-all" quality section was broken into five paragraphs. During the discussion of this revision, magazines asked the board to explain its philosophy in establishing quality factors, especially as it applied to specific subscription production methods.

"If we could follow every subscription solicitor or mailed offer around and see how it performs and how the subscriber acts," Managing Director Stanley Clague answered on behalf of the board, "we could form a good idea of how much reader interest is implied in each subscription. That being impossible, we have to depend on reason and knowledge of human nature. The various plans by which publications secure subscriptions are set forth in ABC reports. It is not the function of the ABC to pass judgment on any of these methods, but to give the facts upon which advertisers can decide as to how well the publication meets their views in its methods."

Coming off the restraints of World War I, publishers' circulation building efforts flourished as each sought to provide the large "box-car" numbers demanded by advertisers. Many of these efforts were suspect, if not in their provisions, then in the methods in which they were carried out. As publishers developed new subscription marketing programs, competitors, supported by advertisers and agencies, demanded to see the resulting circulation production identified and shown separately. Even after the 1920 magazine report format revision, with much of the data split between five sections, the key sources paragraph included 29 questions covering 13 different areas of circulation production methods.

By 1923, the expansion of these data caused buyers to complain of overkill, and they asked ABC to consolidate some of the production source information. Thomas H. Beck, *Collier's Weekly*, petitioned the board to eliminate separate listings in the paragraph for sales through installment programs. "The fact that each subscriber pays 50 percent of the regular price initially," he pointed out, "qualifies the subscription as net paid under the Bureau's rules. To show these separately simply puts the Bureau in the position of raising the question of their value to the advertiser, and this is not ABC's purpose."

M.E. Douglas, *Saturday Evening Post*, rebutted Beck's request with a two-hour presentation on the excesses of installment sales programs. "The plain fact is that the installment method patently differs from other methods and for that reason advertisers are entitled to have the facts about it."

Pointing out that his competitor had added a million and a half subscriptions through the installment plan in less than two years, Douglas said that, under ABC rules, "if only 50 percent of the annual price is collected, these subscriptions may be carried in net paid totals for 18 months (6 months in arrears) without any provision in the forms for disclosure of the number so carried in arrears."

Citing numerous cases of "unscrupulous actions," Douglas told the directors, "The method, as it is practiced today, is to send out sales crews with instructions to get subscriptions from whomever and with whatever means necessary, and to follow them in a few months with high-handed installment payment collector crews, using whatever threats necessary, giving truth to the old saying, 'a dollar down and a deputy sheriff the next week.'"

Installment subscriptions continued as a separate total. Other sources were added. In 1926, business publications called for a reformatting of this information, to split up the oversized paragraph, to substitute actual figures for percentages, and to make reporting of answers mandatory. While this was under consideration, representatives of the American Association of Advertising Agencies told the board, "We feel that it would add to the clearness and value of your reports on magazine

**Davis monitored the
magazines' "XYZ" committee
efforts in defining channel
of subscription sales.**

circulation if the numbers of new and
renewal subscriptions were shown by
the various circulation-getting methods.
It would be more useful if these were
included in a single section of the report."

During a review, the board was
forced to accept the fact that ABC reports
contained a conglomerated mass of
miscellaneous data that was scattered
throughout in a manner that was
difficult to follow. One thing had been
added here and another there. Subjects
directly associated or closely affiliated
were dealt with in different paragraphs
that were often distantly separated from
one another. Then, too, descriptive
captions were phrased in the parlance
of the industry—terms that were not
understood by many advertising buyers.

The board appointed a committee of
Fred R. Davis, General Electric Co., and
Edward T. Hall, Ralston Purina Co., in
1927 to undertake the task of revising
the report formats of periodical members. Members of each of the three
divisions, likewise, appointed working committees. The magazine
members' dubbed their group the "XYZ" committee, an appellation
chosen to differentiate it from the board's official ABC committee.

Four principles guided the committees in their work: (1) that all
subscriptions received during the report period would be analyzed by
sources and methods; (2) associated or closely affiliated information
would be covered in the same or adjacent paragraphs; (3) terminology
would use language better understood by advertising buyers; and (4)
subscriptions produced by sources fundamentally alike were to be
catalogued in ABC reports in the same manner.

In the new formats adopted in 1928, the listing of "primary
sources" became "channels of subscription sales." Under the new
paragraph, subscription production was broadly divided into two categories—sold by mail and sold by salesmen—with such refining subdivisions
as the board might deem desirable as an aid to proper evaluation.

167

This basic structure for reporting new and renewal magazine subscription production sources, with minor refinements, remained unchanged until 1951. The "channels of subscription sales" in each of the periodical reports were reviewed, principally to ensure concurrence with existing policies and practices. At the recommendations of directors Benjamin Allen, Curtis Publishing Co., and W.H. Eaton, *American Home Magazine*, the board agreed that all subscriptions known to have been sold by mail, regardless of the originating source, were to be classified in one place in magazine reports (rather than shown separately by originating source). The board also combined the separate listings of subscriptions received from catalogue agencies and independent individual subscription salesmen. The magazines had told the board that they were unable to segregate these as between those sold by mail, door-to-door, or telephone solicitation without "undue burden and inordinate expense."

In 1954, Managing Director James N. Shryock told the board, "I am convinced that only a small percentage of buyers of space use the ABC reports because there is so much material in them as to make their use difficult and time-consuming. It seems to me that the Bureau would benefit very much by limiting the reports issued by the Bureau to those facts which are actually used."

Sweet: Not much faith in report simplification program.

Director Charles E. Sweet, Capper Publications, in answering Shryock's comments privately, agreed. "On simplifying the Bureau's reports, I do not have too much faith in getting many changes. You have a small, hard core of buyers who study meticulously ABC statements and reports, and they will object at each turn. However, the cold facts in the case are that few buyers or sellers pay any attention to most of the Bureau's information except when some competitor is trying to desperately to make a sales point out of something. In the 1920s, salesmen spent a lot of their time arguing over subscription selling methods. That period is long past and only once in a while the issue springs up temporarily."

Efforts to effect simplifications and clarifications in ABC reports during the mid-1950s did result in additional consolidations and new terminology in the channels of subscription sales paragraph, but no substantial changes. Most of these simplifications represented publisher input and had little to do with buyer enlightenment or efforts to encourage buyers to refer to these data more frequently.

The installment sales issue reappeared in the 1960s when paid-during-service subscription programs came back in vogue. Publishers who didn't use paid-during-service promotions resurrected the images of the 1920s in competing against those who did. Eventually, media buyers began looking for information on these sales in ABC reports only to learn there was no way to ascertain the figures. Depending upon the manner in which the paid-during-service programs were set up, some or all of this subscription production might be included within the totals for "ordered by mail," "catalog agencies and individual agents," and "publisher's own and other publishers' salesmen" sales channels.

Buyers seek data on "sweepstakes" production.

A similar situation arose when advertisers and agencies began asking questions about subscriptions obtained through "sweepstakes" promotions. While subscribing was not normally a prerequisite for winning, buyers were concerned that the lure of large lottery prizes affected the participating magazines' circulation audiences. This production was reported in ABC reports along with all other mail-produced subscriptions.

In 1984, the ABC magazine buyer advisory committee, a member group reporting to the advertiser and advertising agency directors, called for a review of the information in reports on channels of subscription sales. They asked the board to consider a more detailed breakdown. "Currently, all subscriber direct request circulation is reported as a unit within the paragraph on channels of subscription sales in ABC reports. The committee feels it would be valuable to buyers to be able to have this channel broken out further into clearing house [the source of most sweepstake production] subscriptions, television direct request subscriptions, blow-in cards, and publisher's own direct request. This information would make the Publisher's Statement a more useful document."

The magazines were divided on providing this additional detail. Most opposed the buyers' request. At the 1986 ABC annual meeting, Susan Allyn, *Weight Watchers Magazine*, said the buyers "are asking us to reveal more and more proprietary information that, once revealed, will not help, but only serve to confuse them. They're asking us to reveal all our marketing strategies to our competitors." John Thornton, *Forbes*, agreed: "Each time we are asked to give more detail, we are asked to give more of the game away to the competition. That's bad enough. But the real damage is that each change becomes an occasion for a magazine's circulation strategy being called into question."

Stephen Childs, *Texas Monthly*, suggested that attempts to use the ABC report data to measure magazine readership was akin to "trying to fit a round peg in a square hole. The proper place to address that issue is in third party subscriber studies." He proposed that before more detailed breakdowns of channels of subscription sales are considered, "advertising agencies should make it mandatory for all entry level media people to take a one-day intensive course on ABC—how an ABC statement is prepared, how an audit is done, and what the information on the statement means. Just as we need to help advertisers understand our business, advertisers and their agencies would do well to help us learn more about theirs, particularly as it relates to ABC Publisher's Statements. I honestly can't believe that our mutual understanding, or the dialogue between publishers and advertisers will be furthered by an arbitrary undressing of the channeled sales."

Supporters form association • Membership totals reflect competitive pressures • Successfully plead paid circulation eligibility standard • Comparability with other auditing services • Members vote themselves mandatory renewal percentages.

During the 1913 meeting of the Associated Advertising Clubs of America, Mason Britton, representative of the Federation of Trade Press Associations, spoke of the efforts of business publications to meet the requests of advertisers for reliable circulation data. "The National Trade Press Association is now being formed. No publication can join this which will not give a statement of its circulation and tell from where, whence, and how their circulation is obtained." He urged advertisers to meet this movement half-way by standardizing circulation requests and patronizing "these honest publishers."

In a 1965 interview, the retired McGraw-Hill Publishing Co. executive and long-time ABC business publication director recalled his experiences. "It was always a highly competitive publishing industry, with probably more dogs than cats. I could tell you a thousand stories of funny operations. Legitimate publishers welcomed and fought for anything that would expose the charlatans and their false claims. We didn't object to fair competition, and that's why we supported the idea of audited circulation reports."

The Associated Business Publications, an outgrowth of the National Trade Press Association, exerted a strong influence on the development of ABC business publication standards over the years. It set ABC membership as requirement for its own members and, within two years of the founding of ABC, Jesse H. Neal, ABP manager, proudly announced that 55 of that association's 73 members had either been audited or were awaiting their initial audit.

ABP members were behind the drive in 1922 to establish a paid standard for ABC eligibility and passionately promoted the audited paid publication position. Its members also supported the 1926 adoption of ABC rules requiring uniform occupational and business circulation analyses for business publications serving the same fields or markets. When the American Business Publications and the National Business Press, an association formed primarily by free circulation publications, were merged in 1965, the resulting American Business Press (renamed the Association of Business Publishers in 1985) adopted a neutral position on circulation practices and auditing services.

As early as 1935, the National Industrial Advertisers Association (now the Business/Professional Advertising Association) offered the ABC board suggestions on how the Audit Bureau's business publication reports might be improved. Specifically, they sought information on the number of companies and separate establishments each publication reached and breakdowns of circulation by counties, industrial categories, and vocational functions. The board agreed with a special study committee that the unit coverage data would add substantial cost to publications at a time of economic depression; that it already required uniform breakdowns by industrial

> *"No publication can join which won't tell from where, whence, and how their circulation is obtained."*

and business classifications; and the optional additional information on subscribers' "titles or positions" would only be duplicated by the addition of functions. The question of a breakdown of subscriber circulation by counties was submitted to a poll of buyer members and drew only minor interest. In later contacts, NIAA representatives were forcefully involved in the comparability issue.

Membership

Fifty-five business publications were represented at the Audit Bureau's organization meeting. Membership in this division climbed to 129 by the end of ABC's second year and reached 218 in 1920. Except for the period of severe economic conditions in the early 1930s, business publication membership continued to climb at a steady but much slower pace and reached a high of 373 (351 in the U.S. and 22 in Canada) in 1953.

The establishment of free distribution publication auditing services in the U.S. and Canada had no early effect on ABC business publication membership growth, since these services accepted only those publications that could not meet ABC's 50 percent paid requirement. This changed in 1952 when ABC responded to advertiser pressures to audit all business publication data by increasing paid eligibility requirements to 70 percent. Business Publication Audit of Circulations removed its requirement of no more than 50 percent and began to offer its services to both free and paid publications.

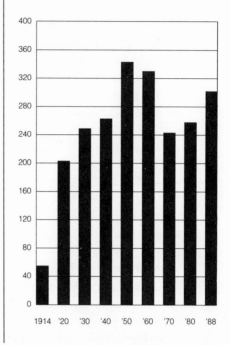

Business Publication Membership

The dramatic increase in business publications following the end of World War II was largely due to free distribution. To meet this competition, many added free distribution to their market coverage, dropping below the 70 percent minimum. Others, dissatisfied with ABC's uniform business or occupational classifications, moved to other services where the disciplines were less demanding. When membership in the division had dropped to 338 in 1962, the board tried to stem the defections by introducing an optional form to allow publishers to report on a limited amount of nonpaid distribution sent to the field served.

Unfortunately, while many publications took advantage of this option, it only momentarily halted the slide. In 1970, the board modified the bylaws to allow each division to set its own eligibility standards. It further approved a request that business publications with at least 70 percent paid and/or nonpaid direct request circulation be eligible for membership. The optional Paid and Direct Request Publisher's Statement was introduced early the following year. This action had the effect of stemming the business publication defections, with divisional membership total going from a low of 239 in 1971 to 261 in 1981 (when the paid and nonpaid direct request option standard was dropped from 70 percent to 50) and to the 1988 total of 302 (289 in the U.S. and 13 in Canada).

Board Representation

Throughout ABC history, the business publication division has been represented on the board of directors by two directors. It has never sought additional representation, content over the years to focus member input to these directors through the Associated Business Publications and, later, through a very active advisory committee. Along with monthly meetings with the directors to review member proposals, the committee has sponsored an ongoing series of recordkeeping clinics, encouraging liaison with people within the circulation staffs of ABC member publications.

Paid Versus Free

Three factors weighed heavily in the business publications' decision to seek a paid circulation membership eligibility standard for ABC publishers and to continue the subject as a controversial issue during the years since.

First was the fact that the nature of free distribution operations made it impossible for such publications to meet the same degree of accountability and intensive auditing standards as paid circulation publications. The Audit Bureau had made no effort to upgrade its standards for free distribution publications through the 1922 decision to set a paid requirement. While alternate free distribution verification services were begun in the United States and in Canada in the 1930s, efforts to seriously upgrade their standards did not take place until the early 1950s, and only after buyers were convinced that ABC would never change its paid policy.

Second was the ABC publishers' fear of unrestricted free publication competition and the liberal use of unpaid to supplement paid circulation by member publications. This was the major reason why newspapers, farm publications, and, to a lesser extent, magazines supported the paid requirement and fought most attempts to have it removed. Business publications saw free competitors stacking up impressive totals and were concerned that unpaid breakdowns in member reports would allow competitors to enhance more salable occupational categories. So long as ABC audited paid circulation represented an added value in the minds of advertisers and advertising agencies, publishers perceived their membership as a form of protection.

174

The third factor was the indecisiveness on the part of media buyers. Many who supported the paid standard when it was introduced went on to equate an ABC audited paid figure with that of the total distribution of a free publication. It wasn't until the late 1920s that buyers began to concern themselves about the verification of the free distribution they were buying.

The ABC standard provided that a member publication must have at least 50 percent of its total distribution qualify as paid circulation under the Bureau's rules. How the remaining 50 percent were used was up to each publication. The standard went into effect in 1924, and some member business publications immediately began to exploit the ABC audited, but not defined, free portions of their distributions.

During the 1927 annual meeting, representatives of some Canadian business publications complained that competitors were using the total extent of the free allowance in the rules each issue. They claimed that "as circulations are small in Canada, it is less burdensome to load up with a big percentage of free distribution." The board was asked to consider a special, higher standard for Canada or make a determination as to how frequently a publication should be permitted to exploit the free half of the ABC standard.

The board ran into considerable opposition the following June when it raised the 50 percent level to 75 percent, a move the directors said would minimize the Canadian members' problem and affect "few others as it is unusual for a publication with paid circulation to distribute more than 25 percent free copies."

The action had the immediate effect of placating advertisers and agencies who were beginning to call for analyses of business publication members' free distribution, since members were permitted less of it. But contrary to the board's assumption, it was almost impossible for most publishers to comply with the new standard. In October 1918, the bylaw was changed back to 50 percent or more qualifying as paid, "plus advertiser copies (one copy only to each advertiser), advertising copies, and correspondent copies" equaling or exceeding 20 percent, or a total of these categories of at least 70 percent. A year later, bulk sales were permitted to be included within the 20 percent total.

While the board and members danced around the prevailing issue, advertisers and agencies began getting restless. Buyers approached the Canadian Business Publishers Association early in October 1928 with a proposal that an alternate auditing service for free publications be established. The proposal was a major agenda item at the annual meeting of the Association of Canadian Advertisers later that month. In mid-1929, Managing Director Orlando Harn told the board, "The question of auditing publications of free circulation is a live one in some quarters and is brought to the Bureau from time to time. The most acute and persistent recurrence of the subject is from Canada, and I find that the rumors of a desire, on the part of Canadian advertisers at least, for a Canadian auditing organization have their origin largely in the fact of a check on these so-called controlled circulation publications.

"I have received within the month from three independent sources the suggestion that it might be well to establish a subsidiary of the ABC with an entirely different name, for the purpose of giving advertisers such authoritative information about free circulation publications as may be possible under the circumstances of their methods of distribution. The advocates of this plan, especially two from Canada, believe that the establishment of such an organization under the control of the ABC would prevent the establishment of a rival organization which might in time draw into its fold some of the publications now members of the ABC as well as some who are now eligible to join the ABC. They feel that if the ABC does not preempt this field an independent organization may spring up which would put up no bars against the admission of paid circulation publications, and the opening wedge would be established for publications which ought to be in the ABC to enter the other organization and achieve prestige without being subjected to the rigorous examinations and standards which the ABC requires."

Publishers "asleep at the switch" when 70 percent eligibility rule is approved?

The board took no action on the managing director's warning and on reconsideration at the following meeting voted unanimously to lay the issue on the table. At the 1930 annual meeting, advertiser members recommended to the board that efforts be instituted to "find some way of auditing the circulations of free business publications."

Sales Management magazine reported in May 1931 that Frank L. Avery, Federated Business Publications, was organizing in New York the Controlled Circulation Audit, "a bureau for collecting and checking circulation data on controlled or free media."

In September 1931, F.W. Harvey, *Confectioners Journal*, wrote to the board saying that he and other independent business publication publishers "were asleep at the switch" when the 70 percent rule went into effect. During the next audit, he was forced to cut off 1,000 unpaid to the field served to meet the paid eligibility requirement. Harn reported that 33 other publishers were similarly affected. Harvey suggested that the 70 percent rule "puts too great a hardship and too strict a limit on the volume of circulation that an ABC member can have. Every ABC member has a tough time competing with a free distribution publication. The ABC rule benefits very few and harms a great many."

About the time the Audit Bureau was holding its 1931 annual meeting in Chicago, *Advertising Age* carried the announcement that the Controlled Circulation Audit (renamed the Business Publication Audit of Circulations in 1952) had officially been established, headed by Paul B. West, National Carbon Co., founder and chairman of the circulation committee of the Association of National Advertisers and later managing director of the ANA.

The new organization didn't excite Harn very much. "I doubt very much whether they will get very far with the proposition," he told the board. "The controlled circulation publications are evidently hard pressed. Some of our directors feel that if there is to be an organization of that kind, the ABC should control it, but any plan carrying with it the privilege of mentioning the ABC in any way would be very unpopular with the present ABC members."

That fall the board adopted another revision to the paid circulation membership eligibility bylaw, retaining the 50 percent paid but dropping the 70 percent proviso to 60 percent.

When informed of the new action, *Confectioners Journal*, who had asked for the reduction several years earlier, called it "too late and too little. Economic conditions have made paid subscriptions hard to maintain. We must supplement this with carefully screened free controlled circulation in order to compete with the other papers in the field. As an ABC member, only our paid portion was reported in *Standard Rate & Data* while our non-ABC competitors were given credit for their total distribution. Membership became a liability and, like other papers, we resigned for our own protection."

At the annual meeting two years later, advertisers and agencies petitioned the board to make the occupational analyses of business publication members' unpaid distribution mandatory as it was for the paid circulation. Business publications agreed to lay the proposal on the table, and the general membership sent the whole issue back to the board for consideration.

At its December 1934 meeting, the board agreed to permit publishers the option of reporting an occupational analysis of their unpaid distribution in the explanatory paragraph of their ABC reports. When management advised that such a breakdown "would be nearly impossible to check," the board agreed to add a qualifying statement to the effect that the breakdown was the claim of the publisher and "this free circulation is not audited or in any way verified by the Bureau." Management was asked to prepare a new rule to implement this policy.

The next meeting of the board was most unusual. Management did present a seriously flawed text for a rule, but, before it was considered, Managing Director Harn stepped out from behind the traditional neutrality of management to lecture to its buyer sponsors. "Any step which encourages the serious consideration by advertisers of free circulation strikes at the prestige of paid circulation. Do you want to drive out of existence or cripple the paid circulation publication? That is the question advertisers must face and face soon. The breakdown of the paid distribution is rigidly audited by means of documentary evidence supplied by the subscriber. No such evidence exists, ordinarily, in connection with the free distribution. There is no more probability of the free breakdown being correct than there is of any other circulation that has been audited. I think it about time that advertisers and agencies seriously consider the inconsistency in their severe attitude toward paid circulation and their great tolerance toward free distribution. Management does not recommend the occupational breakdown of free distribution in business paper Publisher's Statements, and we are opposed to any such breakdown in Audit Reports." Following the lecture, the board voted to lay the subject on the table.

Director L.R. Greene, Tuckett Tobacco Co., Ltd., reported at the board's June 1934 meeting that advertisers and publishers in Canada were making headway in setting up a more efficient audit there of business publications with controlled circulation. The Association of Canadian Advertisers sought ABC's cooperation in this effort. Greene felt the advertisers and publishers were prepared to "go it alone" if ABC declined. The board declined any invitation to "in anyway appear to sponsor such an audit," but did agree to have an ABC representative offer assistance to ACA in establishing an independent effort.

Stunned that the ABC board "does not recognize the problems the bitter, uncontrolled competition existing among many of the trade and technical paper publishers is causing advertisers in Canada," B.W.

Keightley, Canadian Industries Ltd. and chairman of ACA's business publication committee, called for independent action. By the fall of 1936, ACA had brought together a tri-partite board and used its offices to organize the Canadian Circulation Audit Board.

Advertisers favor, agencies oppose, publishers resist efforts for ABC to audit and report free distribution publications.

ABC's reaction to this upstart auditing service is characterized by two Canadian members of the Audit Bureau's board. W.J.J Butler, *Globe and Mail*, called ACA's action "a mischievous and dangerous procedure." Harry Rimmer, Canadian General Electric Co. and a past president of the ACA, said "there is no occasion for us to be alarmed at the activities of the Canadian Circulation Audit Board. The possibility of it ever being competitive with the ABC is so remote that I do not think it is worth worrying about. There are a great many small trade papers in Canada that probably under no circumstances would ever be either eligible or financially able to join ABC. Whether we like it or not, they will stay in business. To get them to supply a CCAB audit is a step in the right direction in establishing the principle of audited circulation."

Again, at the annual meeting that year and the following, resolutions were passed expressing buyer interest in the auditing of unpaid publications and publisher resistance. At the 1936 annual meeting, advertisers asked the board to find "some machinery that would include the inclusion of controlled free circulation trade papers, business papers exclusively, in the Audit Bureau." Advertising agency members recommended that membership not be extended to free publications. The business publication members voted to ask the board to convene an ad hoc committee to "investigate the desirability and feasibility of auditing circulation of business papers having less than 50 percent paid," reporting back to the members in time for a full membership vote on the issue at the 1937 annual meeting.

H.H. Kynett, Aitkin-Kynett Co., whose eloquent pro-paid position had influenced several advertising agency division votes in the past, was named chairman of the free business publication audit study committee. Questionnaires were sent to advertiser, agency, and business publication members for their views on the issue. Rumors of a possible ABC move towards membership for free distribution publications caused an outpouring of opposition from newspaper members, even after the board assured members that only business publications were being considered.

H.H. Kynett and
William Hart shared
views on the issue
of ABC audit of
unpaid.

Kynett presented the committee's findings at the business publication meeting that fall. While the results of the questionnaires were presented without recommendation, Kynett declared that they strengthened his "opposition to the admission of free circulation publications. I cannot state too strongly my belief that the introduction of anything that could possibly weaken the value of net paid circulation as a basis for publishing would be a fatal thing for the Bureau. I would like to know as a buyer of space why the very high integrity of a net paid subscription list, which when it relates to a newspaper, to a farm paper, or to a general magazine is the heartbeat of their existence, all of the sudden becomes a matter that is quite different and probably of no importance in the business paper field."

A resolution presented by Charles B. Groomes, *Editor & Publisher*, calling on ABC "in convention assembled to reaffirm its policy of auditing only publications with net paid circulations in accordance with present bylaws," was passed by a vote of 161 to 14 in the business publication division. Later, at the general session, the same resolution was approved without a dissenting vote.

During 1939 through the war years of the 1940s, increased competition from free distribution business publications was taking its toll on the ABC membership. By 1944, 45 business publications had left ABC; 22 resigned when they added substantial free distribution, 6 were dropped by board action when audits determined they no longer met ABC paid eligibility requirements, 10 were consolidated with free distribution publications, and 7 went out of business, the victims of free distribution competition.

Buyers, at least those active in helping to establish ABC policy, weren't very helpful in finding a solution to these members concerns. As chairman of the Association of National Advertisers, Harold B. Thomas, The Centaur Co., urged the board to permit ABC business publications to report occupational and geographic analyses of their unpaid circulation. Business publication members also asked for this option. Twice the advertiser division and once the advertising agency division passed opposing resolutions. In one, advertisers said "that inasmuch as the Bureau is organized to audit only paid circulation, any breakdown in the unpaid circulation is not auditable, and therefore not within the province of the Bureau."

Doesn't see ABC sacrificing any of its principles.

With the end of the war, industry turned to the neglected needs of consumers. Industrial expansion in the United States and Canada brought with it increased opportunities for business publications. Most new publications were established through free distribution, and the competitive pressures on ABC members were dramatically increased.

George V. Laughton, Maclean-Hunter Publishing Co., called the board's attention to the practice of advertising agencies of crediting ABC business publications with only their paid circulation, while crediting free distribution publications with their total distribution. "To serve the advertiser, all ABC business papers must carry some amount of controlled, but we can get no credit for this in our statements. You say that we cannot report this information since the Bureau can't audit these figures because there was no payment. I maintain that the Bureau already audits unpaid figures. The auditor can check the occupational classification of a controlled unit of circulation just as easily, and by exactly the same process, as he would a paid order. He can certainly count the geographical distribution of the controlled circulation. It doesn't seem to me that the ABC would sacrifice any of its principles whatsoever in identifying this controlled circulation in the ABC report."

Two years later, at the 1947 annual meeting, business publications unanimously requested the board to exempt them from the provision of the bylaws that provided that "no analysis or breakdown of unpaid distribution shall be allowed" in ABC reports. On a motion from William A. Hart, E.I. du Pont de Nemours & Co., the board unanimously voted that no change be made in the existing rule.

Pressure to resolve the issue in favor of the occupational and geographical breakdowns of member business publications' unpaid distribution came from all sides during the following year. The National Industrial Advertisers Association told the directors that buyers could not properly evaluate ABC publications without this information. Deep differences existed between members of the board. Discussion at the board's December 1948 meeting was typical of this divisiveness on the issue—buyers versus publishers and publishers versus publishers.

The board had earlier granted its business publication committee approval to create standards for auditing an occupational analysis of the unpaid portion of member's distribution—that beyond the "at least 50 percent paid"—going to persons in the field served. A "dry run" test had been successfully completed on a New York publication during the course of its regular audit. By a three to two vote, the committee recommended to the full board that the new standards be "touched up by management's experience," and that they be applied on a larger test with the cooperation of several Maclean-Hunter publications in Canada. The discussion quickly turned from the recommendation to a debate on paid versus free.

Speaking against the test audits and in opposition to any occupational breakdown of free in business publication members' reports, James E. Blackburn, McGraw-Hill Publishing Co., called the buyers' requests "much ado about nothing, since unpaid represents less than 4.2 percent of ABC business publications' total distribution." He said the issue was not solely one of members of his division, "but a growth that, if approved, will spread to the throw-away newspapers and free distribution magazines and farm papers. I think the ABC recognition of free will exact a hardship on those who have done their business on a paid circulation standard. They can't manipulate their coverage between business categories, but their competitors can. To adopt the breakdowns of unpaid, we would be interpreted as making a declaration of war—that ABC is trying to raid the other audit bureaus. Buyers should be alarmed at the business ethics of the publisher who charges one fellow and gives it away to the next.

182

James Blackburn checks notes with Stanley R. Clague, Alan Wolcott, and E. Ross Gamble.

"I don't think the ABC can operate successfully for very long with two sets of standards—a very exacting one for paid and a not so exacting one for free. The issue was voted down by the business publications at the last annual meeting 174 to 46, which should tell us all something."

Peter M. Fahrendorf, Chilton Co. and a fellow business publication director and a proponent of the free breakdown, reminded the board that Blackburn had solicited proxy votes on behalf of his candidacy as a director. "Without consulting with these members on this issue, Jim cast more than 150 of his own and the proxy votes he held against the proposal."

H.H. Kynett, Aitkin-Kynett Co., the other member of the committee's minority, spoke of a survey of agencies that he had conducted. "A few are very enthusiastic for ABC to provide these breakdowns. Some agencies are opposed to any consideration of it. I find the great majority are, shall we say, indifferent. If I felt there was an outpouring of space buyer sentiment for this proposition of ABC auditing free, I would not oppose it. I could be convinced if I felt the majority of buyers would make intelligent use of the information, which I don't."

Bernard Duffy, Batten, Barton, Durstine & Osborn, and E. Ross Gamble, Leo Burnett Co., both recognized as skilled media analysts, jumped on Kynett's remarks. "I might be a dumb media buyer," Duffy said, "but we are auditing free circulation right now. Any publisher with at least 50 percent paid and not more than 50 percent free can qualify for membership now. All we are suggesting is that these business publications tell us what in hell half their total distribution is all about, and I don't think that's a dumb thing to be asking."

Gamble said he "agreed with Mr. Duffy and did not agree with Mr. Kynett. Just because he feels there are a lot of dumb space buyers, important information should not be withheld from those who do use it. The intelligent space buyer is entitled to all the information he can get; the dumb space buyer will not use ABC reports anyway."

The original recommendation to carry out the test audits on Canadian publications survived a vote with Chairman Thomson breaking a tie. Two publisher directors lined up with the buyers in favor; two buyers joined those who opposed.

In seeking an answer, the board compounded the problem in 1948 when it unanimously voted to set the Audit Bureau's paid membership eligibility requirement at a straight 50 percent of total distribution, eliminating restrictions on the type of free distribution to be represented by the remaining 50 percent. This opened the way for all publication members to add more unexplained unpaid distribution.

Blackburn's response was to recommend consideration of raising the existing paid standard of 50 percent "to at least 75 or 80 percent. This would help to eliminate the buyers' concern for a free distribution breakdown because there wouldn't be much of it to analyze."

The buyers' problems of evaluating competing paid and free business publications, and ABC's seeming inability to come to grips with the issue, caused

Duffy: "Might be a dumb media buyer."

ANA's Paul West and his counterpart at the American Association of Advertising Agencies, Frederick R. Gamble, to urge the board to find a solution. West offered ANA's offices in bringing buyers and ABC publishers together to seek a solution. The AAAA committee on business papers took the position that "advertising as a whole will be advanced if advertisers and agencies have full information about the circulations of business publications, both paid and unpaid."

"Dry-run" unpaid audit completed; results never released.

Harold Wilt, J. Walter Thompson Co. and chairman of the AAAA committee, visited with Hart and other ABC directors to plead the buyers' case. ABC chairman Philip L. Thomson, Western Electric Co., replied to these appeals, indicating that while the Audit Bureau was interested and desired to help, the board did not feel that it should take the initiative in forming such an industry committee.

Hart's committee and ABC management continued to work on standards for auditing free distribution. A "dry-run" audit was made of an occupational breakdown of the unpaid distribution of a member publication during the course of its regular audit, but the results were never released beyond the board. Further action on actual test audits was lost in subsequent board and member controversy.

Early in 1950, the board's business publication committee offered two optional "solutions to the problem facing ABC members." The first recommendation was a rehash of a suggestion several years earlier that business publication members be permitted to report an occupational breakdown of their unpaid distribution in a statement separate of and on different colored paper than the standard Publisher's Statement. The special report was to "recognize that there are no standards to govern free distribution or the circumstances under which it is distributed. The analyses are to be made, if desired, of free distribution, per se, and without any limiting standards. It will carry a statement by the publisher accepting sole responsibility" for the accuracy of the figures. Absolutely no reference was to be made linking ABC to the data. This recommendation was soundly defeated by the board.

The second recommendation, an effort to reduce the amount of unpaid a member could carry and, supposedly, pacify the buyers' concern for more information on this distribution, suggested that the Audit Bureau's paid eligibility standard once again be raised from 50 percent to 70 percent of total distribution. This latter action was approved.

A "statement of policy by the Association of National Advertisers on circulation audits" made it clear to the board that buyers felt the action was more an evasion than a solution to their problems in attempting to make valid comparisons between competing ABC publications, as well as those verified by other auditing services.

In answering the ANA appeal, Chairman Thomson wrote, "No action should ever be taken that might jeopardize the continued reliability and accuracy of ABC data, and it is the opinion of the majority of the ABC board that every proposal which has been considered to date might, if adopted, be a step toward such jeopardy, with consequences extending far beyond the business publication field.

"In an effort to reduce the area of unpaid circulation and to strengthen further the standards which experience has developed to be the only practical measurement for auditing, the ABC board has passed an amendment to the bylaws raising the circulation requirement for membership of any publication from 50 percent to 70 percent paid."

In their 1950 divisional meetings, buyers continued their plea for breakdowns of business publication members' free distribution. Magazines and farm publications expressed their agreement with the board's action in raising the paid requirement. Members and applicants with more than 50 percent paid but less than 70 percent were given the option of provisional membership by agreeing to meet the new requirement within three years.

However well-intentioned or, for some directors, self-interested, the board's lack of decisive action on the issue had several consequences. Rebuffed by ABC in seeking a solution to their problems in evaluating business publications, industrial advertisers and agencies turned their efforts towards strengthening the other audit bureaus, Business Publications Audit of Circulation in the United States and Canadian Circulation Audit Board in Canada. Secondly, major publishing companies, long influential paid circulation purists, were purchasing successful free distribution publications. These factors, plus the high cost of shaving free from their distributions to meet the 70 percent standard, caused many publications to change their attitudes and drop their ABC memberships to join alternate auditing services.

Members urged to "explore with courage whether old ways are still good enough."

The Audit Bureau's relations with industrial media buyers had slipped so low that the directors openly sought speaking assignments on the annual conventions of the ANA, AAAA, and NIAA "to show in a positive manner why the board makes the decisions it does, either affirmative or negative, to avoid the implication of inaction or having a defensive attitude."

Instead, outgoing chairman of the ANA, Edward G. Gerbic, Johnson and Johnson, was invited to speak at the Audit Bureau's 1955 annual meeting. As a representative of ANA, "but more especially as a long-time member of this association, I believe ABC must be prepared to consider laying aside some of its old ways of doing business. You must explore with courage whether some of the old ways are still good enough to meet today's pressing needs." Among the old ways that advertisers felt needed to be changed in order to help ABC reports fulfill their function to better advantage, Gerbic told the members, was that there "be an analysis of the unpaid circulations of ABC business publications. To the clear-headed and statesmanlike individuals, I appeal to you to close ranks among yourselves and your contemporaries so that we can successfully meet the vital challenge the coming years present all buyers and sellers together."

During 1956, the board conducted another survey of members on the question of including an optional breakdown of unpaid circulation in the reports of business publications. Buyers strongly favored the proposal; publishers, including the business publications, strongly opposed it. Resolutions from the publisher divisions at the annual meeting that fall called for raising the paid circulation requirement, with newspapers going so far as to propose it as high as 90 percent, plus suggesting that reference to "unpaid distribution in ABC reports be limited to a listing of the percentage of such unpaid to total distribution."

The board's policy committee recommended that the percentage paid should not be raised; ABC should recognize that "publishers, in varying degree, require some unpaid distribution for efficient operation of their business; and it is the business of the Bureau to measure and report on all such distribution."

A special committee on business publications was appointed, but this time things were a little different. Early in 1957, Thomas B. Haire, Haire Publishing Co., was elected to the board to fill the vacancy created by the retirement of James Blackburn. Within six months, Haire had developed a proposed breakdown for reporting the unpaid circulation of member business publications and, with the help of ABC staff, had worked out preliminary audit standards.

As if on cue, advertiser and advertising agency members used the annual
meeting to once again urge ABC "to
take action to provide an analysis of
the unpaid portion of the circulation of
business papers." At its next meeting
a month later, the board put the final
touches on Haire's proposal and, without
dissenting vote, adopted the plan for
implementation in the June 1958 Publisher's Statements. The analysis was a
cautious step. For the first time since
1922, the Audit Bureau was able to
announce that it could and would audit
the unpaid circulation of its member
business publications.

But it wasn't enough to satisfy
industrial media buyers. Backed by
representations from the ANA, AAAA,
and NIAA, advertiser and advertising

*Haire had a plan for reporting
unpaid in ABC reports.*

agency members unanimously voted in 1959 to once again express the
feeling "that all circulation of business publications should be audited
and classified."

Attitudes change. By this time most business publication members
desperately wanted to provide the unpaid breakdowns the buyers were
calling for. Many publication companies had acquired free distribution
publications or had been economically forced to add free distribution to
their paid circulation coverage of the fields they served. Newspapers,
whose support they had sought in establishing the paid circulation
membership standard more than 30 years earlier and who had staunchly
defended that position in the years since, now were the business publications' adversary.

The pressure from industrial advertisers and from member
business publications prompted directors Thomas Haire, Haire Publishing Co., and William D. Littleford, Billboard Publishing Co., to propose in
December 1959 that the board "consider the elimination of the 70 percent
rule for business publications and audit paid circulation and unpaid
distribution." Newspaper directors countered during the discussion of
that proposal a few months later with an alternate resolution that "all

Littleford: "Consider elimination of 70 percent rule."

reference to unpaid distribution be eliminated from business publication reports." The latter was actually approved in June 1960, but rescinded three months later, when a third alternative was recommended.

Haire recommended "that in the future, business publication members be allowed to elect to have complete information on their distribution reported" on "a blue Statement form similar to the present one to be available to those who use free distribution rotating for the purpose of building paid circulation and such free distribution reported in quantity only; or a different colored Statement form available to publishers who use free distribution on a fixed free basis to supplement the market coverage of their paid circulation and with a breakdown of the unpaid distribution comparable to paid circulation including occupational and geographical analyses." The board voted 21 to 5 (all newspaper directors) to approve the new optional paid and unpaid form and changes in the existing paid circulation form with an effective date for their use as June 30, 1961.

Advertiser and advertising agency members hailed the action as a positive forward step by the Audit Bureau. Business publications looked to the action as an answer, at least for the moment, to their problems. Newspapers, however, passed a lengthy resolution that ended, "In view of the opposition that has developed among newspaper members of the Audit Bureau of Circulations, it is further strongly and unanimously urged that the action taken by the board on this matter be rescinded by the board at its next meeting." Author of the resolution and a pro-paid advocate, Lyle W. McFetridge, Tulsa, Oklahoma, Newspaper Printing Co., was elected to the board on his pledge to cause ABC to carry out the newspaper resolution.

The annual meeting was followed with a barrage of letters and telegrams from newspaper publishers in the United States and Canada appealing to the board to reconsider the action. In the final board vote to

McFetridge led newspapers in opposing business publication reporting of free circulation.

establish the new optional paid and free form for business publications, only the newspaper directors opposed it. The new form was introduced on schedule with 26 publishers electing its optional use and 12 more indicating plans to use it during the succeeding six-month Publisher's Statement period.

Speaking to the Dotted Line Club of Chicago, William D. Littleford warned publishers not to rush out and add free distribution simply for the sake of building up their ABC figures. "The use of any quantity of unpaid distribution, any extensive dilution of paid circulation, makes it almost impossible to maintain, let alone build, paid circulation."

To meet the competition of a growing number of free distribution publications, many ABC members added unpaid to supplement their market coverage, now that such coverage could be reported and broken down in their Publisher's Statements and Audit Reports. And, as Littleford warned, they were having increasing problems maintaining ABC paid circulation requirements. Several times in the mid-1960s the board's business publication committee, pointing to a declining membership, called on the board to approve the elimination of the 70 percent standard for business publications.

In 1966, another board committee, seeking to find new and better ways for ABC to serve the advertising and publishing industry, was asked to study the implications inherent in extending auditing services to unpaid publications. After 20 "very controversial" months of study, William Weilbacher, C.J. LaRoche and Co., reported for the committee that it had been unable to reach a consensus. In announcing that this subject had been removed from the board's agenda, Chairman William H. Ewen, The Borden Co., said that the issue had prompted a great deal of dialogue between members and the directors. "Opinions have crystal-lized, and it is now indicated that a clear majority of the membership is opposed to the auditing of nonpaid distribution. The board's decision, therefore, is in the proper democratic tradition. Further debate becomes both unnecessary and a waste of time."

But, two years later, it was back on the board's agenda and presented for an advisory vote by the full membership at the 1969 annual meeting. The question of establishing separate and different standards of membership eligibility for business publications was defeated by a vote of 1,123 to 525, with newspapers and magazines solidly with the majority. Behind the vote was the recommendation that the 70 percent paid standard be eliminated for the business publications. A breakdown of the vote indicated that despite the overwhelming numbers against the separate standards, it was actually approved by the business publication, advertiser, advertising agency, and farm publication divisions—only newspapers and magazines opposed.

In January 1970, the board's business publication committee, headed by J. Elton Tuohig, McGraw-Hill Publications Co., told the directors, "Changes in the economics and marketplaces served by business publications have dictated the need for nonpaid as well as paid circulation business publications, resulting in the increasing demand by

Tuohig: Marketplace dictating need for change.

advertisers and their agencies for greater comparability of audited circulation data and, preferably, a single auditing organization to serve all business publications most effectively. The committee resolves that the 70 percent paid eligibility requirement be rescinded for business publications only," and "requests the Chairman activate appropriate machinery to determine the means by which the needs of all members can be met." An ad hoc committee, reflecting the various membership classes and varying member opinions, was established by the board.

The ad hoc committee reported in April that, after several lengthy meetings, it "was unable, compatible with the vote of the majority of the membership, to find an acceptable and reasonable compromise that would bring satisfaction to the expressed needs of a troubled minority. With sincere regret, the committee reports that it cannot recommend a compromise at this time."

As the directors once again began to push the issue off the table, Chairman Fred Heckel, United Air Lines, told the board "something ought to be done—certainly started—today to resolve this issue. There is no question but that this is a difficult problem. It has survived because it is difficult. The perpetuation of indecision is often synonymous with organizational suicide." He spent nearly a half hour in an attempt to clarify positions expressed on the issue, and on the responsibilities of directors to take early action.

Heckel: "Perpetuation of indecision often synonymous with suicide."

The directors argued points of view for another three hours. Finally, Touhig told the board that the business publication committee would put before the directors at its next meeting a resolution asking for a board vote on the rescission of the 70 percent requirement for business publications only.

In June, the committee offered two motions: That the board recognize that membership eligibility requirements of each publisher division may be different, and that any board action to implement such a different standard could be rescinded only by a majority vote of the affected publisher division and the advertiser and advertising agency divisions. The motion was carried by a vote of 17 to 9.

The second motion asked that the bylaws be amended to specify that membership eligibility requirements for business publications only be a total circulation of at least 70 percent paid and/or nonpaid direct request from the recipient for delivery as mail. This motion was carried by a vote of 17 to 6. Both actions were unanimously reaffirmed by the board at its September meeting, becoming effective with the period ending December 31, 1970. A new third form of business publication

Publisher's Statement was developed for those members who qualified under the rule with less than 70 percent paid.

In September 1981, the board approved a new requirement for those wishing to qualify with nonpaid direct request, dropping the requirement from 70 percent to 50 percent paid and/or direct request.

A year later, the board approved its business publication committee's request that the 50 percent requirement be eliminated for a period of 18 months after acceptance as provisional members for those publications seeking to use the paid and/or direct request form. If they did not qualify for regular membership after that time, they were to be automatically dropped from ABC. This provision was approved by the business publication members at the 1982 annual meeting and became effective the following year.

On a higher plane of standards and sophistication of auditing practices, to be sure, and after more than 60 years of often bitter division and debate, free distribution business publications could qualify for membership in the Audit Bureau.

Comparability

The dramatic industrial changes that followed World War II in the late 1940s and early 1950s unleashed an equally dramatic proliferation of business publications in the United States and Canada. To meet competitive pressures, historically committed paid publication companies began to reassess their positions, switching to free distribution and to other circulation verification services.

The loss of commonality between ABC reports and standards and those of the other services brought appeals from the NIAA and the American Association of Advertising Agencies for comparability between the reports and practices of the services, particularly dealing with the business and occupational breakdown.

These efforts were opposed by many ABC business publication members, who pointed out that the Audit Bureau already required comparability between its own members serving the same field or market, while the other services encouraged their participants to establish their own analysis classifications. They further reminded the buyers that only a fifth of the all business publications in the United States were supplying any circulation verification at all, and addressing this issue might be more important.

At the 1959 meeting of the National Industrial Advertisers Association, William A. Marsteller, Marsteller, Rickard, Gebhardt and Reed, Inc., proposed that comparability could only be achieved if advertisers, advertising agencies, and business publications joined together to establish a new auditing organization, "specifically to provide a single comparable audit of business publication circulation." The ABC board replied that it was "actively interested in exploring methods of providing for information to buyers of media and of rendering greater service to publishers" within its own standards. In deference to its membership, "ABC believes that it can best serve the industry by continuing to audit and report the circulations of all publications which can meet the high standards and circulation recordkeeping requirements of the Audit Bureau."

Upset by the lack of overt action by other industry groups to test the Marsteller suggestion, the Chemical Advertisers Group of New York wrote both the ABC and Business Publication Audit of Circulations boards in 1962 suggesting that an exploratory meeting be set. All agreed, but an hour prior to the planned meeting, BPA representatives released a statement to the advertising press. The strongly worded statement, and conditions it set for BPA participation in the exploratory talks, precluded much in the way of an objective discussion.

In 1968, another call came for the consolidation of all business publication auditing services to merge into a single unit. Arthur E. Earley, Meldrum & Fewsmith and chairman of the BPA board, invited various interested associations to discuss the project. The joint committee for audit comparability failed to make any headway and, in 1971, ABC recommended that its efforts either be discontinued or placed under the jurisdiction of the Association of Industrial Advertisers (as the NIAA was renamed). Despite AIA backing and a continuing series of meetings, the discussions seldom got beyond informational exchanges.

No single audit; work for comparability of reports, rules, and procedures.

Richard Christian, Marsteller, Inc., revived the issue of comparability in 1981. Conceding that a single audit of business publication circulations was not feasible under current attitudes, he told members at the annual meeting that he felt comparability of reports, rules, and audit procedures for audit bureaus was attainable. He proposed changes in the rules and reporting procedures that governed the reporting of business publication data.

Under the leadership of William J. Mackey, Rumrill-Hoyt, Inc.,
the comparability committee of the Media Comparability Council took
on the assignment of bringing rules, procedures, and reports of business
publication members of the ABC and BPA into closer conformity. By late
fall of 1982, the committee made 19 proposals to the two audit bureaus
aimed at providing advertising buyers with a more comparable way to
evaluate competitive business publications. The proposals, ten of which
directly affected ABC members, dealt with new definitions and terminology, reporting formats, and additional information.

The committee's proposals were adopted by the ABC board in early
1983. Work began immediately to implement the changes with rules
revisions, which were subsequently phased in over a three-year period.

Renewal Percentage

When they voted in the mandatory reporting of a subscription renewal
percentage in 1923, most business publication members did not understand the implications of what they were voting for. Up to this point,
publishers had the option of answering the question in one of four
methods: a percentage based on complete figures, supported by original
orders; a percentage based on the analysis of a single issue; a percentage
based on a modified "on and off " record; and "Actual figures not available." Sixty-five percent of the business publication members answered
the question with the latter method.

In the years immediately following implementation of the new
requirement, some 60 publishers requested and were granted exceptions
to the rule because they did not maintain adequate records to permit the
verification of the renewal percentages they were reporting.

With the adoption of the mandatory reporting, permissable
methods were cut from four to two. The fact that different publications
figured their renewals on different bases and changed their methods
from year to year led the business publication division, in 1926, to
demand the establishment of "a standardized method of calculating
the renewal percentages."

The board turned to a philosophically split staff for advice. Ed
Chandler, the Audit Bureau's chief auditor in Chicago, favored analyzing
the condition of the circulation as of a given issue and dividing the
number of renewals shown on that issue by the number of subscribers
as represented by that issue. William Hoffman, manager of the Audit

Bureau's eastern regional staff in New York, favored the figuring of the total number of renewals during the entire 12-month audit period against the total expirations of the period. After hearing both staff members debate the methods at its June 1927 meeting, the board adopted Hoffman's recommendation.

"To comply with this rule," the new rule's instructions said, "a publisher must keep a record of his expirations and a record of renewals. A proof list of expirations must be kept for each expiration date. ["Expiration" means the date the subscription expires and not the date it is discontinued.] If expiration notices are addressed from stencils, then proof copy may be run at the same time the notices are addressed. If the notices are addressed from a card it will be necessary to typewrite or hand-write the list when the expiration notices are addressed. Renewals can be checked to these proof lists, or a column can be provided in the cash book for renewals."

"Considerable dissatisfaction with the system" arose almost immediately. "By dividing the renewals received during the year by expirations during that year, an inaccurate picture might, and often does, arise," the business publication advisory committee told the board. The board suspended implementation of the single standard and, once again, began the quest for a new and acceptable system for figuring renewal percentages.

In June 1936, the board adopted another new method that divided renewals for the period into total subscriptions for the same period. While the method accomplished the mission of economy of recordkeeping and auditing, it failed to show the percentage of those who had renewed, and the publication which was getting a large number of new subscribers each period would show up badly in renewal percentage, even though the actual percentage of expiring subscribers who renewed might be high. Member protests were numerous, and the board rescinded its action in September.

By the time of the annual meeting, many members were in favor of rescinding the whole mandatory provision. Out of the meeting, however, came a resolution requesting the board to adopt the "exact method" or the "accurate method." This method required that each renewal in a period be matched to its own expiration. This method of determining renewal percentages was adopted at the board's next meeting, to become effective with the December 1938 Publisher's Statement. The procedure was now called the "specific method" when a new rule added that all publishers were required to compute renewal percentages for the same 12-month period.

Complaints were received from publishers regarding the cost of complying with the standard, and, at the 1940 annual meeting, business publications passed a resolution favoring "the analysis on a one-issue basis in figuring renewal percentages, for the

Renewal percent exceptions fire up board, member discussions.

purpose of simplifying records and cutting down on the work involved by the present method, and for showing renewal percentages as of a more recent date." After discussions with members of the business publication division, the board responded to the resolution by saying that "no further study, looking to change in the method of figuring renewal percentages, is desirable or necessary at this time." Again, the board was faced with a number of requests for exceptions and granted them.

The 12-month versus a single issue question was raised again in 1942 and 1943. The board met with proponents of each side. During the full-day discussion, it was repeatedly called to the directors' attention that "certain concessions had been made in connection with the method by which records had been kept by publishers." Following the meeting, William A. Hart, E.I. du Pont de Nemours & Co. and chairman of the board's business publication forms and practices committee, criticized management for permitting these "concessions" to exist. Managing Director James N. Shryock reminded the directors that it was they, and not management, who had granted the exceptions.

In 1952, after business publications again asked that the procedure for figuring renewals be restudied, the board queried members on their preference of three methods. The answers were inconclusive, and the board continued the "specific method."

The mandatory provision in the rules applying to business publications was questioned again in 1962, 1967, 1972, 1974, and 1977. When the issue was discussed in the 1974 divisional meeting, "a very strong majority consensus indicated that the mandatory renewal percentage rule should continue." Managing Director Alan T. Wolcott expressed concern in 1974 over the frequency with which business publications were requesting exceptions to the renewal percentage rule and with which the board was granting these exceptions. To stem the flow, the board adopted a policy in 1975 to include an explanatory statement in the reports of publishers where exceptions had been granted, including references to the period covered by the exception, a full statement of the reasons for the exception, and a notation on previous exceptions granted to the publication. The 1977 question of the mandatory provision came as a result of the excessive number of exception requests and a study of the appropriateness of the rule, the enforceability of the rule, and possible negative effects of granting or denying such requests. The business publication member advisory committee was asked "to provide specific reasons why renewal data reporting should not be made optional for business publications." The advisory committee recommended that the rules remain unchanged.

Other than modifications to reflect changes in the Audit Bureau's business publication membership eligibility rules (the first making renewal percentages mandatory for paid circulation to the field served only, and then applying the mandatory provision to publications with 50 percent or more paid circulation), and despite the many efforts and thousands of hours of discussion aimed at changing both the mandatory provision and the method of computing renewal percentages, the rule remains substantially as it was when first adopted in 1937.

Farm Publications: ABC an Aid to Profitability

8

Beset with costly circulation practices • APA supports
Audit Bureau • Membership traces agricultural economy
• A directorship goes to magazines • Snookered over bulk
sales decision • Efforts to define agricultural markets,
circulation coverage.

Governor S.R. McKelvie, *Nebraska Farmer*, told an early meeting of ABC
farm publication members, "Except that we are all interested, one way or
another, in agriculture, we are often about as different from one another
as are magazines from trade papers."

The farm publication industry has frequently wrestled with its
identity, sometimes serving as the voice and instructor for business
segments of U.S. and Canadian agriculture; sometimes serving as an
entertainment vehicle for rural families; and sometimes some of each.
Several years later, during a discussion of circulation breakdowns, H.G.
Eisert, *American Poultry Journal*, wrote to the ABC board, suggesting
that "specialized farm papers, such as poultry, dairy, fruit culture, beef
cattle, swine, etc., be listed separately within the division and be exempted from those rules and regulations directed to those farm papers
directed to general farmers and their families."

Of the 52 charter ABC farm publication members, 9 served agricultural businesses, 3 were directed to interests of farm wives, and the
remainder carried a variety of information of general interest to farmers
and their families.

There was another long-standing problem in the farm publication
industry that caused differences and actually spurred many publishers
to welcome the formation of the Audit Bureau. Farmers and ranchers in
many states and provinces were served by several competing publications. Of the 43 original ABC farm publication members that served the
general interests of farmers, 30 were state publications and 13 were

Butler: "Give advertisers a fair shake for their money."

regional or national publications. Adding to these, an estimated 500 unaudited periodicals and weekly newspapers serving farm interests posed situations of intense competition.

Farm publications used about every circulation promotion practice in the book to encourage subscription sales. Subscription prices were pegged low and long-term sales offers were encouraged through the use of premiums, insurance, and travel plans. Subscriptions were frequently tied in with sales of grain to elevator companies and stock and crops to cooperatives. Solicitors, who travelled from farm to farm selling, among other things, subscriptions, readily accepted produce or poultry in lieu of money. This remuneration for what was called "chicken circulation" was carried to the next town and sold. Frequently, solicitors received any money collected for subscriptions as pay for their efforts.

One of the strongest advocates of the Audit Bureau was Burridge C. Butler, *Prairie Farmer*. "Lest we wish to destroy ourselves, we must change these unprofitable circulation building methods. This new movement offers hope in controlling these practices and giving prestige to those publishers among us who wish to give the advertisers a fair shake for their money."

The agricultural industries of the U.S. and Canada have changed dramatically over the years. Improvements in transportation and communications and the extension of electrical services have more closely allied farm family interests to those of its urban neighbors. Farm publications have both served to advance and benefit from greater sophistication in all aspects of the agricultural industry.

Economics forced farmers to recognize the need for better business practices. As Butler and others predicted, the Audit Bureau helped farm publication members eliminate the uneconomic circulation practices their industry had grown up with.

200

Agricultural Associations

Like their business publication brethren, farm publication publishers organized in an attempt to improve their medium in the eyes of advertisers and to "put distance between the honest magazine and those published by those men of less integrity."

The Agricultural Publishers Association strongly supported the formation of the Audit Bureau. Its representatives served on the committee that developed ABC's initial standards and the farm publication Publisher's Statement forms. Officers and members of APA have often been called upon by ABC directors for advice and counsel relative to proposed changes in farm publication rules and services.

Together with the Agricultural Circulation Managers Association, APA called the Audit Bureau board's attention in 1950 to "a need for a new method that will more accurately identify farm and nonfarm circulation in ABC reports." A joint committee of the three groups worked for over a year to produce an alternative to the then-existing optional circulation breakdown by rural free delivery postal designations to identify farm coverage. APA members initially objected to the proposals their officers helped frame as "being too costly and unworkable." This was later resolved with APA support of the Audit Bureau's proposed adoption of the Nielsen ABCD county-size analyses and the use of supplementary reports covering subscriber farm demographics.

Membership

Fifty-two farm publications were represented at the Audit Bureau's organizational meeting. Except for periods following each World War when numbers of farm publications increased, generally, membership in this division has reflected the

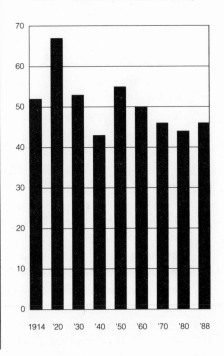

Farm Publication Membership

declining number of farm families in the U.S. and Canada. The decline in farm publication membership also reflects increased pressure on publishers to turn to free distribution to supplement market coverage. Changes in transportation patterns also brought urban cultures and media to rural lifestyles.

Farm publication membership reached a high of 84 in 1921. It dropped to a low of 40 members in 1983. Recent rule changes that permit farm publications to report and break down free portions of their circulations and new efforts to serve market segments have brought membership in this division to a 1988 total of 46 (39 in the U.S. and 7 in Canada).

Board Representation

As with other media divisions, farm publications were represented on the Audit Bureau's original board by two directors. Despite the relatively small number of members in this division, this was justified initially to give recognition to publications located in the East and the West. Over the years, the justification was to assure representation for the national publications and the state and regional publications. As economic conditions changed, and with them a lessening difference between these types of publishing operations, the need for two directors declined. In 1973, the farm publication division gave up one of its directorships to the far more numerous members of the magazine division.

Throughout the ABC history, farm publication member publishers have been a closely knit community, with communications focused through the Agricultural Publishers Association. From time to time, advisory committees and task forces have served to supplement member dialogue in review of board discussions.

Bulk Sales

"Plain and simply, we got snookered." Looking back on the farm publications' 1929 decision, Marco Morrow, Capper Publications, explained that "unfortunately this division adopted a resolution agreeing to the proposition that bulk subscriptions be thrown out of net paid. We thought the resolution was intended to apply to all divisions. We were speaking of general policy, but the Board complied with our request and applied it to us and not to the magazines or business papers.

Morrow: "We got snookered."

"That issue came out of the newspaper division due to publishers in New York selling papers to hotels at ridiculous prices. They got squabbling among themselves and we got caught up."

What Morrow said several years after the fact is undoubtedly true. He was there. He had been an ABC director for ten years before the division's action and knew farm publications were not above bulk sales excesses. In the campaigns during the 1920s to achieve circulation supremacy, farm publication publishers loaded up with quantity sales to livestock commission companies, grain dealers, implement manufacturers, and other suppliers. One publisher reported that he did not know how many "deals we have going, but I do know that each gives us no less than 500, 600, and 700 names."

Advertiser members had asked in 1926 that bulk sales be eliminated from paid circulation totals in the ABC reports of all publications. The farm publication division asked that this request be tabled. When the subject was brought before the annual meeting again in 1929, farm publications went beyond their newspaper counterparts by moving bulk sales from paid to unpaid in their reports. The depressed economy of the early 1930s limited the market for bulk sales efforts, but it was back on the farm publication agenda in 1937 with a divisional resolution to the board "that the farm paper form be so changed as to include bulk circulation in net paid." During board discussion that followed receipt of this resolution, the farm publication directors advised that they had talked about the question with various agricultural publishers and, since there had been no particular interest in it, they recommended the proposal be laid on the table.

E.M. Holiday, *Western Producer*, Saskatoon, raised the subject again at the 1939 divisional meeting. His resolution was to have farm publication bulk reported in paid, in the same manner as was being done for magazines. F.W. Taylor, *Progressive Farmer*, opposed the proposal saying, "Bulk circulation is subject to abuses and that is one of the reasons why we voted it out. I would be against any change in the present rule." The resolution to restore bulk sales to paid circulation in ABC farm publication reports was defeated.

During a general review and clarification of bulk sales rules the following year, the board did make a change in how farm publications were to report their quantity sales. Bulk was separated from other unpaid and reported separate of but beneath the "total net paid excluding bulk" listing.

Coming out of the World War II period, specialized ABC farm publications were feeling the competitive squeeze from an increasing number of free distribution farm and business publications. Informal discussions of

Watt: Want bulk classified and reported as paid.

bulk sales surfaced from time to time, and, in 1957, the board approved a rule change permitting farm publications to report mail subscriptions— quantity sales to companies for distribution to their employees—as paid.

In 1960, Leslie A. Watt, *Poultry Tribune*, presented the board with a resolution on behalf of 15 members, requesting that bulk sales be classified as paid in ABC farm publication reports.

The proposal was presented to the divisional meeting for guidance, and the members voted to table it. At the board meeting following this session, Director Richard Babcock, *Farm Journal*, reported that the farm publication committee "was in unanimous agreement with the division's vote and that no further action would be taken unless the subject was again brought up."

Bulk sales did come up again in 1964, in conjunction with a format change allowing "unpaid including bulk sales" to be reported in addition to paid in issue-by-issue breakdowns of farm publications.

Agricultural Markets

Marco Morrow, Capper Publications, once called the farm publication
division "a unique blend of the best characteristics of magazines and
trade papers. Our advertising customers know us and our markets and,
therefore, don't complicate our lives with the types of requests they make
of these other publications."

As approved in the summer of 1914, ABC's original report formats
provided for farm publication members to identify the rural/urban nature
of their subscription circulation. It also allowed for publishers to report
an editorial statement as to the markets their publications were serving.

The original report formats included a paragraph for farm publication publishers to show a breakdown of subscription circulation (first
by percentages and later by percentages and actual totals) by: "On all
R.F.D. routes and to Post Offices in towns under 1,000; to Post Offices
in towns over 1,000 and under 2,500; and to Post Offices in towns over
2,500." The problem was that very few publishers "fully realized the
importance of answers to the question on the distribution of circulation.
A considerable percentage have answered Paragraph 12 in their Publisher's Statements by 'Actual Figures Not Available.'" In 1920, the
board made this breakdown mandatory, based on an analysis of an
actual issue. The date of the issue was to be optional with the publisher.

Advertisers' attention was diverted by concerns over forced
circulation during most of the 1920s. At the 1927 meeting of advertiser
members, however, complaints were registered about the statements
publishers were allowed to make concerning their markets and the
ability of their farm publications to serve these markets.

The board approved new formats for farm publication reports in
1929. Major change was to add population group categories for subscription analysis and to eliminate the rural delivery break out. Copies delivered by "rural free delivery" were reported separately within the breakdown of total distribution by states and provinces.

Part of this format change involved moving the publisher's own
definition of the publication's market from the explanatory information
to the first page introductory information, and subjected this to ABC
staff review. The review wasn't much because at the 1933 annual
meeting advertising agencies resolved "that the answers [to the 'field
served' paragraph] should be confined to a brief description of a few

words," and that staff should eliminate promotional claims. The board noted the buyers' request but took no further action.

In 1931, the board approved an extension to the rule on the analysis of subscription circulation by population groups. It was optional for farm publications to supply a breakdown of "circulation other than subscriptions" unless such an analysis was furnished advertisers outside of ABC, in which case a similar analysis would become mandatory.

H.G. Eisert, *American Poultry Journal*, wrote the board two years later to ask that all of the poultry publications be exempted from reporting a population group breakdown and to show a separate tabulation of copies delivered by R.F.D. All seven farm publication members serving that industry agreed with Eisert, pointing out that such breakdowns were not worth the cost since the "location of hatcheries and poultry raisers is well known to advertisers and not given to R.F.D. and non-R.F.D. identification." Both advertisers in these publications and a poll of all other farm publication members agreed with Eisert's request, and the board approved the group exemption.

Except for these poultry publications, the analysis of single copy sales, in addition to subscription circulation, was made mandatory in 1944. The poultry publication exemption was rescinded in 1947. After farm publication discussion at the annual meeting, the board approved a rule change making the mandatory analysis of an actual issue a requirement at least once every five years instead of annually, and intervening analyses could be based upon percentages developed in the actual count and applied to the circulation totals for those years.

Criticism of ABC's reliance on rural mail delivery as an indication of farm interest was voiced by both publishers and buyers. At its March 1948 meeting, the board voted to urge the U.S. Post Office Department and the Bureau of the Census "to devise a separate designation for farms as distinguished from nonfarms on R.F.D. routes as a means of providing the advertising and publishing industry with an accurate enumeration of farms." The reply was that such a breakdown by either agency "just wasn't feasible."

Board tells farm publications to aid in helping solve their own market definition problems.

The 1950 meeting of farm publication members requested that a committee representing ABC, the Agricultural Publishers Association, and the Agricultural Circulation Managers Association "to develop a new method that will more accurately identify farm and nonfarm circulation" for reporting in ABC reports. Under the chairmanship of Leslie A. Watt, *Poultry Tribune*, the committee met frequently during 1951, only to report in October that "objection had been raised to various plans which had been presented to the Agricultural Publishers Association as being too costly and unworkable. The subject was presented to the farm publication divisional meeting and no particular interest had been shown by the members."

By 1957, rural postal delivery was virtually useless as an indication of the on-farm market. Post-World War II housing booms and urban spread gobbled up farms faster than post offices could replace rural delivery. After 43 years as the Audit Bureau's indicator of farm circulation, the board polled farm publication members and, with their overwhelming concurrence, dropped all reference to rural delivery from ABC reports. A special board committee worked through most of 1958 to develop a survey procedure for determining the farm interests of farm publication subscribers.

Pilot surveys were completed on *The Ohio Farmer* and *The Farm Journal*, reviewed by the technical committee of the Advertising Research Foundation, and submitted to the farm publication members for reaction. The replies, at approximately a seven to one ratio, indicated the members' feeling that a plan costing $500 to $600 a year would not provide information of relative value. George C. Dibert, J. Walter Thompson Co. and chairman of the special committee, recommended "that the Audit Bureau take no further action until the farm publication members take a greater interest in solving this problem of identifying their markets." The board concurred and discharged the committee. It further made the reporting of circulation by population groups optional.

Robert Palmer, Cunningham and Walsh Inc., told farm publication members at their 1960 meeting that attrition in agriculture would pose challenging times for farm publications. "With the emergence of the large farmer as practically the sole market for agricultural goods and services, there will be a continuing reappraisal of advertisers' marketing objectives to allow for greater concentration on this key group. If you are to play an important part in the coming scheme of things, you must be able to document your subscribers' interest in agriculture." He suggested that farm publications provide this documentation through questionnaires, "subject to and reported through the ABC audit."

At the same annual meeting, advertising agency members called on the board to replace the population group breakdowns of magazines and farm publications, for those reporting this, with either county-city size definitions or some other form of standard metropolitan area analyses. A joint magazine-farm publication committee went to work on the suggestion. In 1962, the board approved an optional farm publication report analysis, breaking down circulation by six county population-size groupings within U.S. Standard Metropolitan Statistical Areas. Circulation outside the SMSAs was analyzed and reported within four county groupings, classified according to the percentage of urban population in each. The action eliminated the long-time breakdown reporting circulation by city-size groupings for U.S. farm publications. The new breakdown did not affect Canadian members.

Some farm publications provided advertisers with their circulation analyses by selected counties. The procedure used in compiling circulation data for the county population size groupings supplied counts by individual counties as a by-product.

The board's farm publication committee, seeking new areas to improve ABC services, suggested that county circulation breakdowns be made a part of ABC reports. The members concurred at the 1965 meeting, approving a resolution that this be offered as an optional service. The county-by-county breakdown of a single issue's total paid circulation by counties receiving 25 or more copies was approved as optional audited Supplemental Data Reports the following year. Within two years, 12 farm publications were reporting the county data.

The concept of subscriber documentation, suggested by Palmer at the 1960 farm publication meeting, came up again in 1966. This time it was raised by *Fortune Magazine* in a request for ABC verification of its subscriber identification program. Granting the request opened the way to similar verifications of supplemental "other data" for other magazines and farm publications. *The Farm Journal*'s request that its Top Operator edition be reported and audited was granted in 1969. That same year, *Successful Farming*'s request for a Supplemental Data Report identifying subscribers by degree of indicated farm interest and detailed data on crop and livestock interest was granted. A decision in 1971 to include an analysis of demographic

County-by-county circulation reports and demographic data offer farm publishers added service options.

editions in the ABC FAS-FAX reports for farm publications encouraged a number of U.S. and Canadian farm publications to follow the *Successful Farming* lead in showing the degree of subscriber farm interest, occupation, and crop and livestock demographics.

Today's market coverage breakdown for U.S. and Canadian farm publications follows the population group analysis adopted for magazines in 1973. At the publisher's option, paid circulation is broken down by counties grouped by ABCD size, with A the most heavily populated and D the least. The breakdown includes the number of counties in each grouping, percent of population represented by the grouping, totals of subscription and single copy sales and percents of total, and total circulation and percent of total within each grouping.

As they have since 1914, farm publications report a mandatory analysis of circulation by states and/or provinces.

Organization Relies on Dedicated Direction and Operation

9

Control vested in elected board of directors • Day-to-day operation and accomplishing ABC objectives • Work of management and staff • Service improvements react to needs changes, new technology • The Audit Bureau of Marketing Services experiment.

"So far as I can call to mind, the Audit Bureau of Circulations is the only institution in North America in which the producer and the consumer, the manufacturer and the customer, the seller and the buyer, have voluntarily sat down together and have cooperated, harmoniously and with good feeling, in establishing standards of practice," the Honorable Arthur Capper, U.S. Senator from Kansas and publisher of a number of farm publications, told the members in 1938. "ABC was something new in trade relations in 1914. We had long given lip service to the idea that buyer and seller have mutual interests; but the ABC made that vague theory an actuality. This is all the more significant because the Bureau came into being, not upon compulsion, not through government edict, but through the voluntary action of men of integrity who saw that decency and fairness and honorable dealing were prime essentials of business.

"Most of us members assume that the Bureau is doing a fairly good job and let it go at that. We take it for granted. We vaguely wonder why its auditors have to be so persnickety about some of our own perfectly legitimate practices, and when our esteemed contemporary down the street gets away with murder. We grouch about the quarterly bills and yell our heads off if there is a charge for 'excess costs'—but that's all a part of our regular routine.

"In reality we take the Bureau as 'one of those things' that God, or Fate, or Custom has wished upon us, and we suppose it's necessary and all right. Yet, despite the lackadaisical attitude on the part of too many of us members, it is high time to salute the dedicated directors and staff who deserve much of the credit that the Bureau has persisted all these years. And in all that time, through their direction and operation, it has grown in prestige, in influence, and in value of its services to the business world."

Board of Directors

As one member put it, the May 20-21, 1914, organizational meeting of the Audit Bureau of Circulations sounded "like a convention of amateur parliamentarians and curbstone lawyers." Covering the better part of two days, discussion of a proposed nine article "constitution and bylaws" for the new organization elicited no less than 70 motions to amend and motions to amend motions.

Article V of the proposal was to establish a board of directors (then called a "board of control") composed of 11 advertiser representatives, and 2 each representatives of advertising agencies, newspapers, magazines, farm publications, and business publications, for a 21-member board and with directors to be nominated by members of their respective divisions. Newspapers challenged this arrangement, first moving that they be granted 3 directors and the farm publications 1; then that newspapers should have "at least" 5 representatives on the board; and, finally, that all divisions, including advertisers, have equal representation.

"Effort to gain an unfair advantage will split this association."

Using the same logic put forth by the newspapers, other members suggested similar increases in representation for their divisions. At one point, it would have taken a board of no less than 51 members, nearly 11 percent of the total membership, to accommodate all suggestions.

Merton C. Robbins, *Iron Age*, questioned the whole discussion, suggesting "it has a tendency towards an effort to gain an unfair advantage which will ultimately split this association if allowed to continue. None of us should question the right of advertisers to a controlling voice in its affairs. It seems to me that aside from this, this body is based more upon the theory on which our United States Senate is organized, viz. a representation from each unit, the two senators from each state, whether it the State of Texas or the State of Rhode Island. It is upon that basis, as outlined in the original prospectus, that many of us have joined this association."

With little more discussion, the members approved the board structure as suggested in the proposed constitution. It further provided that "the power to in anyway alter this constitution and bylaws shall be vested solely in the board of control, to be effective only after confirmation by a majority of Division A (advertiser) members, ratified by two-thirds of the membership on voting upon such alteration."

This provision proved extremely difficult for the board. New standards, as well as amendments to existing rules had to be held for annual meetings before they could be implemented or were rescinded. In an overhaul of bylaws, approved at the 1919 annual meeting, rules and bylaws were separated and the board's position enhanced. The new bylaws gave the board the power to "make, publish, and enforce such rules and regulations as they may deem necessary for the proper conduct of the business of the Bureau," with such rules in full force and effect until rescinded by the board or a two-thirds vote of the membership voting on the proposition. A change in the amend-

Board's authority to establish, change standards offset by member vote to rescind actions.

ments article eliminated the need to first submit bylaw alterations to the advertiser division but retained the ratification by at least two-thirds of members voting on the proposition to become effective.

Over the years, the members have approved a number of bylaw changes aimed at increasing the effectiveness of the board by granting the directors more control over the organization. In a 1934 revision, the two-thirds override provision for the members was changed to a simple majority at any regularly called annual or special meeting of the members. This changed, however, when travel restrictions during the World War II years prevented the holding of an annual meeting. In 1944, the members approved revisions that retained the right of a majority to override the board on the repeal, modification, alteration, or amendment of rules or standards but granted full authority to the board to make or repeal bylaws, substantially as these provisions currently exist.

As has been noted in previous chapters, the composition and size of the ABC board has changed over the years:

	1914	1918	1926	1935	1953	1956	1969	1973	1987
Advertiser	11	11*	13	12	11	11	11	11	10**
Advertising Agency	2	2	2	3	4	6*	7	7	8**
Newspaper									
Daily	2	4	4	6*	6	6	7	7	7
Weekly						1	1	1	1
Magazine	2	2	2	2	2	2	2	3	3
Farm Publication	2	2	2	2	2	2	2	1	1
Business Publication	2	2	2	2	2	2	2	2	2
Periodical at Large						1*	1	1	1
	21	23	25	27	27	31	33	33	33

* 1 Canadian directorship specified.   ** 2 Canadian directorships specified.

Through the earlier years of the Audit Bureau, its board met the first Friday of each month in Chicago (with the exception of quarterly meetings in New York), and the executive committee met weekly. Over the years, the frequency of regular board meetings was cut to bimonthly, then to five times a year, and, since 1972, four times a year. From time to time, the board has met in special meetings, usually to provide additional time to give in-depth attention to a specific agenda.

The first board officers—president, first and second vice presidents, secretary, and treasurer—were elected by the members attending the organizing convention. Thereafter, officers were elected by their fellow directors at each board's organizational meeting held immediately following the close of the annual meeting of members. The term "chairman" was added to that of "president," and the dual title was used until 1954 when the staff executive was designated "president and managing director." Along with the other officers, the current board includes four vice-chairmen.

Much of the board's work is carried out through committee discussions. Along with the executive committee, the 1914 board had committees on standard forms and audits, data, and membership. Today's board has 14 standing or liaison committees. These committees regularly meet during the course of the board meeting but, when necessary, are called into session between these meetings.

Through most of the Audit Bureau's history, directors have been aided in their discussions through the efforts of advisory committees, divisional committees, and liaison committees of allied associations. The committees extend the board members' communications into the general membership or to specific constituencies within the membership. Today, 12 advisory or liaison committees serve to enhance member dialogue in the board's efforts to identify and meet industry needs.

Management and Staff

Distrust was evident in most discussions of the Audit Bureau's initial bylaws in 1914. This was displayed in debates over the manner in which the managing director was to be selected and the extent of that person's responsibilities. The constitution committee proposed that the managing director be appointed by the board and that duties of the office include the direction of general operations of ABC, including the making of all contracts on behalf of ABC (the latter subject to board approval).

Publishers were generally suspicious of the type of individual an advertiser-controlled board might choose and sought one-year terms for the office, with the right of the membership to approve or reject the board's choice each year.

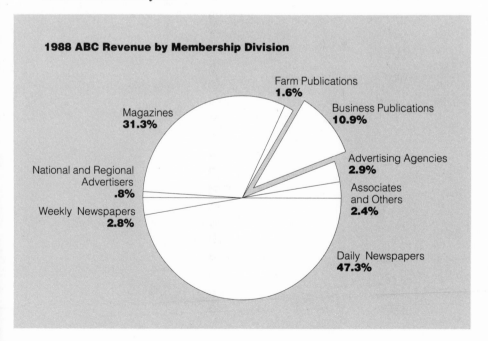

1988 ABC Revenue by Membership Division

Farm Publications **1.6%**

Business Publications **10.9%**

Magazines **31.3%**

Advertising Agencies **2.9%**

National and Regional Advertisers **.8%**

Associates and Others **2.4%**

Weekly Newspapers **2.8%**

Daily Newspapers **47.3%**

Advertiser leaders indicated their support for Russell R. Whitman, a former Hearst newspaper executive who had headed up the efforts that led to the organization meeting.

While this placated some publisher members, it upset representatives of newspapers that competed with Hearst-owned newspapers, and who feared Whitman would not exercise his duties without showing favoritism. The original bylaws were adopted and Whitman appointed, but only after a four-hour debate and the assurance that the board's selection of ABC's first managing director would be submitted for membership approval.

The bylaws giving the board authority to appoint the managing director and designating responsibilities for that office remained substantially unchanged until 1949. The board then clarified and expanded the responsibilities to bring the bylaws into compliance with the evolved operating practices.

Additionally, the board assigned the managing director the duty and responsibility "to interpret and enforce the rules and standards" fixed by the board, to investigate charges or accusations against members, conduct special investigations, make reports and recommendations relating to offenses and punishments, employ and discharge employees, and to provide assistance to the board's secretary.

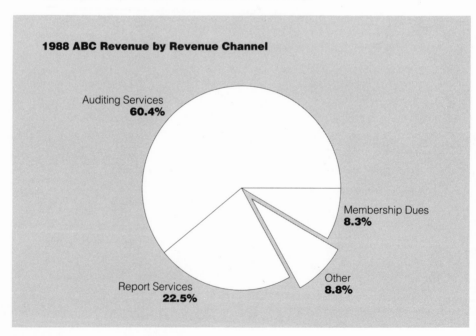

1988 ABC Revenue by Revenue Channel

Auditing Services
60.4%

Membership Dues
8.3%

Other
8.8%

Report Services
22.5%

Despite the early concerns over the appointment of the managing director, the integrity and impartiality of ABC's management and staff have never been seriously challenged during the organization's 75-year history.

With an assistant and three employees, Whitman's first task was to prepare and distribute standard circulation reporting forms. This was accomplished within ten weeks of the organization meeting. Slow publisher response in filing these forms and returns with incomplete information provided staff with an opportunity to become familiar with Publisher's Statement production and afforded Whitman the time to concentrate on developing a field auditing staff.

By mid-August, Whitman was only able to engage four auditors "with the required practical knowledge of making circulation examinations and who also were considered as possessing the necessary high standard of character and reliability demanded by the Bureau in this work." These men formed the base of the field auditing staff; before beginning the field work, they spent a month in the ABC office going over the Publisher's Statements, becoming familiar with Audit Bureau's bylaws and rules, and in formulating a standard code of auditing procedure. When each of these auditors initiated his first circulation audit on September 21, he was accompanied by an auditor trainee. As the trainees became competent, they were added to the staff and other trainees were hired.

Between September 1914 and the annual meeting of members the following June (less than nine months), the field staff included 33 qualified auditors and 7 trainees. In addition to the work done by these men, the services of five certified public accounting firms were being used. During that same period, 321 audits had been completed, with another 63 in progress. In its second year of operation, Whitman reported the completion of 724 audits, with another 78 in process.

Growth of the ABC staff over the years reflects the growth in membership, increase in the number and complexity of circulation audits, and expansion of services. As of August 31, 1988, the end of the fiscal year, the ABC staff totaled 225 employees. This included 107 field auditors and 11 auditing trainees. By the end of that year, 2,435 audits had been completed, and another 309 were in process.

From its earliest days, part of the management and auditing staff was headquartered in New York City, as a means of recognizing the eastern organizers and in an effort to economize on auditor travel costs.

Following a management change in that office in 1920, the New York staff became increasingly independent of the Chicago headquarters, especially during the period that Orlando Harn served as managing director. With the 1956 death of William Hoffman, manager of that office for 26 years, the total auditing staff was brought under Chicago management and the New York operation de-emphasized to the status of an Eastern Member Service office. A similar liaison office had been established in Toronto for Canadian members in 1953.

ABC's headquarters facilities have improved considerably since Whitman shared a loaned office at Montgomery Ward & Co. in Chicago. The organization moved to "new and spacious" rental quarters within a month of its founding meeting, the first of what would be five moves. In 1979, after losing its lease in the building that had housed ABC headquarters for nearly 30 years and a search of possible new quarters in Chicago, the board approved the purchase of property in northwest suburban Schaumburg and the development of a new 32,400-square-foot building designed specifically to ABC operational requirements. The move to the current headquarters building was made in August 1980.

By the end of the first year of operation, the 15-person ABC "duplicating" department staff had mimeographed and mailed 2,754 quarterly Publisher's Statements and 170 Audit Reports, totalling 701,863 copies. Growth the following year required staff to seek help from outside printing sources, and, in 1919, the board authorized the acquisition of letterpress equipment to enable management to bring production of all reports within the Audit Bureau's direct control. ABC's current typesetting and printing facilities are efficient, accounting for the production of all the various printed reports—well over 12 million impressions a year.

As happened with many organizations, the "computer age" arrived before management and staff were adequately prepared, and the long-range ABC implications of the computer were neither understood or realistically anticipated.

By 1962, computers were being used by increasing numbers of media planners and publishers, enough so that members were asking the board to revise ABC reports and provide new services that would make these data more compatible with this equipment. The board's policy committee asked staff to study possible changes in ABC reporting formats. Later that year, a board computer task force was established to determine the extent of computer use by the member companies and the

Headquarters moved in 1980 from Chicago's Loop to ABC's own building in the suburbs.

relationship of this use to ABC data. The staff report to the policy committee in 1963 proposed that because computer use in the industry was so occasional and use so fragmented, it would be impractical to restructure ABC reports. The task force came to a similar conclusion and made no recommendation, other than to advise management to "keep alert to the possibilities."

A management recommendation to the board's finance committee in 1967 re-introduced the computer subject. Management justified a proposed lease of an in-house small mainframe computer on the basis of improved internal accounting and member service records, and only incidentally suggested the equipment might at some time be used for application to additional services to members. The committee and the board approved the proposal to computerize these records, and authorized management to select and contract for the necessary equipment. The equipment was in place in the fall of 1968, with the accounting system being converted and with the conversion and selective access of magazine and farm publication county circulation data to follow.

In 1970, Managing Director Alan T. Wolcott reported to the board that the computer was functioning well but that "the first year and a half of computer operations was an extremely difficult period, involving the transition of much of our internal accounting work." Work now was progressing on ABC's county circulation data bank reports.

After "an extremely difficult" start, ABC's computer operations were gradually expanded. Major change in equipment and systems in 1989 puts organization "on cutting edge" of service progress.

While several additional new services became possible because of the computer, data processing technology and use in the industry moved faster than the Audit Bureau. Progress at ABC was inhibited by traditional management concern over costs and a built-in conservative attitude. Early after his appointment as managing director, M. David Keil established a staff computer task force, with representatives from each department. Its preliminary report was ready in 1983, but, due to concentration on the Trenton litigation, board action on the report was deferred.

Management used 1984 and 1985 to prepare staff for a future deeply committed to advancing electronic technologies. Keil stressed quality control and consistency in all departments, with special

emphasis on personnel recruitment, training, and evaluation. Organizational charts were changed, particularly in the auditing department, providing expanded staff control and staff and member liaison.

While all departments, aided by consultants, became more comfortable with and explored new possibilities of computer use, the board agreed to make ABC's 75th anniversary in 1989 the target date for shedding the ABC staff of its "green eyeshade" image. With the acquisition of new equipment and systems, and mentally and organizationally prepared, the Audit Bureau is entering a period of new services and service improvements.

The potential encompasses not only publisher member communication of data to ABC electronically and headquarter's staff verification and review of these data, but an electronic linkage through the functions of hard copy report production and distribution, the availability of diskette report formats, and direct access to increased quantities of historical data on member publications.

Member Report Services

The first ABC standard circulation blanks went to all publication members to be filled out on July 29, 1914. Publishers were slow in returning their statements because of wartime personnel shortages. The information required on the blanks was new in the case of most publications, and new records had to be installed. In many instances, the blanks received by ABC were incomplete and had to be returned—frequently six or eight times—before they were accepted. By the end of the Audit Bureau's first fiscal year, April 30, 1915, quarterly Publisher's Statements were being issued on 688 member publications.

Justifying these statement claims was more of a problem for publishers. The growing ABC field auditing staff, supplemented by personnel from five public accounting firms, completed only 170 audits between September 1914 and the end of the first fiscal year. Managing Director Russell R. Whitman reported to the first annual meeting that audit work "was rendered slower on account of the condition of the publisher's records in many cases, and on account of the fact that our auditors were instructed to give every assistance possible to publishers in helping them to install adequate and sufficient circulation records and systems."

With greater familiarity of ABC requirements came increased data for buyers. The quarterly frequency for Publisher's Statements was changed to semi-annual, and, during the organization's second fiscal year, reports on nearly 1,200 individual member publications were distributed, along with 745 Audit Reports. The information in these reports as well as the terminology and format by which it is reported have changed over the years, reflecting the reaction of obsolete practices and the need for new facts.

Data provided through the semi-annual Publisher's Statements and the Audit Reports, which verify or correct these publisher's claims, remain the basis of the Audit Bureau's member report services.

Blue Books

Early in 1923, Managing Director Stanley Clague reported he was meeting advertiser and advertising agency membership resistance from those who claimed they could get ABC data through rate and data digests and directories. He also reported that he had received "a number

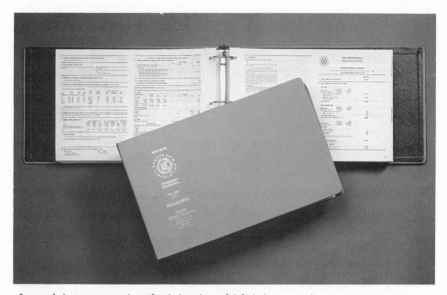

of complaints concerning the injustice which it is declared is being done to publisher members by the use, in Standard Rate and Data Service, of their ABC figures in conjunction with claimed figures of publications which are not members of the Bureau."

The ABC Blue Book service attempted to answer demand for more compact data libraries.

A "Blue Book" committee was established to study whether ABC should publish a directory of its own member publications, including information on them similar to that provided by SRDS for all publications, and refuse other digests and directories permission to carry ABC circulation data. SRDS countered with an agreement to identify the circulation figures of ABC members in a different typeface, carry an ABC comment on each page, and to identify each member's listing with the ABC membership insigne. "When these changes have been carried out," SRDS told the committee, "the total space devoted to the promotion of ABC ideals will consume the equivalent of 30 pages of ABC advertising, which we gladly contribute to the cause."

With the committee's approval, Clague pursued a plan to develop special interest in the reports of member publications. In September 1924, periodical Publisher's Statements issued for the period ended June 30 were bound and sent, without charge, to all advertiser and advertising agency members. The board approved a similar plan for binding and sending complete sets of newspaper Publisher's Statements to buyers.

The viability of this gratis Blue Book service was questioned in 1927. A poll of buyer members indicated that these volumes were being used effectively by 80 percent of the recipients, and the suggestion was made that the periodical volume be separated into individual books covering magazines, business publications, and farm publications.

Supplemental Data Reports

The promises of new marketing data retrieval planned into the 1960 U.S. census and the potential of computer technology to manipulate these data for media planning use created a demand that ABC review its reports for utility in "the new era." An early conclusion was that the magazine and farm publication breakdown of circulation by population groups was out of sync with the growing interest of buyers in county-size analyses. Advertising agency members sent the board a resolution specifically requesting it replace the exiting analysis with "either Nielsen county-city sized definitions or some other form of standard metropolitan area breakdown."

For those U.S. magazines for whom this breakdown was required (those with over 100,000 paid circulation) and those U.S. magazines (those under 100,000 circulation) and all farm publications for which the breakdown was optional, the board adopted a new analysis in 1962. This provided for an optional allocation of paid circulation figures by county groupings within U.S. Standard Metropolitan Statistical Areas and for distribution outside such areas by county groups according to the percentage of urban population. A similar analysis, based on Canadian groupings, was also developed and offered.

During the process of developing data for this breakdown, publishers were required to compile circulation figures by counties, using an ABC circulation analyses workbook. With advertising agencies continuing to seek county-by-county circulation figures and many publishers providing them either independently or through a Magazine Advertising Bureau service, it was only a matter of time before an optional county circulation Supplemental Data Report service was adopted by the board. The difference between this service and the breakdowns provided independently or through MAB was the assurance of the ABC audit.

In early 1967, Managing Director Alan T. Wolcott announced that the first Supplemental Data Report for magazines and farm publications had been processed and released. This report contained a county analysis of the circulation of *Better Homes and Gardens*. Within weeks, additional magazines and farm publications joined the optional service.

While the initial Supplemental Data Report service dealt with the county-by-county breakdown of magazine and farm publication circulation, later use has been expanded to include such other information as subscriber demographics, subscriber farm crop demographics, verified data from business publication readership research, etc.

Data Bank Services

"Give us an Oregon button," suggested George Simko, Benton & Bowles, Inc., during an ABC-sponsored media buyer focus interview seeking to identify new service opportunities in the mid-1960s. "ABC could save us time and frustration if it could provide comparative magazine coverage analyses based on our needs and our market definitions. We give you a list of counties or states, and ABC tells us what circulation each of the magazines we have under consideration has in the area."

Simko's comment was typical of a number of suggestions from buyers. With ABC's computer experience advancing and the county-by-county

County circulation reports for magazines and farm publications got ABC in line to establish Data Bank services.

Paid Circulation in Counties by States

based on March 28, 1988 issue:

ALABAMA TOTAL PAID	21,175	ALABAMA (Cont'd)		ARIZONA (Cont'd)		ARKANSAS (Cont'd)	
COUNTY	CIRCULATION	COUNTY	CIRCULATION	COUNTY	CIRCULATION	COUNTY	CIRCULATION
AUTAUGA	164	LOWNDES	41	SANTA CRUZ	212	JEFFERSON	328
BALDWIN	579	MACON	162	YAVAPAI	908	JOHNSON	63
BARBOUR	109	MADISON	1,757	YUMA	635	LAFAYETTE	18
BIBB	48	MARENGO	108	BALANCE IN STATE		LAWRENCE	66
BLOUNT	89	MARION	137	Total	32,182	LEE	39
BULLOCK	45	MARSHALL	326			LINCOLN	35
BUTLER	89	MOBILE	2,098	ARKANSAS		LITTLE RIVER	49
CALHOUN	565	MONROE	86	TOTAL PAID	10,091	LOGAN	55
CHAMBERS	120	MONTGOMERY	1,513			LONOKE	118
CHEROKEE	48	MORGAN	493	ARKANSAS	75	MADISON	27
CHILTON	98	PERRY	57	ASHLEY	114	MARION	38
CHOCTAW	57	PICKENS	60	BAXTER	137	MILLER	11
CLARKE	110	PIKE	128	BENTON	497	MISSISSIPPI	279
CLAY	32	RANDOLPH	47	BOONE	125	MONROE	39
CLEBURNE	23	RUSSELL	192	BRADLEY	37	MONTGOMERY	26
COFFEE	243	ST. CLAIR	147	CALHOUN	9	NEVADA	21
COLBERT	204	SHELBY	370	CARROLL	84	NEWTON	13
CONECUH	53	SUMTER	67	CHICOT	55	OUACHITA	163
COOSA	21	TALLADEGA	255	CLARK	83	PERRY	25
COVINGTON	141	TALLAPOOSA	142	CLAY	43	PHILLIPS	130
CRENSHAW	41	TUSCALOOSA	865	CLEBURNE	65	PIKE	33
CULLMAN	256	WALKER	255	CLEVELAND	15	POINSETT	59
DALE	457	WASHINGTON	48	COLUMBIA	114	POLK	65
DALLAS	326	WILCOX	43	CONWAY	85	POPE	164
DE KALB	188	WINSTON	71	CRAIGHEAD	277	PRAIRIE	24
		BALANCE IN STATE		CRAWFORD	115	PULASKI	2,391

Supplemental Data Report service operational, the board agreed early in 1968 to establish a computerized bank of these data, and make this circulation information available in hardcopy and computer-readable punch card formats. Information on 12 magazines and 10 farm publications was available by late summer of 1968, and another 48 publications had indicated their desire to participate in the Audit Bureau's new Circulation Data Bank service.

Despite the relatively small amount of data available, and the fact that information on separate publications was not merged by ABC, orders for 29 punch card sets were ordered the first month of operation. The first specialized Data Bank report, for Hunt-Wesson Foods, analyzed the circulations of 12 magazines by the advertiser's dealer territories to show household coverage for several schedules under consideration. Within the first ten months, information on 43 publications was included and requests for 199 punch card decks and over a dozen printouts had been received.

The merging of circulation data on several publications to provide comparative analyses by user-designated geographical areas and the inclusion of related census-based information came when the Magazine Advertising Bureau's Magazine Advertising Coverage Service was absorbed by the ABC Circulation Data Bank service in the fall of 1969.

As the number of publisher participants in the ABC Data Bank service and requests for specialized computer-generated reports grew, so did the efforts to expand the types and availabilities of data in meeting the individual needs of buyer members. User-supplied information on media rates and confidential proprietary data on product distribution, sales, leased product data, and coupon redemption projections were incorporated into the requests of individual buyers. County-by-county data for all daily and weekly newspapers were added to the Data Bank service in 1970, U.S. 1970 Census tapes in 1971 and Market Statistics "Survey of Buying Power" data in 1972, and, more recently, increasing amounts of ABC historical information on magazines and farm publications.

Increased base and flexibility of Data Bank service help save time and cost for media buyers.

In 1984, ABC Data Bank information was made available on-line through outside services. Recognizing the tremendous growth of the use of personal computers by media planners, Data Bank information was made available on computer diskettes early in 1984.

During 1988, ABC's Data Bank services staff responded to 1,195 requests for specialized and stock reports and diskettes from both media buyer and publisher members. The service includes ABC circulation data by counties (or equivalent), Areas of Dominant Influence, Dominant Marketing Areas, and Metropolitan Statistical Areas for 201 U.S. periodicals and 1,645 U.S. and Canadian daily and weekly newspapers. It also has available a five-year history of all Publisher's Statement data for the periodical participants.

FAS-FAX Reports

The industry's need for quick updates of publisher members' circulation data and the impractical, high cost of adding staff and production capacity to meet the surge of Publisher's Statements following each of the four reporting periods each year (March 31 and September 30 for newspapers, and June 30 and December 31 for periodicals) produced criticism during much of the Audit Bureau's history.

Publisher's Statements are reviewed, typeset, printed, and distributed following the close of each reporting period in the order of their receipt at ABC headquarters. Those received nearest to the deadline for filing may be released as much as three months following the end of the report period.

In response to an increasing number of complaints, management proposed in 1962 the creation of a new report that would publish a digest of the key data from the publishers' claims for release quickly after the filing deadlines. The board vetoed the suggestion because the data input for the volume would be drawn from statements that had not yet been reviewed by the house auditing staff.

The proposal was reintroduced in 1968 as part of an effort to find new service uses for the ABC computer. After a review of publishers input versus the released Publisher's Statement figures revealed relatively infrequent and, for the most part, insignificant differences, the board agreed to authorize the new service. The first volumes of the FAS-FAX Reports covering frequency, updated household and latest circulation figures for each market area, and total circulation for this period and the comparable period of the previous year for each U.S. and Canadian daily newspaper member were released November 14, 1969, exactly two weeks following the deadline for filing semi-annual Publisher's Statements.

PRELIMINARY FIGURES AS FILED WITH AUDIT BUREAU OF CIRCULATIONS SUBJECT TO AUDIT

Newspaper / Area	Edition	CZ OR NDM OH'S	CIRC	RATIO CIRC/OH'S %	RTZ OR NDM OH'S	CIRC	RATIO CIRC/OH'S %	TOTAL NDM OR CZ & RTZ OH'S	CIRC	TOTAL CIRCULATION AS OF 9/30/88	TOTAL CIRCULATION AS OF 9/30/87
NEW JERSEY											
HIGHTSTOWN (MERCER CO.)											
RACING FORM	MON									49,965	48,980
RACING FORM	M (TU-F)									43,713	45,867
RACING FORM	SAT									73,497	77,264
RACING FORM	SUN									35,059	35,639
JERSEY CITY (HUDSON CO.)											
JOURNAL	E (M-F)	195,200	54,740	28.04	167,900	2,184	1.30	363,100	56,924	57,275	56,719
JOURNAL	SAT E		53,472	27.39		2,202	1.31		55,674	56,012	54,451
MILLVILLE (CUMBERLAND CO.)											
DAILY (4-1-88 to 5-22-88)	E	9,900	5,216	52.69	5,000	999	19.98	14,900	6,215	6,437	6,294
MORRISTOWN-PARSIPPANY (MORRIS CO.)											
RECORD	M (M-F)	131,200#	50,311	38.35	131,200			131,200	50,311	56,878	58,117
RECORD	SAT	#	47,122	35.92					47,122	53,536	54,975
RECORD	SUN	#	57,365	43.72					57,365	66,592	69,040
NEW BRUNSWICK (MIDDLESEX CO.)											
CENTRAL HOME NEWS	E	72,900	30,929	42.43	82,300	18,435	22.40	155,200	49,364	57,076	60,033
CENTRAL HOME NEWS	SUN		34,264	47.00		22,047	26.79		56,311	67,505	74,010
NEWARK (ESSEX CO.)											
STAR-LEDGER	M (M-F)	367,300	160,723	43.76	1,607,500	290,970	18.10	1,974,800	451,693	462,084	467,549
STAR-LEDGER	SAT M		141,703	38.58		267,283	16.63		408,986	419,392	427,237
STAR-LEDGER	SUN		195,917	53.34		443,449	27.59		639,366	665,085	673,799
NEWTON (SUSSEX CO.)											
HERALD	E (M-F)	48,600#	17,116	35.22				48,600	17,116	18,022	18,516
HERALD	SUN	#	23,380	48.11					23,380	25,418	25,961
PASSAIC CO.-UNION CO.-HUDSON CO.-MORRIS CO.-BERGEN CO.											
NORTH JERSEY NWSPS.	CMB DLY	911,300			911,300			911,300		139,743	153,266
NORTH JERSEY NWSPS.	M		78,271	8.59					78,271	109,546	76,716
NORTH JERSEY NWSPS.	E									30,197	76,550
NORTH JERSEY NWSPS.	SUN		54,001	5.93					54,001	54,880	64,703
TRENTON (MERCER CO.)											
TIMES	M	97,200	41,287	42.48	162,600	27,498	16.91	259,800	68,785	75,682	69,504
TIMES	SUN		48,964	50.37		33,062	20.33		82,026	89,042	86,776
TRENTONIAN	M (M-F)		47,434	48.80		16,441	10.11		63,875	68,405	69,405
TRENTONIAN	SAT		44,255	45.53		16,472	10.13		60,727	65,569	66,689
TRENTONIAN	SUN		44,023	45.29		14,774	9.09		58,797	63,753	65,319

(a) CITY OF PUBLICATION
\# NEWSPAPER DESIGNATED MARKET
∴ CHANGE IN PUBLISHING PLAN

*AVERAGES FOR 3 MONTHS

55

FAS-FAX reports
substantially
reduced the time
between filing of
these data and the
availability of
current figures.

The FAS-FAX Reports for daily newspapers met with such enthusiastic response that the board immediately authorized similar types of reports for magazines, farm publications, and business publications covering the December 31, 1969, Publisher's Statement period. A volume for ABC weekly newspaper members was added to cover the period ending March 31 that year.

In subsequent years, the deadline for filing semi-annual newspaper Publisher's Statement data was reduced from 30 days following the close of the period to 15 days. This made possible the production and distribution of FAS-FAX Reports two weeks earlier, and getting information to media planners that much earlier.

An immediate success, FAS-FAX Report service had the effect of alleviating the criticisms of the necessary lag time in processing and printing ABC Publisher's Statements.

Canadian Newspaper FACTBOOK

While several independent services extracted ABC newspaper data in single-volume circulation, household, and market data analyses by counties and major market areas in the United States, a similar review of Canadian newspapers did not exist. At the request of Canadian media buyers, the Audit Bureau's directors and staff began a review of such a service early in 1971.

With the help of input from 28 advertising agencies and the assistance of the Montreal chapter of the Media Directors' Council, ABC introduced the Canadian Newspaper FACTBOOK the following August as an annual service. Initially covering only daily newspaper members, the volume contained a breakdown of each newspaper's circulation averages and latest household estimates by market areas and by counties; by Metropolitan and Major Urban areas by number of households, circulation, and coverage of newspapers serving the market; and rankings by newspaper circulation size and by household numbers.

Canadian weekly newspaper member data were added to the FACTBOOK in the 1972 edition. A review of the service by media buyers in 1988 to ensure it met the needs of advertisers and advertising agencies resulted in several format and content changes.

Coupon Distribution Verification

Advertiser use of merchandising coupons increased dramatically during the 1970s, to a point that by 1979 the industry estimated nearly 73 billion coupons were being carried annually in newspapers alone—run of press, free-standing inserts, and as supplements. The down side of coupon-bearing advertising was the multi-faceted problem of misredemption, which was estimated then to cost advertisers as much as $150 million a year without benefit of compensating product sales.

Since publications were the primary coupon distribution vehicles, advertiser members urged ABC to consider possible standards aimed at restricting the potential for misredemption and an auditing service verification of distribution and disposition of left-over and unsold copies of publications containing coupons.

Newspapers carried an estimated 77 percent of all merchandising coupons, so they were the focus of the board's consideration. Concern centered on areas where the potential for sizeable misredemption existed—loss of bulk quantities of free-standing inserts prior to publication, increased distribution on heavy coupon days, etc.

Coupon Distribution Verification service helped concentrate concern on protecting advertisers' merchandising efforts.

Cooperating with the Audit Bureau were the Grocery Manufacturers Association and the American Society of Industrial Security. After considerable review, a plan and standards were approved early in 1980 calling for start-up costs to be charged 70 percent against participating advertisers, 10 percent against participating advertising agencies, and 20 percent against participating newspaper publishers.

In the voluntary program, participating publishers were questioned through a publisher's statement on practices and procedures used by their newspapers on handling the storage and disposition of copies of free-standing inserts, advertising supplements, and newspaper copies containing run of press coupons that were not distributed or sold. Verifications of these statements were conducted at the time of the annual ABC circulation audit. During the first month, 5 advertisers, 6 advertising agencies, and 73 newspapers (including 5 in Canada) signed up for the program.

ABC's first Coupon Distribution Verification Reports, covering eight daily and four Sunday newspapers, were completed and distributed in January 1981. After its first six months of operation, George Simko, Benton & Bowles and chairman of the board's forward planning committee, reported the program "has caused many publishers to institute stringent practices to protect stored coupon sections and free-standing inserts from pilferage. And it has resulted in many publishers taking another look at the validity of increased draws on heavy coupon days. More publishers are conscientiously upgrading their practices in the handling of returns and other unsold copies."

By the end of the first 18 months the service was in operation, 122 reports verification reports had been issued covering the coupon handling practices of more than 150 newspapers in the United States and Canada. A coupon users forum was organized in 1983 to provide an ongoing opportunity for service participants to discuss report use and advise on data needs and potential report changes. A Canadian coupon users group was organized in 1986.

Today's ABC Coupon Distribution Verification Service participation includes 160 newspapers (131 U.S. and 29 Canadian) on whom annual verifications are made, 37 advertisers, 19 advertising agencies, 5 coupon suppliers, and 4 coupon redemption centers. Along with the growth of participation in this program, its success can be measured by a dramatically increased awareness of coupon misredemption problems and the tightening of coupon handling practices throughout the industry.

Magazine Trend Report

For many years, the Audit Bureau supplied circulation data and tabulations for the periodic magazine and business publication Circulation and Rate Trend Reports published by the Association of National Advertisers. When the ANA decided to eliminate the service in 1979, the Audit Bureau, at the request of advertiser and magazine members, revised and added the magazine volume to its regular report service offerings.

Initially covering ABC magazines with at least 300,000 circulation and an annual advertising revenue of at least $2 million, the first issue of the ABC Magazine Trend Report was distributed in the spring of 1980. It included five-year tabulations on 80 magazines grouped by general interest categories and by average paid circulation, percent of subscription and single copy sales, subscription sales, basic prices, and cost per thousand circulation rates. It also contained norms for each market grouping to which individual magazine's histories could be compared.

Advertising rate base data, for those magazines reporting a rate base or circulation guarantee, were added in the second edition that fall. In 1983, the advertising prerequisite was halved, and 46 Canadian ABC magazine members were added to the 98 U.S. magazines included in the trend report.

A popular service today, the Magazine Trend Report provides basic reference information for media planners needing a quick reference guide to tracking circulation and rate changes.

Magazine Market Coverage Reports

"ABC should turn its attention to the time-consuming problems of numbers-crunching at agencies," Bernard Guggenheim, Campbell Ewald, suggested in 1982. "An aid to early media planning, and to answer frequent day to day questions, would be a quick-reference volume of U.S. magazine circulations by major marketing area definitions."

A review of his suggestion among other media buyers indicated widespread interest and resulted in the 1983 introduction of the series of three ABC Magazine Market Coverage Reports. Each report, broken down by Areas of Dominant Influence, Designated Market Areas, and Standard Metropolitan Statistical Areas, contained a list of the 150 magazines and farm publications participating in the ABC Data Bank with total typical-issue circulation, an alphabetical list of markets, and a ranked list of markets by ABC-estimated households.

In 1984, ABC expanded the series, with three volumes relating individual publications to the three market areas and three volumes listing data on publications serving the individual market areas.

Broadcast

As leader in the field of media circulation verification, the Audit Bureau many times has been asked to consider expanding its services beyond the scope of its original print orientation. Over the years, the board, staff, and special task forces have studied a variety of these, seriously or otherwise, ranging from blotter, calendar, and telephone book distribution to radio and television audiences.

Broadcast audience measurements were probably considered more often than most. The introduction and growth of radio in the 1920s was dramatic, but the medium did not become a serious competitor for advertising revenues until the formation of broadcasting systems. Based on the impressive claims of radio reach and the excitement of the new medium, advertisers were eager to get on board. Measurement indices as to what their money was actually buying came as an afterthought. When it was proposed that the Audit Bureau consider establishing some uniform standards during the depression era of the early 1930s, the organization was deeply involved in problems of its own members, especially the newspapers.

The question of possible services in the area of television audience measurements arose during U.S. Congressional investigations in the late 1950s. Frequent criticisms of the television industry for not having "ABC accuracy" brought about board and staff studies with advertisers and broadcast networks, only to reveal that no new measurement services were desired.

When the board's computer task force began its preliminary studies to learn how electronic data processing would impact on ABC's future, one of its suggestions was the possible verification of broadcast advertising reports. From 1963 until it was removed from the board's agenda in 1968, a ranging review of possibilities of broadcast services was conducted, but none was considered feasible for ABC.

The question of possible ABC involvement in community antenna television service measurements was raised briefly by the board's projects evaluation committee in 1967. The possible auditing of television commercial performance was proposed in 1974 during a meeting of representatives of the American Association of Advertising Agencies, the Association of National Advertisers, and ABC directors but was dismissed based on earlier studies.

Ostrow: Can cable television meet the same standards as print media?

The increasing importance of cable television to advertisers brought it back to the board's agenda in 1975, and efforts to probe its value were made during meetings with AAAA and ANA representatives in 1976 and 1978. The discussions indicated support for ABC to offer a service to verify the subscriber data of cable television networks.

It wasn't until 1981 that an advertiser and advertising agency asked for the actual exploration of the potential cable service. Under the guidance of a cable television study task force headed by ABC Director Joseph W. Ostrow, Young & Rubicam Inc., standards were developed and a test verification was conducted with the cooperation of the Cable News Network of the Turner Broadcast System. The test verification of subscribers in a sample of the local cable systems carrying CNN was proved feasible, and, in 1983, ABC announced the availability of this as an experimental service.

While ABC proved it could verify cable subscriber records just as it could audit the circulation records of print media, media buyers were more concerned with audience figures. Since audience figures were larger and more impressive than subscriber figures, cable systems showed little interest in the ABC service. The final blow to the Audit Bureau's efforts came when outside services began to develop and publish projected audience data for the cable systems.

Audit Bureau of Marketing Services

ABC's most aggressive effort to expand its services to the advertising industry began in 1965, nearly a year after members overwhelmingly approved a charter change to permit such action. James B. Kobak, from the consulting firm of J.K. Lasser and Co., provided guidance for board planning by recommending that ABC "adopt a progressive service-oriented philosophy," suggesting that the Audit Bureau could "audit market research studies (without doing the actual research), radio and television data, direct mail lists, trade shows, outdoor audience exposure, free distribution of print media, and many other fields."

The Lasser report further stated "ABC is the logical vehicle for setting standards and performing audits in other fields because of its spotless reputation for integrity, its size, its very competent staff, and its many years of experience. It is well organized to take over additional duties. The marketing community would be ill-advised if it did not take advantage of the ABC."

During the year following the 1964 charter changes, ABC tested the feasibility of broadening its services into other areas of marketing measurement. In cooperation with the Association of National Advertisers, it determined the viability of verifying the registered attendance at trade shows. In cooperation with the Advertising Research Foundation and the Industrial Advertising Research Institute, ABC determined the practicality of verifying audience measurement procedures.

A pioneering audit of the registered attendance at a trade show was conducted by the ABC staff in February 1965. Format for the audit report of the attendance was developed by the trade show committee of the ANA. Two additional trade show attendance audits were conducted later that year.

In September 1965, ABC Chairman Kenneth Laird, Tatham-Laird & Kudner, Inc., reported that the board had taken "the first positive

Most aggressive effort to expand industry services.

steps in the direction of having the Audit Bureau make its services available for auditing various types of auditable market and circulation data," actions which enable ABC to implement the intent of the membership in approving the 1964 charter changes.

First action was to establish a projects evaluation committee and an organizational structure, through which the directors could examine the organization's "broadest possible service capability."

At the recommendation of the committee the following January, the board approved the creation of an affiliated corporation to conduct experimental audits for the ABC and provide auditing services in fields not traditionally within the Audit Bureau's historic purview. Through the creation of the ABC board-controlled new corporation, the Audit Bureau of Marketing Services, the board felt that auditing services could be expanded without disturbing ABC's operations and its basic concept of facts without opinion.

While ABMS was being organized, the Audit Bureau's board authorized trial audit of direct mail lists, under the guidance of the projects evaluation committee and with the cooperation of the Direct Mail Advertising Association. Again at the recommendation of the committee, the board authorized management to proceed with experimental plans to verify "other data" of business publications as a possible new service. It was pointed out that "other data" could include such information as number of subscribers or recipients added and dropped; retention percentages; cost per thousand index; total number of pages published by editorial, paid display advertising, and paid classified; number of advertisers; reader service cards; requests for reprints; and page sizes. Early on the ABMS agenda was the exploration with the Outdoor Advertising Association of Canada of the possibile verification of outdoor advertising data, another service that was later instituted.

During this same period, a number of studies were underway that led to changes in existing report services. The county-by-county break-downs of magazine and farm publication circulation were being discussed. Similarly, market area concepts for newspapers were under-going changes. The whole issue of the incorporation of demographic data in ABC reports was being debated. And the Audit Bureau released its first unit count audit report for business publications.

With so many new service discussions going on, it was natural for some publishers, particularly newspaper members, to suspect that ABMS was designed to be "the surrogate for ABC's auditing of free distribution magazines and newspapers." The board of the new affiliate tried to still this criticism by a statement that ABMS would not entertain any consideration of the audit of free publications. The ABC board made no such statement, however, and was deeply into the discussion of the audit of free distribution publications, a discussion that was finally terminated in the spring of 1967.

Newspapers continued to question the whole concept of ABMS and the Audit Bureau's expansion into service areas for media other than paid print publications. At their 1966 divisional meeting, newspaper members created their own "Review Committee" to "study all the new activities undertaken or proposed to be undertaken by the ABC or ABMS" and report its recommendations to the membership. In effect, the review committee duplicated an existing divisional committee that reported on behalf of the members to the newspaper directors.

Prior to the 1967 annual meeting, the review committee publicized its intention of killing off ABMS and any ABC consideration of services to other than paid print media.

Newspapers invited members from other divisions to join its debate on the issue. Vote on a resolution to ask the board to dissolve ABMS by newspaper members passed 896 to 267. In contradictory resolutions, members of the advertiser and advertising agency division unanimously urged the continued growth of ABMS.

The beginning of the end for ABMS came with the approval of an emphasis on paid print media explorations and a two-year evaluation of existing ABMS services, "and for phasing out any activity if it is not found to meet demonstrated needs of a substantial segment of the ABC membership." Both the ABMS and ABC boards agreed that "despite support from major advertiser and advertising agency organizations, and from buyer membership divisions within ABC, general industry support by either buyers or media for ABMS-offered services has been disappointingly scant."

Less than a year following the review committee's resolution, the board of the ABMS adopted action to phase out the Audit Bureau's affiliate "within the next 24 months." It was officially disbanded in June 1970. During its life, the Audit Bureau of Marketing Services pioneered standards for and conducted 18 trade show registered attendance audits, 7 direct mail list audits, 112 outdoor traffic count audits.

ABC Considers Its Purpose

Defining association's objectives • Charter change opens new service opportunities • Statement reaffirms Audit Bureau's mission • Looking to the future.

Those attending the organization meeting of the Audit Bureau of Circulations spent more than three hours the morning of May 20, 1914, in attempting to define the mission of their association. They finally agreed that the objects should be:

"To make examinations by qualified auditors or independent auditing concerns of all bills and other records considered by the board of control necessary to ascertain all facts with regard to circulation of any and all newspapers, magazines, agricultural, trade, technical, and class, or other publications which are members of this association, and for the determination of data for the benefit of advertisers, agents, and publishers. Each report issued to members shall embrace facts bearing on the quantity, quality, and distribution of circulation, thereby enabling quality as well as quantity to be established. Facts without opinions are to be reported."

In developing the Audit Bureau's first publication of the bylaws, rules, and regulations in 1919, the board proposed a clarification of the language of the original constitution. With the members' approval that year, the objects were revised to: "The objects of the Audit Bureau of Circulations shall be to issue standardized statements of the circulation of publisher members; to verify the figures shown in these statements by auditors' examinations of any and all records considered by the Bureau to be necessary; and to disseminate data for the benefit of advertisers, advertising agents, and publishers." The reference to the contents of reports was shifted from the bylaws to the rules and regulations.

Caught up in the fervor to eliminate free distribution publications from ABC membership, the newspaper division unanimously resolved that the objects be changed to include only paid circulation. The proposal was defeated at the general meeting the following day, when it was pointed out that its acceptance would eliminate any reference to the unpaid portion of the member publishers' own distribution and would have the effect of setting any membership eligibility provision at 100 percent paid.

The advertisers' effort to have advertising rates included in ABC reports in 1924, successfully fought by newspaper members, brought another brief change in the Audit Bureau's objects two years later. Suspicious of the buyers' control of bylaw and rule changes, and the possibility that advertising rates and other data might be mandated without publisher approval, newspapers resolved to add the word "only" following "circulation" in the objects.

The change was overwhelmingly approved at the general session. In the process of implementing this change, it became evident that the objects were too restrictive, eliminating such mutually desired information as census data and market definitions from ABC reports.

A re-codification of the bylaws and rules in 1949 returned the contents section of the original objects to the opening bylaw. The action added a second paragraph to the objects: "Each Publisher's Statement and each Audit Report issued to members shall embrace figures and facts bearing on the quantity, quality, distribution of circulation, and circulation methods; thereby enabling quality as well as quantity to be established. The figures in the Audit Report shall be those verified by Bureau auditors. Facts without opinion, to be reported."

Charter Change

The early 1960s was a period of great exploration for the advertising industry. The promise of the 1960 U.S. census data and the excitement of new electronic data processing equipment possibilities caused buyers and publishers to seek new and improved data opportunities. ABC's response was to generate new service discussions through board and member task forces and advisory committees.

In 1963, ABC Chairman Robert W. Boggs, Union Carbide Corp., challenged the members. "Over the years there have been repeated calls for the creation of authenticated complete audience measurement and,

more recently, for the measurement or
validation of data regarding billboards
and trade shows. Also, there have been
frequent comments on the procedures
used in print media as compared to
broadcast media.

"I wish that I could report to you at
this time that ABC is ready to perform
all of these services, but I cannot.
Certainly the industry recognizes the
Audit Bureau as the logical leader in
this field. I believe that the time has
come when the decision must be made
as to whether these should be areas of
ABC service, a decision really, as to the
future course of ABC. It seems appropriate that our 50th year should be the year
of decision."

That it was. At the 1964 annual
meeting, members voted 1,662 to 43 to
approve a charter amendment to permit
the organization to explore ways of

*Boggs: ABC's "50th year
should be a year of decision."*

broadening its services to the advertising industry. The charter changes
eliminated the earlier "circulation data only" restriction and, in its place,
added "circulation data or other data" reported by a member.

Chairman Kenneth Laird, Tatham-Laird, Inc., assured members
that there would be no rush to expand ABC services, but warned that
many in the industry felt the Audit Bureau "has erred in the past on the
side of standpatism. I believe we can expect from the board a thoughtful
evaluation of ways in which it can better meet its responsibilities in an
era of change." Broadcast, readership and audience exposure, trade
show attendance, and outdoor advertising data were areas advertisers
were seeking better, verified data, he suggested.

Special study committees probed for new service concepts, both
outside ABC's traditional print media orientation and for existing
members. In 1965, the Audit Bureau completed its first trade show
audit (International Automotive Service Industries); verified certain
magazine comparative readership research (Alfred Politz Research on
five members); introduced the "unit count" audit for business publication

Laird: Many feel ABC "has erred on the side of standpatism."

members (*National Bottlers' Gazette*); hired the J.K. Lasser firm to do an in-depth study of ABC services and potential; began a review of demographics and new market analyses for newspapers and the verification of free distribution business publications; and established a new Projects Evaluation committee to study the expansion of ABC service.

The following year, the board established a new affiliate, the ill-fated Audit Bureau of Marketing Services, feeling additional verification service exploration could be expanded through this new corporation "without a departure from the Audit Bureau's basic concept of facts without opinion."

ABC introduced supplementary data reports for "other data" on business publications, and county by county analysis of circulation for magazines and business publications. In 1966, directly and through ABMS, the Audit Bureau expanded into services to direct mail list (MacArthur Enterprises, Inc.), outdoor (Outdoor Advertising Association of Canada), subscriber identification (*Fortune Magazine*), and annually updated population and occupied housing estimates.

With the dissolution of the ABMS experiment, the board agreed to "aggressively investigate important new projects in order to expand the Audit Bureau's services to areas of advertising and marketing information which, though auditable, are not currently served by ABC." It created a new Marketing Services committee, saying its thrust would be given to efforts for greater service to the industry.

While advances were made in member services in the following years, the introduction of FAS-FAX reports, the Canadian Newspaper FACTBOOK, the Magazine Trend reports, the Coupon Distribution Verification service, and the Magazine Market Coverage reports, to name a few, the mission of the Audit Bureau was once again clearly print media oriented. Despite efforts to expand the scope of ABC's functions through industry task forces, a revised marketing service committee, and the creation of a new forward planning committee, and despite extensive exploration of newspaper audience and cable television subscriber data verification, the Audit Bureau's purpose is almost completely that of reporting and verifying print media circulation.

Mission Statement

In 1988, on the eve of the Audit Bureau's 75th anniversary, the board adopted a statement, attempting to define the organization's mission to serve as a benchmark for future planning.

The statement says:

Our Mission:

ABC is dedicated to being the preeminent self-regulatory auditing organization, responsible to advertisers, advertising agencies, and the media they use, for the verification and dissemination of our members' circulation data and other information for the benefit of the advertising marketplace in the United States and Canada.

Our Core Beliefs:

To accomplish this mission, we renew our commitment to ABC's charter statement, "facts without opinion," and to the following Core Beliefs that have built our reputation since 1914 for maintaining the highest standards of professionalism and integrity.

WE BELIEVE it is the people of ABC—our Members, our Board of Directors, and our Staff—who will preserve our credibility, established and maintained through our commitment to the highest levels of integrity and objectivity.

WE BELIEVE we must actively identify the needs of our industry, and develop qualification requirements, verification standards, and reporting services that respond to those needs.

WE BELIEVE we must provide a forum that allows for a balance of interest between the buyers and sellers of advertising within a not-for-profit organization.

WE BELIEVE we must continue our commitment to the development of technological resources that enhance the accuracy, breadth, and timeliness of our verification and reporting services in a manner which is cost effective for our members.

These Core Beliefs will not be compromised.

The Future

The mission statement defines the Audit Bureau's fundamental function, saying in effect that the organization has been in the business of auditing and reporting circulation facts and other data of its publisher members for 75 years, that ABC is the best at it, and that the services ABC provides are valuable to the industry.

The 1964 ABC charter change was adopted largely on the premise that the organization needed to expand and extend its services within itself but, more importantly, to enlarge and encompass other media and media measurements.

Perhaps taking its cue from changes in overall business philosophy during recent years, the 1988 mission statement projects for the future the belief that what ABC has been it should continue to be—that it should not stray far from its fundamental function. While the statement does not preclude service extensions to other media and media measurements, it defines the scope of such considerations to the verification, auditing, and reporting functions.

One of the great strengths of the Audit Bureau over the years has been its conservative approach to change, the detailed exploration of all nuances before taking action. This suggests that it will probably not be doing anything in the foreseeable future that it does not do now, just more of it and in improved ways. The rapid pace of change in the advertising and publishing marketplace, however, places on ABC's future the need to recognize these changes earlier, and to be prepared to adjust its rules and requirements to them.

Already in place are member advisory and liaison committees, which serve to extend the eyes and ears of the board and staff. Since the importance of ABC membership to publishers rests squarely upon the value advertisers and advertising agencies place on the data this affiliation makes possible, the dramatically increased involvement of buyers in recent years is significant. Maintenance and extension of this member involvement will be important to the organization as it seeks to understand and react to changes.

The advertising and publishing industry has witnessed massive technological changes during the last decade. The numbers crunching that used to take media planners days has been reduced to minutes. Personal computers have replaced calculators and typewriters, enabling planners to consider more detailed information in their evaluations.

The impact of new technology on ABC's future will enormously test the organization's ability to respond to an accelerating pace of change. Management and staff have already completed, or are planning and developing, new computer readable data formats, direct on-line user access to ABC data, direct publisher access for computer input of circulation data, computer use in speeding auditing, technical review, report production, and data dissemination functions, and increasing amounts of historical data for comparative analyses. In addition to the challenge of providing accurate data faster and with increased access, ABC will be faced with the buyer need to analyze circulation data within smaller marketing increments.

Attitudes change with new economic conditions and marketing practices. These will cause ABC to re-think historic positions and adapt rules and procedures to new situations. Bulk circulation, shunted to the inside of newspaper reports, has been redefined and returned to front page prominence in recently adopted formats. The

Future offers new challenges, test of ability to respond.

growing use of nonpaid circulation by newspapers, magazines, and farm publications has already brought pressure on the Audit Bureau to reconsider its paid eligibility requirements. The introduction and acceptance of new advertising vehicles, new media forms and practices whose distribution methods are susceptible to audit, and the accompanying demands of buyers for authoritative data will offer new opportunities and test ABC's print orientation.

On its 75th anniversary, the Audit Bureau of Circulations stands on the experience of past accomplishments but, more importantly, is already committed to the future. Membership involvement is at a high level. The board is providing effective leadership, dedicated to protecting historic ABC values while proactively challenging old issues and exploring new opportunities. The ABC is financially strong. The staff is organized, trained, and equipped to the standards of professionalism required to respond to the demands of rapidly changing conditions.

The people of the Audit Bureau—its members, its directors, and its staff—look to the future from a position of strength, new vitality, and determination, rooted in the simple promise begun in 1914—objectivity and integrity; facts without opinion.

Officers and Directors 1914–1989

Chairmen of the Board

Louis Bruch
American Radiator Co.
Chicago, Illinois
May 20, 1914–June 6, 1918

Edward S. Babcox
Firestone Tire & Rubber Co.
Akron, Ohio
June 7, 1918–Jan. 10, 1919

Lewis B. Jones
Eastman Kodak Co.
Rochester, New York
Feb. 7, 1919–Oct. 15, 1920

Orlando C. Harn
National Lead Co.
New York, New York
Oct. 15, 1920–Feb. 4, 1927

Philip L. Thomson
Western Electric Co.
New York, New York
Feb. 4, 1927–Oct. 27, 1950

Harold H. Kynett
Aitkin-Kynett Co., Inc.
Philadelphia, Pennsylvania
Oct. 27, 1950–Oct. 24, 1952

William A. Hart
E.I. du Pont de Nemours & Co.
Wilmington, Delaware
Oct. 24, 1952–Oct. 22, 1954

John H. Platt
Kraft Foods Co.
Chicago, Illinois
Oct. 22, 1954–Oct. 21, 1955

George C. Dibert
J. Walter Thompson Co.
Chicago, Illinois
Oct. 21, 1955–Oct. 18, 1957

Walter P. Lantz
Bristol-Myers Co.
New York, New York
Oct. 18, 1957–Oct. 23, 1959

William R. Farrell
Monsanto Co.
St. Louis, Missouri
Oct. 23, 1959–Oct. 20, 1961

Robert W. Boggs
Union Carbide Corp.
New York, New York
Oct. 20, 1961–Oct. 22, 1963

Kenneth Laird
Tatham-Laird & Kudner, Inc.
Chicago, Illinois
Oct. 22, 1963–Oct. 20, 1965

William H. Ewen
The Borden Co.
New York, New York
Oct. 20, 1965–Oct. 20, 1967

Warren Reynolds
Ronalds-Reynolds Co.
Toronto, Ontario
Oct. 20, 1967–Oct. 21, 1969

F.W. Heckel
United Air Lines
Chicago, Illinois
Oct. 23, 1969–Oct. 21, 1971

Paul H. Willis
Carnation Co.
Los Angeles, California
Oct. 21, 1971–Oct. 18, 1973

Herbert A. Lehrter
Hiram Walker Inc.
Detroit, Michigan
Oct. 18, 1973–Oct. 23, 1975

Clinton Thompson
J.C. Penney Co., Inc.
New York, New York
Oct. 23, 1975–Nov. 10, 1977

James J. Tommaney
Case & McGrath, Inc.,
New York, New York
Nov. 10, 1977–Nov. 9, 1978

William M. Claggett
Ralston Purina Co.
St. Louis, Missouri
Nov. 9, 1978–Nov. 5, 1981

Charles A. Tucker
R.J. Reynolds Tobacco Co.
Winston-Salem,
   North Carolina
Nov. 5, 1981–Nov. 10, 1983

Donald G. Goldstrom
Armstrong World
   Industries, Inc.
Lancaster, Pennsylvania
Nov. 10, 1983–Nov. 1, 1985

David K. Braun
General Foods Corp.
White Plains, New York
Nov. 1, 1985–Nov. 13, 1987

Robert J. Galloway
Campbell Soup Co., Ltd.
Toronto, Ontario
Nov. 13, 1987–

Vice-Chairmen

Curtis P. Brady
Woman's World
Chicago, Illinois
May 20, 1914–Oct. 30, 1917

Alfred W. Erickson
The Erickson Co.
New York, New York
May 20, 1914–Oct. 28, 1921

W. Laughlin
Armour & Co.
Chicago, Illinois
June 7, 1918–Mar. 6, 1925

Henry W. Schott
Montgomery Ward & Co.
Chicago, Illinois
June 7, 1918–Oct. 20, 1922

Ernest I. Mitchell
Mitchell-Faust Advertising Co.
Chicago, Illinois
Oct. 28, 1921–Oct. 21, 1927

Fred R. Davis
General Electric Co.
Schenectady, New York
Oct. 20, 1922–Dec. 26, 1940

John Murray Gibbon
Canadian Pacific Railway Co.
Montreal, Quebec
Oct. 16, 1925–Oct. 21, 1927

Stanley R. Latshaw
Butterick Publishing Co.
New York, New York
Oct. 21, 1927–Oct. 16, 1936

David B. Plum
Record
Troy, New York
Oct. 21, 1927–Oct. 21, 1932

Ralph Starr Butler
General Foods Corp.
New York, New York
Oct. 21, 1932–Oct. 16, 1947

Fred Bohen
Successful Farming
Des Moines, Iowa
Oct. 16, 1936–Oct. 21, 1949

Harold H. Kynett
Aitkin-Kynett Co., Inc.
Philadelphia, Pennsylvania
Feb. 22, 1941–Oct. 27, 1950

E. Roy Hatton
Detroit Free Press
Detroit, Michigan
Oct. 16, 1947–May 30, 1960

Robert M. Gray
Esso Standard Oil Co.
New York, New York
Oct. 21, 1949–Oct. 26, 1951

William A. Hart
E.I. du Pont de Nemours & Co.
Wilmington, Delaware
Oct. 27, 1950–Oct. 24, 1952

Harland H. Rimmer
Canadian General
   Electric Co., Ltd.
Toronto, Ontario
Oct. 26, 1951–Oct. 20, 1961

John H. Platt
Kraft Foods Co.
Chicago, Illinois
Oct. 24, 1952–Oct. 22, 1954

George C. Dibert
J. Walter Thompson Co.
Chicago, Illinois
Oct. 22, 1954–Oct. 21, 1955

Walter P. Lantz
Bristol-Myers Co.
New York, New York
Oct. 21, 1955–Oct. 18, 1957

Carleton Healy
Hiram Walker & Son Inc.
Detroit, Michigan
Oct. 18, 1957–Oct. 23, 1959

John H. Platt
Kraft Foods Co.
Chicago, Illinois
Oct. 21, 1960–June 13, 1962

Donald F. Hunter
Maclean-Hunter
   Publishing Co., Ltd.
Toronto, Ontario
Oct. 20, 1961–Oct. 21, 1964

Kenneth Laird
Tatham-Laird & Kudner, Inc.
Chicago, Illinois
Oct. 20, 1961–Oct. 22, 1963

Lester A. Walker
Fremont Tribune
Fremont, Nebraska
Oct. 24, 1962–Feb. 15, 1966
Kearney Daily Hub
Kearney, Nebraska
Mar. 1, 1966–Oct. 19, 1967

William H. Ewen
The Borden Co.
New York, New York
Oct. 22, 1963–Oct. 20, 1965

Warren Reynolds
Ronalds-Reynolds Co.
Toronto, Ontario
Oct. 21, 1964–Oct. 20, 1967

Harry F. Schroeter
National Biscuit Co.
New York, New York
Oct. 20, 1965–Oct. 21, 1969

Richard J. Babcock
Farm Journal
Philadelphia, Pennsylvania
Oct. 20, 1967–Oct. 21, 1971

William M. Weilbacher
Jack Tinker & Partners, Inc.
New York, New York
Oct. 20, 1967–Jan, 14, 1971

Paul H. Willis
Carnation Co.
Los Angeles, California
Oct. 23, 1969–Oct. 21, 1971

Herbert A. Lehrter
Hiram Walker Inc.
Detroit, Michigan
Oct. 21, 1971–Oct. 18, 1973

John R. Miller
Hearst Magazines
New York, New York
Oct. 21, 1971–Nov. 7, 1974

James J. Tommaney
LaRoche, McCaffrey and
McCall, Inc.
New York, New York
Oct. 21, 1971–Nov. 10, 1977

Clinton Thompson
J.C. Penney Co., Inc.
New York, New York
Oct. 18, 1973–Oct. 23, 1975

R.I. McCracken
The Times Herald
Norristown, Pennsylvania
Nov. 7, 1974–Nov. 9, 1978

William M. Claggett
Ralston Purina Co.
St. Louis, Missouri
Oct. 23, 1975–Nov. 9, 1978

Jules P. Fine
Ogilvy & Mather, Inc.
New York, New York
Nov. 10, 1977–Nov. 9, 1978

George J. Simko
Benton & Bowles, Inc.
New York, New York
Nov. 9, 1978–Nov. 11, 1982

Peter W. Hunter
McConnell Advertising Ltd.
Toronto, Ontario
Nov. 6, 1980–Sept. 7, 1982
Cockfield Brown, Inc.
Toronto, Ontario
Sept. 8, 1982–June 22, 1983

Charles A. Tucker
R.J. Reynolds Tobacco Co.
Winston-Salem,
    North Carolina
Nov. 6, 1980–Nov. 5, 1981

Lloyd M. Hodgkinson
Maclean-Hunter Ltd.
Toronto, Ontario
Nov. 8, 1979–Oct. 31, 1984

Donald G. Goldstrom
Armstrong World
    Industries, Inc.
Lancaster, Pennsylvania
Nov. 2, 1981–Nov. 8, 1982

Robert B. Funkhouser
Carnation Co.
Los Angeles, California
Nov. 8, 1982–Oct. 31, 1985

David K. Braun
General Foods Corp.
White Plains, New York
Nov. 11, 1983–Nov. 1, 1985

Michael D. Drexler
Doyle Dane Bernbach, Inc.
New York, New York
Nov. 11, 1983–Nov. 14, 1986

Grover J. Friend
Calkins Newspapers
Levittown, Pennsylvania
Nov. 1, 1984–Nov. 12, 1985

William S. Campbell
Hearst Magazines
New York, New York
Nov. 2, 1985–Nov. 13, 1986

Robert J. Galloway
Campbell Soup Co., Ltd.
Toronto, Ontario
Nov. 2, 1985–Nov. 12, 1987

Michael E.G. Kirby
Xerox Corp.
Stamford, Connecticut
Nov. 2, 1985–Nov. 12, 1987

Paul F. McPherson
McGraw-Hill Publications
New York, New York
Nov. 14, 1986–Nov. 3, 1988

Michael D. Moore
DMB&B
New York, New York
Nov. 14, 1986–

Sanford Buchsbaum
Stevens & Buchsbaum
New York, New York
Nov. 12, 1987–

Dan F. Pearson
RJR Nabisco, Inc.
Winston-Salem,
    North Carolina
Nov. 12, 1987–

Robert E. Riordan
Family Media, Inc.
New York, New York
Nov. 3, 1988–

Secretaries

Henry Dumont
Pacific Coast Borax Co.
Chicago, Illinois
May 20, 1914–June 18, 1915

M.F. Harris
Armour & Co.
Chicago, Illinois
June 18, 1915–June 1, 1917

Lafayette Young, Jr.
Des Moines Capital
Des Moines, Iowa
June 1, 1917–June 20, 1919

Walter A. Strong
Daily News
Chicago, Illinois
June 20, 1919–Oct. 21, 1927

Ernest I. Mitchell
Mitchell-Faust Advertising Co.
Chicago, Illinois
Oct. 21, 1927–Oct. 24, 1930

T.F. Driscoll
Armour & Co.
Chiacgo, Illinois
Oct. 24, 1930–Feb. 7, 1936

G.R. Schaffer
Marshall Field & Co.
Chicago, Illinois
Feb. 7, 1936–Oct. 18, 1946

John H. Platt
Kraft Foods Co.
Chicago, Illinois
Oct. 18, 1946–Oct. 24, 1952

Vernon D. Beatty
Swift & Co.
Chicago, Illinois
Oct. 24, 1952–Mar. 7, 1953

Wesley I. Nunn
Standard Oil Co. (Indiana)
Chicago, Illinois
Mar. 7, 1953–June 21, 1953

Stanley R. Clague
Modern Hospital
  Publishing Co.
Chicago, Illinois
June 21, 1953–Oct. 23, 1959

Sam O. Shapiro
Look Magazine
New York, New York
Oct. 23, 1959–Oct. 20, 1965

John R. Miller
Hearst Magazines
New York, New York
Oct. 20, 1965–Oct. 21, 1971

Preston W. Balmer
Regina Leader-Post
Saskatoon Star-Phoenix
Toronto, Ontario
Oct. 21, 1971–Nov. 7, 1974

J. Elton Tuohig
McGraw-Hill Publications Co.
New York, New York
Nov. 7, 1974–Aug. 25, 1976

Clement W. Kohlman
American Cyanamid Co.
Bound Brook, New Jersey
Aug. 25, 1976–Nov. 6, 1980

Jack A. Wishard
The Procter & Gamble Co.
Cincinnati, Ohio
Nov. 6, 1980–Nov. 2, 1981

Peter J. Spengler
Bristol-Myers Co.
New York, New York
Nov. 2, 1981–Nov. 8, 1982

Michael D. Drexler
Doyle Dane Bernbach Inc.
New York, New York
Nov. 8, 1982–Nov. 10, 1983

Sanford Buchsbaum
Revlon, Inc.
New York, New York
Nov. 10, 1983–Nov. 1, 1985

Michael D. Moore
Benton & Bowles, Inc.
New York, New York
Nov. 1, 1985–Nov. 13, 1986

Joseph W. Ostrow
Young & Rubicam Inc.
New York, New York
Nov. 14, 1986–Mar. 31, 1987
Foote, Cone & Belding
New York, New York
Apr. 1, 1987–

Treasurers

Hopewell L. Rogers
Daily News
Chicago, Illinois
May 20, 1914–June 1, 1917

William H. Field
Chicago Tribune
Chicago, Illinois
June 1, 1917–Jan. 24, 1918

S.C. Stewart
Stewart-Davis Advertising
  Agency
Chicago, Illinois
Jan. 24, 1918–Apr. 23, 1918

Ernest R. Shaw
Power Plan Engineering
Chicago, Illinois
Apr. 23, 1918–Jan. 12, 1938

E. Ross Gamble
Leo Burnett Co. Inc.
Chicago, Illinois
Jan. 12, 1938–Mar. 16, 1960

George C. Dibert
J. Walter Thompson Co.
Chicago, Illinois
Mar. 16, 1960–Dec. 4, 1964

Ray Weber
Swift & Co.
Chicago, Illinois
Dec. 4, 1964–Jan. 14, 1966

Richard J. Babcock
Farm Journal
Philadelphia, Pennsylvania
Jan. 14, 1966–Oct. 20, 1967

Donald B. Abert
The Journal Company
Milwaukee, Wisconsin
Oct. 20, 1967–Nov. 6, 1974

250

Lloyd M. Hodgkinson
Maclean-Hunter Ltd.
Toronto, Ontario
Nov. 7, 1974–Nov. 10, 1978

David Kruidenier
Register & Tribune
Des Moines, Iowa
Nov. 10, 1978–Nov. 1, 1984

Lloyd M. Hodgkinson
Maclean-Hunter Ltd.
Toronto, Ontario
Nov. 1, 1984–Nov. 1, 1985

Grover J. Friend
Calkins Newspapers
Levittown, Pennsylvania
Nov. 1, 1985–

Advertiser Directors

Armstrong, Kim
AT&T Communications
Bedminster, New Jersey
Oct. 31, 1985–

Ashby, W.S.
Western Clock Co.
LaSalle, Illinois
Oct. 16, 1925–Oct. 20, 1926

Babcox, Edward S.
Firestone Tire & Rubber Co.
Akron, Ohio
June 7, 1918–Jan. 10, 1919

Baker, Roger W.W.
IBM Corp.
White Plains, New York
Feb. 23, 1987–Feb. 24, 1988
American Brands, Inc.
Old Greenwich, Connecticut
May 17, 1989–

Baldwin, Stanley E.
Willard Storage Battery Co.
Cleveland, Ohio
Mar. 15, 1927–Oct. 18, 1935

Beard, David F.
Reynolds Metals Co.
Richmond, Virginia
June 22, 1961–Oct. 19, 1967

Beatty, Vernon D.
Swift & Co.
Chicago, Illinois
Feb. 21, 1941–Mar. 7, 1953

Bell, Franklin
H.J. Heinz Co.
Pittsburgh, Pennsylvania
Oct. 20, 1933–Oct. 19, 1934

Boggs, Robert W.
Union Carbide Corp.
New York, New York
June 28, 1957–Oct. 19, 1968

Botsford, Henry C.
General Motors Corp.
Detroit, Michigan
Oct. 23, 1953–Mar. 2, 1956

Bowers, John R.
Ford Motor Co.
Detroit, Michigan
Nov. 10, 1977–July 1, 1982

Boynton, James F.
JCPenney Co., Inc.
New York, New York
June 10, 1981–Nov. 3, 1988

Bramble, B.H.
Canadian Chewing
  Gum Co., Ltd.
Toronto, Ontario
Sept. 10, 1918–Apr. 29, 1927

Braun, David K.
General Foods USA
White Plains, New York
Nov. 6, 1980–

Bristol, Lee H.
Bristol-Myers Co.
New York, New York
Feb. 15, 1929–Apr. 25, 1930

Brown, Allan
Bakelite Co.
Div. of Union Carbide &
  Carbon Corp.
New York, New York
Oct. 27, 1950–Oct. 26, 1951

Bruch, Louis
American Radiator Co.
Chicago, Illinois
May 20, 1914–June 6, 1918

Buchsbaum, Sanford
Revlon, Inc.
New York, New York
Aug. 14, 1980–Nov. 13, 1986

Budd, Rex M.
Campbell Soup Co.
Camden, New Jersey
Oct. 21, 1960–Jan. 10, 1968

Burnett, Verne E.
General Motors Corp.
Detroit, Michigan
Oct. 22, 1926–Jan. 24, 1930

Butler, Ralph Starr
U.S. Rubber Co.
New York, New York
Oct. 20, 1922–Mar. 6, 1925
Postum Cereal Co.
New York, New York
Oct. 20, 1926–Mar. 5, 1948

Carson, James O.
H.J. Heinz Co.
Pittsburgh, Pennsylvania
Oct. 20, 1939–Apr. 17, 1942

Chapin, Howard M.
General Foods Corp.
New York, New York
Sept. 21, 1950–Oct. 24, 1952

251

Cherry, Walter B.
Merrell-Soule Co.
Syracuse, New York
Jan. 7, 1915–Jan. 10, 1919

Claggett, William M.
Ralston Purina Co.
St. Louis, Missouri
Sept. 17, 1970–July 15, 1986

Connolly, William N.
S.C. Johnson & Son, Inc.
Racine, Wisconsin
Oct. 26, 1951–July 9, 1961

Conybeare, S.E.
Armstrong Cork Co.
Lancaster, Pennsylvania
Apr. 29, 1927–Mar. 11, 1932

Cora, William J.
Sears, Roebuck and Co.
Chicago, Illinois
Feb. 23, 1987–Aug. 10, 1988

Crites, Lowry H.
General Mills, Inc.
Minneapolis, Minnesota
Oct. 27, 1950–Sept. 10, 1954

Cushing, George W.
Hudson Motor Car Co.
Detroit, Michigan
Mar. 14, 1919–Feb. 24, 1922

Davis, Fred R.
General Electric Co.
Schenectady, New York
May 20, 1914–Dec. 26, 1940

Dineen, J.W.
General Motors Corp.
Detroit, Michigan
Oct. 18, 1935–Oct. 20, 1939

Dobbs, Samuel C.
Coca-Cola Co.
Atlanta, Georgia
Nov. 19, 1915–June 7, 1918

Douglas, Donald B.
Quaker Oats Co.
Chicago, Illinois
Oct. 21, 1932–Apr. 23, 1937

Driscoll, T.F.
Armour & Co.
Chicago, Illinois
Oct. 22, 1926–Feb. 7, 1936

Dryden, W.H.
Sears, Roebuck and Co.
Chicago, Illinois
Oct. 24, 1930–Feb. 5, 1932

Dumont, Henry
Pacific Coast Borax Co.
Chicago, Illinois
May 20, 1914–June 18, 1915

Eller, Russel Z.
California Fruit Growers
   Exchange
Los Angeles, California
Oct. 19, 1945–Oct. 24, 1962

Ellison, Paul S.
Sylvania Electric Products
New York, New York
Dec. 6, 1946–June 26, 1948

Elting, Victor, Jr.
Quaker Oats Co.
Chicago, Illinois
Mar. 18, 1959–June 13, 1961

Ewen, William H.
The Borden Co.
New York, New York
June 22, 1956–Oct. 21, 1960
Mar. 9, 1962–Oct. 21, 1971

Farrell, William R.
Monsanto Co.
St. Louis, Missouri
Oct. 21, 1955–Sept. 15, 1965

Foss, John
Canadian Canners, Ltd.
Toronto, Ontario
June 23, 1976–Aug. 9, 1979

Fowler, George S.
Colgate & Co.
New York, New York
June 7, 1918–Oct. 15, 1920

Funkhouser, Robert
Carnation Co.
Los Angeles, California
Aug. 24, 1976–Oct. 31, 1985

Galloway, Robert J.
Campbell Soup Co., Ltd.
Toronto, Ontario
Aug. 9, 1979–

Garceau, Yvan
Dairy Bureau of Canada
Montreal, Quebec
Aug. 10, 1988–

Gasparro, Anthony M.
The Great Atlantic &
   Pacific Tea Co., Inc.
Montvale, New Jersey
Nov. 3, 1988–

Gettig, Blair R.
Aluminum Co. of America
Pittsburgh, Pennsylvania
Aug. 10, 1982–Mar. 8, 1986

Gibbon, John M.
Canadian Pacific Railway Co.
Montreal, Quebec
Oct. 20, 1922–Nov. 18, 1927

Glasier, John F.
Ford Motor Co. of Canada
Oakville, Ontario
Dec. 8, 1961–June 24, 1976

Goldstrom, Donald G.
Armstrong World
   Industries, Inc.
Lancaster, Pennsylvania
Oct. 23, 1975–May 18, 1989

Goldthwaite, C.F.
Canadian National Railways
Montreal, Quebec
Oct. 25, 1929–Oct. 21, 1932

Grandin, Frank C.
Postum Cereal Co.
Battle Creek, Michigan
May 20, 1914–July 25, 1919

Gray, Robert M.
Esso Standard Oil Co.
New York, New York
Sept. 17, 1948–Mar. 7, 1953

Greene, L.R.
Tuckett Tobacco Co., Ltd.
Hamilton, Ontario
Oct. 21, 1932–Feb. 7, 1936

Griffiths, Eben
Socony-Vacuum Corp.
New York, New York
Oct. 20, 1934–Dec. 6, 1946

Guarascio, Philip
General Motors Corp.
Detroit, Michigan
Mar. 8, 1986–

Hall, Edward T.
Ralston Purina Co.
St. Louis, Missouri
Oct. 22, 1926–Jan. 24, 1930

Harding, S. Scott
Sears, Roebuck and Co.
Chicago, Illinois
Aug. 10, 1988–

Harn, Orlando C.
National Lead Co.
New York, New York
May 20, 1914–Feb. 4, 1927

Harris, M.F.
Armour & Co.
Chicago, Illinois
Feb. 16, 1915–Jan. 3, 1918

Hart, John K.
Rexall Drug Co.
St. Louis, Missouri
Oct. 26, 1962–Sept. 13, 1967

Hart, William A.
E.I. du Pont de Nemours & Co.
Wilmington, Delaware
June 10, 1927–Oct. 21, 1955

Harwood, Frank W.
American Tobacco Co.
New York, New York
Mar. 15, 1927–Jan. 18, 1929

Hattwick, Melvin S.
Continental Oil Co.
Houston, Texas
Apr. 6, 1966–Apr. 1, 1973

Hawkins, G.H.E.
N.K. Fairbank Co.
Chicago, Illinois
May 20, 1914–Dec. 3, 1914

Healy, Carleton
Hiram Walker & Sons, Inc.
Detroit, Michigan
Apr. 17, 1942–Oct. 21, 1960

Heckel, Fred W.
United Air Lines
Chicago, Illinois
Sept. 13, 1967–Oct. 18, 1973

Heller, D.W.
Sunkist Growers
Van Nuys, California
Mar. 5, 1975–June 24, 1976

Howard, William H.
Macy's
New York, New York
Dec. 6, 1946–June 25, 1948

Ingraham, Gar K.
Sears, Roebuck and Co.
Chicago, Illinois
Oct. 21, 1971–Nov. 8, 1974

James, William A.
Hudson Motor Car Co.
Detroit, Michigan
Feb. 5, 1932–Oct. 20, 1933

Johnson, A. Dexter
Eastman Kodak Co.
Rochester, New York
Apr. 12, 1968–Sept. 1, 1972

Jones, Lewis B.
Eastman Kodak Co.
Rochester, New York
June 18, 1915–June 21, 1929
May 23, 1930–Aug. 25, 1934

King, L.L.
Goodyear Tire & Rubber Co.
Akron, Ohio
Jan. 10, 1919–Apr. 27, 1921
Feb. 24, 1922–Apr. 29, 1927

Kirby, Michael E.G.
Xerox Corp.
Stamford, Connecticut
Nov. 10, 1983–Nov. 12, 1987

Kissel, Robert G.
Sears, Roebuck and Co.
Chicago, Illinois
Aug. 28, 1975–Mar. 6, 1981

Knowlton, Archa O.
General Foods Corp.
White Plains, New York
Mar. 9, 1973–Aug. 18, 1978

Kohlman, Clement W.
American Cyanamid Co.
Bound Brook, New Jersey
Jan. 12, 1968–Nov. 6, 1980

Lantz, Walter P.
Bristol-Myers Co.
New York, New York
Oct. 23, 1953–Mar. 9, 1961

Laughlin, W.
Armour and Co.
Chicago, Illinois
Feb. 15, 1918–Mar. 6, 1925

Lehrter, Herbert A.
Hiram Walter Inc.
Detroit, Michigan
June 19, 1968–Aug. 18, 1978

Lowy, Felix
Colgate-Palmolive-Peet Co.
Chicago, Illinois
Sept. 18, 1931–Mar. 25, 1933

Lunde, Marvin C.
Sears, Roebuck and Co.
Chicago, Illinois
Sept. 15, 1965–Apr. 4, 1969

Mapes, Emery
Cream of Wheat Co.
Minneapolis, Minnesota
May 20, 1914–June 7, 1918

Martin, John A.
Montgomery Ward & Co.
Chicago, Illinois
Mar. 7, 1953–Oct. 23, 1953

McLean, W.S.
Fisher Body Division
General Motors Corp.
Detroit, Michigan
Oct. 20, 1939–Oct. 24, 1952

McNiven, Malcolm
Coca-Cola USA
Atlanta, Georgia
June 28, 1973–Aug. 24, 1974
The Pillsbury Co.
Minneapolis, Minnesota
Mar. 3, 1976–Aug. 14, 1980

McQueen, L.A.
B.F. Goodrich
Akron, Ohio
Jan. 20, 1928–Oct. 25, 1929

Merritt, Edwin B.
Armour and Co.
Chicago, Illinois
May 20, 1914–Feb. 16, 1915

Morley, J.A.
N.K. Fairbank Co.
Chicago, Illinois
June 7, 1918–July 6, 1918

Moses, Bert
Omega Chemical Co.
New York, New York
May 20, 1914–Nov. 19, 1915

Nejelski, Leo
Swift & Co.
Chicago, Illinois
June 28, 1937–Sept. 22, 1939

Noyes, Harley N.
Oneida Ltd.
Oneida, New York
Oct. 26, 1951–Mar. 24, 1954

Nunn, Wesley I.
Standard Oil Co. (Indiana)
Chicago, Illinois
Oct. 24, 1952–June 20, 1953

Ogle, Arthur H.
Bauer & Black
Chicago, Illinois
Feb. 21, 1930–Oct. 21, 1932

Peabody, Stuart
The Borden Co.
New York, New York
Jan. 24, 1930–Oct. 24, 1930
Oct. 19, 1934–Oct. 18, 1945

Pearson, Dan F.
RJR Nabisco, Inc.
Winston-Salem,
   North Carolina
Oct. 31, 1985–

Perkins, Grafton B.
Lever Brothers
Cambridge, Massachusetts
June 9, 1933–Oct. 22, 1937

Piggott, Robert J.
Pet Milk Co.
St. Louis, Missouri
Sept. 7, 1961–June 26, 1970

Platt, John H.
Kraft Foods Co.
Chicago, Illinois
Oct. 22, 1937–June 13, 1962

Rechholtz, R.A.
R.J. Reynolds Tobacco
Winston-Salem,
   North Carolina
Oct. 19, 1972–Mar. 9, 1973

Richards, D.D.
Sears, Roebuck and Co.
Chicago, Illinois
Feb. 7, 1936–Oct. 27, 1950

Rigby, M.F.
Studebaker Corp. of America
South Bend, Indiana
Oct. 25, 1929–June 18, 1931

Rimmer, Harland H.
Canadian General
   Electric Co., Ltd.
Toronto, Ontario
Feb. 7, 1936–Dec. 7, 1961

Robertson, R.C.
Colgate-Palmolive-Peet Co.
Jersey City, New Jersey
Oct. 24, 1952–Sept. 10, 1953

Rogan, Ralph F.
Procter & Gamble Co.
Cincinnati, Ohio
Sept. 16, 1932–Sept. 18, 1935

Ross, Thomas J.
American Airlines
New York, New York
Nov. 7, 1974–Aug. 27, 1975

Schaeffer, G.R.
Marshall Field & Co.
Chicago, Illinois
Oct. 20, 1933–Dec. 6, 1946

Schott, Henry W.
Montgomery Ward & Co.
Chicago, Illinois
June 7, 1918–Sept. 8, 1922

Schroeter, Harry F.
National Biscuit Co.
New York, New York
Sept. 7, 1961–Sept. 17, 1970

Shallberg, G.A., Jr.
Borg-Warner Corp.
Chicago, Illinois
Sept. 10, 1954–Mar. 18, 1959

Simons, E.W.
James Manufacturing Co.
Fort Atkinson, Wisconsin
May 26, 1921–Sept. 8, 1922

Sizer, Lawrence B.
Marshall Field & Co.
Chicago, Illinois
June 25, 1948–Oct. 26, 1951

Smith, Guy C.
Libby, McNeill & Libby
Chicago, Illinois
June 21, 1929–Oct. 20, 1933

Smith, H. Strong
Bauer & Black Co.
Chicago, Illinois
June 25, 1919–May 26, 1921

Spengler, Peter J.
Bristol-Myers Co.
New York, New York
Aug. 17, 1978–Feb. 23, 1987

Sproull, William
Burroughs Corp.
Detroit, Michigan
Sept. 10, 1954–Mar. 9, 1962

Squier, Fred W.
Pabst Brewing Co.
Milwaukee, Wisconsin
May 20, 1914–Sept. 10, 1918
Jan. 10, 1919–Oct. 28, 1921

Stokes, Charles
Canadian Pacific Railway Co.
Montreal, Quebec
Nov. 18, 1927–Oct. 25, 1929

Sumner, G. Lynn
International Correspondence
  Schools
Scranton, Pennsylvania
Apr. 27, 1921–Nov. 20, 1925

Taylor, E.E.
Carnation Milk Products
Chicago, Illinois
Oct. 28, 1921–Oct. 16, 1925
Postum Cereal Co.
New York, New York
Nov. 20, 1925–Oct. 20, 1926

Thompson, R. Clinton
J.C. Penney Co., Inc.
New York, New York
Oct. 23, 1969–Nov. 10, 1977

Thomson, Philip L.
Western Electric Co.
New York, New York
Oct. 16, 1925–Oct. 27, 1950

Towers, W.K.
Paige-Detroit Motor Car Co.
Detroit, Michigan
Mar. 6, 1925–Nov. 18, 1927

Tucker, Charles
R.J. Reynolds Tobacco Co.
Winston-Salem,
  North Carolina
June 25, 1974–Oct. 31, 1985

Tucker, Frank T.
B.F. Goodrich Co.
Akron, Ohio
Oct. 23, 1953–Oct. 19, 1956

Van Cleave, James W.
Procter & Gamble
Cincinnati, Ohio
Aug. 15, 1986–

Walsh, Arthur H.
American Telephone &
  Telegraph Co.
New York, New York
June 13, 1962–Apr. 12, 1968

Walters, Kenneth L.
General Electric Co.
New York, New York
Oct. 19, 1956–June 28, 1957

Weber, Ray
Swift & Company
Chicago, Illinois
Oct. 21, 1960–Jan. 14, 1966

Wheeler, W.W.
Pompeian Manufacturing Co.
Cleveland, Ohio
Oct. 15, 1920–Oct. 20, 1922
Oct. 18, 1923–Nov. 19, 1926

Willis, Paul H.
Carnation Co.
Los Angeles, California
Oct. 19, 1967–Oct. 22, 1975

Wishard, Jack A.
Procter & Gamble Co.
Cincinnati, Ohio
Nov. 9, 1978–Nov. 10, 1983

Wrigley, William, Jr.
William Wrigley Co.
Chicago, Illinois
May 20, 1914–Nov. 6, 1917

Young, Thomas H.
U.S. Rubber Co.
New York, New York
June 25, 1948–Sept. 21, 1950

Youngreen, C.C.
J.I. Case Plow Works
Racine, Wisconsin
Sept. 8, 1972–Sept. 7, 1923

Advertising Agency Directors

Anderson, James M.
McKim Advertising Ltd.
Toronto, Ontario
Nov. 3, 1988–

Anderson, Richard C.
Needham, Harper &
    Steers, Inc.
Chicago, Illinois
Mar. 6, 1981–Sept. 5, 1984

Brother, Doren P.
Campbell-Ewald Co.
Detroit, Michigan
Apr. 28, 1933–Oct. 19, 1934

Buchsbaum, Sanford
Stevens & Buchsbaum, Inc.
New York, New York
Nov. 13, 1986–

Clague, Stanley
Clague Agency
Chicago, Illinois
May 20, 1914–Jan. 19, 1927

Dean, Sidney W., Jr.
McCann-Erickson, Inc.
New York, New York
Oct. 18, 1957–Oct. 18, 1961

Dibert, George, C.
J. Walter Thompson Co.
Chicago, Illinois
Oct. 23, 1953–Dec. 2, 1964

Dickson, John A.
Mitchell, Faust,
    Dickson & Wieland
Chicago, Illinois
Oct. 24, 1930–Oct. 21, 1932

Dow, Hugh F.
MacLaren:Lintas Ltd.
Toronto, Ontario
Nov. 12, 1987–

Drexler, Michael D.
Doyle Dane Bernbach, Inc.
New York, New York
Nov. 7, 1980–Feb. 23, 1987

Duffy, Bernard C.
Batten, Barton,
    Durstine & Osborn
New York, New York
Oct. 20, 1933–Oct. 21, 1955

D'Arcy, William C.
D'Arcy Advertising Co., Inc.
St. Louis, Missouri
Oct. 21, 1932–Apr. 28, 1933

Erickson, Alfred W.
The Erickson Co.
New York, New York
May 20, 1914–Oct. 28, 1921

Fine, Jules P.
Ogilvy & Mather, Inc.
New York, New York
Apr. 7, 1971–Oct. 31, 1985

Frank, Clinton E.
Clinton E. Frank, Inc.
Chicago, Illinois
Oct. 23, 1969–June 23, 1971

Gamble, E. Ross
Leo Burnett Co.
Chicago, Illinois
Oct. 19, 1934–Mar. 18, 1960

Gordon, Daniel M.
Ruthrauff & Ryan, Inc.
New York, New York
Dec. 6, 1956–Sept. 12, 1957

Gordon, Herbert
Ketchum
    Communications Inc.
Pittsburgh, Pennsylvania
May 11, 1987–

Hermes, Frank J.
The Blackman Co.
New York, New York
Oct. 21, 1927–Oct. 11, 1933

Hine, Walker
Frank Seaman, Inc.
New York, New York
Oct. 28, 1921–Oct. 21, 1927

Hunter, Peter W.
McConnell Advertising Ltd.
Toronto, Ontario
Mar. 7, 1975–Sept. 7, 1982
Cockfield Brown, Inc.
Toronto, Ontario
Sept. 8, 1982–June 22, 1983

Kynett, Harold H.
Aitkin-Kynett Co.
Philadelphia, Pennsylvania
Oct. 18, 1935–Oct. 19, 1967

Laird, Kenneth
Tatham-Laird & Kudner, Inc.
Chicago, Illinois
Mar. 18, 1960–Apr. 4, 1969

Maneloveg, Herbert
Batten, Barton,
    Durstine & Osborn
New York, New York
Oct. 24, 1968–Oct. 20, 1970
McCann-Erickson, Inc.
New York, New York
June 23, 1971–Oct. 18, 1973

McCaffrey, James J.
LaRoche, McCaffrey & McCall
New York, New York
Jan. 15, 1970–Oct. 22, 1970

Meskil, John J.
Warwick Advertising, Inc.
New York, New York
Nov. 10, 1983–

Messner, Fred R.
Michel-Cather, Inc.
New York, New York
Oct. 19, 1972–Sept. 16, 1974
Douglas Turner, Inc.
Newark, New Jersey
Sept. 16, 1974–Mar. 27, 1978
Poppe Tyson Inc.
Mar. 27, 1978–Nov. 13, 1986

Miller, Hal
SSC & B Inc.
New York, New York
Mar. 7, 1973–Mar. 6, 1981

Mitchell, Ernest I.
Mitchell-Faust Advertising Co.
Oct. 15, 1920–Oct. 24, 1930

Moore, Michael D.
DMB&B
New York, New York
Oct. 30, 1984–

Moynihan, J.M.
Campbell-Ewald Co.
Detroit, Michigan
Jan. 14, 1971–Mar. 9, 1973

Ostrow, Joseph W.
Young & Rubicam Inc.
New York, New York
June 9, 1978–Apr. 1, 1987
Foote, Cone & Belding
Apr. 1, 1987–

Reynolds, C. Warren
Ronalds-Reynolds Co.
Toronto, Ontario
Dec. 8, 1961–Mar. 7, 1975

Ronalds, Russell C.
Ronalds Advertising
   Agency, Ltd.
Montreal, Quebec
Dec. 6, 1956–Dec. 7, 1961

Rosen, Marcella
NW Ayer, Inc.
New York, New York
Oct. 31, 1985–

St. Georges, Joseph
Young & Rubicam Inc.
New York, New York
Oct. 19, 1967–Oct. 22, 1968

Sawin, F.B.
Critchfield & Co.
Chicago, Illinois
Oct. 19, 1917–Apr. 18, 1919

Simko, George J.
Benton & Bowles, Inc.
New York, New York
Oct. 18, 1973–Nov. 10, 1983

Steers, William
Needham, Harper & Steers
New York, New York
Oct. 21, 1955–Jan. 15, 1970

Stern, Edward M.
Foote, Cone & Belding, Inc.
Chicago, Illinois
Apr. 4, 1969–Mar. 1, 1978

Stewart, S.C.
Stewart-Davis Advertising Co.
Chicago, Illinois
Nov. 27, 1917–Apr. 23, 1918

Tommaney, James J.
LaRoche, McCaffrey & McCall
New York, New York
Oct. 22, 1970–Nov. 6, 1980

Troup, Paul V.
Lord & Thomas
Chicago, Illinois
Apr. 18, 1919–Oct. 15, 1920

Weilbacher, William
Jack Tinker & Partners, Inc.
New York, New York
Dec. 4, 1964–Jan. 14, 1971

Wittner, Fred
Fred Wittner Co.
New York, New York
Oct. 20, 1961–July 6, 1972

Yeates, Allan B.
Baker, Lovick, Ltd.
Toronto, Ontario
June 22, 1983–Nov. 3, 1988

Magazine Directors

Allen, Benjamin
Curtis Publishing Co.
Philadelphia, Pennsylvania
Oct. 15, 1948–June 20, 1958

Beck, Thomas H.
Crowell Publishing Co.
New York, New York
Jan. 16, 1920–Sept. 8, 1922

Brady, Curtis, P.
Women's World
Chicago, Illinois
May 20, 1914–Oct. 30, 1917

Buttikofer, T.J.
Hearst Magazines
New York, New York
Oct. 16, 1936–Sept. 17, 1937

Campbell, William S.
Hearst Magazines
New York, New York
Nov. 19, 1974–Nov. 13, 1986

Collins, P.S.
Curtis Publishing Co.
Philadelphia, Pennsylvania
June 20, 1919–July 25, 1919

Cook, George E.
Mother's Magazine
New York, New York
Nov. 20, 1917–Nov. 21, 1919

Crocker, Hugh
TV Guide / USA
Radnor, Pennsylvania
Nov. 5, 1981–Feb. 25, 1989

Davis, F.E.
Newsweek
New York, New York
Oct. 23, 1969–Nov. 8, 1979

Deyoe, Allan M.
Golf Digest / Tennis, Inc.
Norwalk, Connecticut
Nov. 8, 1979–Oct. 31, 1985

Eaton, W.H.
American Home Magazine
New York, New York
Oct. 21, 1949–Oct. 23, 1953

Hoyt, Frank C.
The Outlook
New York, New York
May 20, 1914–June 1, 1917

Lacy, Bernard B.
CBS Magazines
New York, New York
Nov. 13, 1986–Oct. 5, 1987
Diamandis
   Communications, Inc.
Oct. 5, 1987–Jan. 4, 1988
Ziff-Davis Publishing Co.
Jan. 4, 1988–

Latshaw, S.R.
Butterick Publishing Co.
New York, New York
July 25, 1919–Sept. 18, 1936

McCombs, G.B.
Curtis Publishing Co.
Philadelphia, Pennsylvania
Oct. 20, 1965–Oct. 21, 1969

Meredith, E.T.
Meredith Publishing Co.
Des Moines, Iowa
Oct. 21, 1927–June 17, 1928

Miller, John R.
Hearst Magazines
New York, New York
June 20, 1958–Oct. 19, 1974

Narber, James R.
Meredith Corp.
Des Moines, Iowa
Oct. 18, 1973–Nov. 5, 1981

Riordan, Robert E.
Family Media Inc.
New York, New York
Oct. 31, 1985–

Shapiro, S.O.
Cowles Magazines, Inc.
New York, New York
Oct. 23, 1953–Oct. 20, 1965

Stone, F.W.
American Review of Reviews
New York, New York
June 1, 1917–June 20, 1919
Parents' Magazine
New York, New York
Sept. 8, 1922–Oct. 15, 1948

Wyman, Phillips
McCall Corp.
New York, New York
Sept. 17, 1937–Oct. 21, 1949

Farm Publication Directors

Allen, W.C.
Dakota Farmer
Aberdeen, South Dakota
Oct. 26, 1928–Oct. 20, 1933

Anderson, Vernon C.
Prairie Farmer Publishing Co.
Chicago, Illinois
Oct. 22, 1970–Oct. 18, 1972

Babcock, R.J.
The Farm Journal
Philadelphia, Pennsylvania
Mar. 18, 1960–Oct. 21, 1971

Boberg, W.E.
The Farmer
St. Paul Minnesota
Oct. 18, 1957–Oct. 20, 1966

Bohen, Fred
Meredith Publishing Co.
Des Moines, Iowa
Oct. 20, 1933–Oct. 21, 1949

Butler, Burridge D.
Prairie Farmer
Chicago, Illinois
May 20, 1914–June 2, 1916

Chronister, Hugh
Harvest Publishing Co.
Cleveland, Ohio
Oct. 19, 1972–Oct. 16, 1973

Cunningham, Emory
Progressive Farmer Co.
Birmingham, Alabama
Oct. 21, 1971–Oct. 22, 1975

Fensler, Robert K.
Nebraska Farmer Co.
Lincoln, Nebraska
Nov. 5, 1981–Oct. 31, 1985

Huey, Paul
Progressive Farmer
Birmingham, Alabama
Oct. 23, 1959–Feb. 4, 1960

Jenkins, Charles F.
The Farm Journal
Philadlephia, Pennsylvania
May 20, 1914–June 1, 1917

Kinderwater, Jack
The Webb Co./*The Farmer*
St. Paul, Minnesota
Oct. 31, 1985–

Klein, Horace C.
The Farmer
St. Paul, Minnesota
Sept. 21, 1928–Oct. 26, 1928

Laing, Neff
Pennsylvania Farmer
Philadelphia, Pennsylvania
Oct. 15, 1920–Mar. 23, 1922

Long, Frank E.
Farmer's Review
Chicago, Illinois
June 2, 1916–Sept. 19, 1919

Lund, Bert O., Jr.
The Webb Co./*The Farmer*
St. Paul, Minnesota
Oct. 23, 1975–Nov. 5, 1981

Milholland, James, Jr.
Home State Farm Publications
Cleveland, Ohio
Oct. 20, 1966–Oct. 22, 1970

Morrow, Marco
Capper Publications, Inc.
Topeka, Kansas
Oct. 17, 1919–Oct. 15, 1942

Rankin, B. Kirk
Southern Agriculturist
Nashville, Tennessee
Mar. 23, 1923–Oct. 21, 1927

Sweet, Charles E.
Capper Publications, Inc.
Topeka, Kansas
Oct. 15, 1942–Oct. 18, 1957

Watt, Leslie A.
Poultry Tribune
Mt. Morris, Illinois
Oct. 21, 1949–Oct. 23, 1959

Whitney, W.A.
Phelps Publishing Co.
Springfield, Massachusetts
June 1, 1917–Oct. 14, 1920
Mar. 23, 1922–Mar. 23, 1923

Canadian Periodical Directors

Drane, Bruce L.
Maclean-Hunter Ltd.
Toronto, Ontario
Oct. 31, 1985–

Hodgkinson, Lloyd M.
Maclean-Hunter Ltd.
Toronto, Ontario
June 21, 1968–Oct. 31, 1985

Hunter, Donald F.
Maclean-Hunter
  Publishing Co.
Toronto, Ontario
Dec. 6, 1956–Mar. 3, 1965

Laurin, Cyrille J.
Maclean-Hunter
  Publishing Co.
Toronto, Ontario
Mar. 3, 1965–June 21, 1968

Business Publication Directors

Aldrich, Paul I.
National Provisioner
Chicago, Illinois
June 24, 1938–Oct. 17, 1941

Blackburn, James E., Jr.
McGraw-Hill Publishing Co.
New York, New York
Oct. 17, 1947–Mar. 8, 1957

Britton, Mason
McGraw-Hill Publishing Co.
New York, New York
June 7, 1918–Sept. 22, 1944

Clague, Stanley R.
Modern Hospital
  Publishing Co.
Chicago, Illinois
Dec. 2, 1949–Oct. 23, 1959

Emery, John R.
Technical Publishing Co.
New York, New York
Nov. 7, 1980–Feb. 25, 1989

Erhlich, Howard
McGraw-Hill Publishing Co.
New York, New Yrok
Oct. 19, 1944–Sept. 19, 1947

Fahrendorf, Peter M.
Chilton Company, Inc.
New York, New York
Oct. 17, 1947–Oct. 21, 1949

Haire, Thomas B.
Haire Publishing Co.
New York, New York
Mar. 8, 1957–Oct. 21, 1960

Henderson, Edward
Business News Publishing Co.
Detroit, Michigan
Oct. 21, 1960–Nov. 8, 1974

Keeney, Frank P.
Keeney Publishing Co.
Chicago, Illinois
Oct. 17, 1941–Oct. 18, 1945

Kusherick, John P.
Chilton Co.
Radnor, Pennsylvania
Nov. 7, 1974–Nov. 6, 1980

Littleford, William D.
Billboard Publishing Co.
New York, New York
Oct. 23, 1959–Oct. 19, 1967

McDermott, Terrence M.
Cahners Publishing Co.
Newton, Massachusetts
May 18, 1989–

McPherson, Paul F.
McGraw-Hill Publishing Co.
New York, New York
Oct. 22, 1976–Nov. 8, 1979
Aug. 19, 1983–Mar. 1, 1989
FM Business Publications, Inc.
Mar. 1, 1989–

Porter, F.D.
National Builder
Chicago, Illinois
May 20, 1914–June 18, 1915

Rice, Kingsley L.
Power Plant Engineering
Chicago, Illinois
Oct. 19, 1945–Sept. 19, 1947

Robbins, Merton C.
Iron Age
New York, New York
May 20, 1914–June 7, 1918

Shaw, Ernest R.
Power Plant Engineering
Chicago, Illinois
June 18, 1915–Jan. 12, 1938

Simpson, Gene W.
McGraw-Hill Publishing Co.
New York, New York
Nov. 8, 1979–Aug. 19, 1983

Slocum, George M.
Automotive News
Detroit Michigan
Oct. 21, 1949–Oct. 30, 1949

Tuohig, J. Elton
McGraw-Hill Publishing Co.
New York, New York
Oct. 19, 1967–Aug. 25, 1976

Newspaper Directors

Abert, Donald B.
The Journal Co.
Milwaukee, Wisconsin
June 17, 1964–Nov. 8, 1974

Baker, Lisle, Jr.
Courier-Journal
Louisville, Kentucky
Oct. 21, 1949–June 26, 1954

Baker-Pearce, Jean
Alliston Press Ltd.
Alliston, Ontario
Nov. 3, 1988–

Balmer, Preston W.
Regina Leader-Post/
Saskatchewan Star
Toronto, Ontario
Sept. 11, 1968–Nov. 9, 1978

Bennett, Edward L.
The Call
Patterson, New Jersey
Oct. 23, 1969–Jan. 15, 1970

Bradford, Tutt S.
Alcoa Daily Times
Maryville, Tennessee
Oct. 19, 1967–Oct. 18, 1972

Bresnahan, John F.
The World
New York, New York
Feb. 17, 1928–Oct. 23, 1931

Brown, Roy A.
Independent-Journal
San Rafael, California
Sept. 13, 1956–June 26, 1963

Bryant, W.B.
Press-Guardian
Patterson, New Jersey
Oct. 22, 1926–Oct. 26, 1928

Burbach, George M.
Post Dispatch
St. Louis, Missouri
Oct. 26, 1928–Apr. 25, 1930

Butler, William J.J.
Globe and Mail
Toronto, Ontario
Oct. 18, 1935–June 19, 1955

Carpenter, Richard W.
Evening & Sunday Bulletin
Philadelphia, Pennsylvania
June 17, 1975–Aug. 30, 1978
Newspaper Agency
San Francisco, California
Sept. 1, 1978–Nov. 5, 1981

Cowles, John
Register & Tribune-Capital
Des Moines, Iowa
Oct. 25, 1929–Oct. 20, 1933

Dampier, Lawrence
The Vancouver Sun
Vancouver, British Columbia
Oct. 20, 1966–Sept. 11, 1968

Dayton, James C.
Journal
New York, New York
Oct. 21, 1927–Feb. 17, 1928

Dear, Walter M.
Jersey Journal
Jersey City, New Jersey
Oct. 21, 1932–Oct. 16, 1936

Emmerich, John O.
Greenwood Commonwealth
Greenwood, Mississippi
Nov. 10, 1983–

Field, William H.
Chicago Tribune
Chicago, Illinois
June 1, 1917–June 7, 1918

Friend, Grover J.
Bucks County Courier-Times
Levittown, Pennsylvania
Nov. 9, 1979–Oct. 31, 1983
Calkins Newspapers
Levittown, Pennsylvania
Nov. 1, 1983–

Gaylord, Edward K.
Oklahoman & Times
Oklahoma City, Oklahoma
Oct. 20, 1933–Oct. 18, 1935

Geoghegan, Frank
The Patriot-Ledger
Quincy, Massachusetts
June 23, 1961–Oct. 20, 1966

Green, Harry
John P. Scripps Newspapers
San Diego, California
June 23, 1965–Oct. 18, 1973

Green, William C., Jr.
The Birmingham News Co.
Birmingham, Alabama
Nov. 5, 1981–Nov. 3, 1988
The Huntsville Times
Huntsville, Alabama
Nov. 3, 1988–

Hatton, E. Roy
Detroit Free Press
Detroit, Michigan
June 2, 1939–May 30, 1961

Hersam, V. Donald, Jr.
New Canaan Advertiser
New Canaan, Connecticut
June 19, 1975–Nov. 10, 1983

Hudson, Buell W.
The Call
Woonsocket, Rhode Island
Oct. 18, 1940–Oct. 18, 1946

Jones, Robert Letts
Copley Newspapers
LaJolla, California
June 26, 1963–June 23, 1965

Joy, Verne
Sentinel
Centralia, Illinois
Oct. 16, 1936–Sept. 12, 1957

Kauffmann, John H.
The Star
Washington, D.C.
Oct. 23, 1969–Mar. 5, 1975

Kennedy, Sam D.
Daily Herald
Columbia, Tennessee
Oct. 19, 1972–Nov. 10, 1983

Kimber, Harry G.
Globe and Mail
Toronto, Ontario
June 19, 1955–Oct. 24, 1958

Kruidenier, David
Register & Tribune
Des Moines, Iowa
Nov. 7, 1974–Oct. 31, 1984

Larone, Kenneth J.
MetroSPAN Ltd.
Toronto, Ontario
Oct. 18, 1973–Mar. 7, 1975

Lincoln, A.G.
Post-Dispatch
St. Louis, Missouri
June 20, 1919–Oct. 20, 1922

Litvany, William M.
Independent Press
Bloomfield, New York
June 21, 1968–Oct. 18, 1973

Lucey, William F.
Eagle-Tribune
Lawrence, Massachusetts
Oct. 18, 1946–Mar. 8, 1957

Macy, J. Noel
Westchester County
 Publishers, Inc.
Yonkers, New York
Oct. 18, 1935–Oct. 18, 1940

McClure, J.W.
Gannett Co.
Rochester, New York
Mar. 5, 1975–June 16, 1975

McCracken, Robert I.
Times Herald
Norristown, Pennsylvania
Oct. 20, 1966–Nov. 6, 1980

McFetridge, Lyle W.
Newspaper Printing Corp.
Tulsa, Oklahoma
June 23, 1961–Oct. 21, 1969

McIntosh, C. Irwin
News Optimist
North Battleford,
 Saskatchewan
Nov. 10, 1983–Sept. 24, 1988

McMillan, Kenneth A.
Toronto Star
Toronto, Ontario
Oct. 21, 1960–Sept. 7, 1963

Mills, Russell
The Ottawa Citizen
Ottawa, Ontario
Nov. 3, 1988–

Moroney, James M., Jr.
A.H. Belo Corp./*Morning News*
Dallas, Texas
Oct. 31, 1984–Nov., 3, 1988

Newell, Frank S.
State-Journal
Frankfort, New York
Oct. 18, 1946–Sept. 23, 1949

Palmer, Harlan G.
Citizen-News
Hollywood, California
June 27, 1947–July 25, 1956

Peters, Charles H.
The Gazette
Montreal, Quebec
Oct. 25, 1963–Oct. 20, 1966

Plum, David B.
Troy Record
Troy, New York
Oct. 20, 1922–Oct. 21, 1932

Powell, Horace
Journal
Atlanta, Georgia
Oct. 18, 1940–Oct. 18, 1946